HUMAN AGGRESSION

MAPPING SOCIAL PSYCHOLOGY

Series Editor: Tony Manstead

HUMAN AGGRESSION

SECOND EDITION

Russell G. Geen

OPEN UNIVERSITY PRESS
Buckingham • Philadelphia

Open University Press
Celtic Court
22 Ballmoor
Buckingham
MK18 1XW

email: enquiries@openup.co.uk
world wide web: www.openup.co.uk

and
325 Chestnut Street
Philadelphia, PA 19106, USA

First edition published 1990
Reprinted 1999

First Published in this second edition 2001

A catalogue record of this book is available from the British Library

ISBN 0 335 20472 4 (hb)   0 335 20471 6 (pb)

Library of Congress Cataloging-in-Publication Data
Geen, Russell G., 1932–
    Human aggression / Russell G. Geen. — 2nd ed.
       p. cm. — (Mapping social psychology series)
    Includes bibliographical references and indexes.
    ISBN 0-335-20472-4 — ISBN 0-335-20471-6 (pbk.)
    1. Aggressiveness. I. Title. II. Series.

    BF575.A3 G43 2001
    302.5′4—dc21
                                                2001021146

Typeset by Graphicraft Limited, Hong Kong
Printed in Great Britain by Biddles Limited, Guildford and Kings Lynn

Dedicated to the memory of my
Father and Mother

CONTENTS

PREFACE

Books about human aggression tend to be of two types. Some are composed according to a particular point of view. These books organize and explicate research findings from a perspective determined by the theory that underlies the approach. Other books are broader, more inclusive and less theory-driven. They structure material along topical lines such as the development of aggression, the social and environmental determinants of aggressive behaviour and strategies for the control of aggression. This book falls somewhere between the two. As a volume in a series of short texts, it does not pretend to be exhaustive in its review. As a book intended for classroom use, it does not aspire to make any innovative contributions to theory. Instead, it reviews a body of literature that has accumulated in the study of one type of human aggression and it organizes the findings of the literature along the lines of a simple process model.

This book is the second edition of Human Aggression, and its has been organized to reflect the state of knowledge on this subject at the beginning of the twenty-first century. Aggression is defined as an act of harmdoing inflicted consciously and intentionally upon an unwilling victim. Traditionally, aggression has been conceptualized as primarily either affective or instrumental in nature, i.e. as either an outburst of behaviour animated by anger or a relatively affect-free action carried out because it serves some other purpose. This distinction forms the basis for a more recent one between proactive aggression, which is instrumental in nature, and reactive aggression, which is a response to some provoking circumstance. Affective aggression is further defined as a response to an aversive change in the person's environment – a provocation – and not to anything internally generated. The relative emphasis of this book is on the analysis of aggression that is reactive and affective, because this is the approach taken by most students of human aggression and violence. Nevertheless, it will also be clear from a perusal of this book that interest in the instrumental nature of aggression has been increasing in recent years, and that instrumental motives (e.g. power and dominance) are heavily involved in the explanation of certain everyday problems of violence, such as spouse abuse and bullying.

It will also be obvious that much of the research and theorizing on affective aggression is addressed to the identification of processes that intervene between provoking conditions and aggressive reactions. Here, too, certain theoretical trends can be seen. The processes that mediate aggression are described in terms of affect, cognition and activation or arousal. Cognition has become the major process on which most mediational models are built, with affect and arousal as important parallel mechanisms. The nature of the cognitive emphasis has changed somewhat from what it once was. In the 1980s, the cognitive analysis of aggression was based mainly on the attribution of meaning to the provoking event. More recently the role of cognition has been couched in terms of such matters as the accuracy of social information processing, with processing deficits serving as the underlying antecedent of aggression in provoking situations, and the mechanisms by which environmental conditions prime aggressive thoughts, feelings and dispositions to act. The level of cognitive analysis has therefore become more detailed and has, as a consequence, increased in predictive power.

The important function of background, or moderator, variables in aggression occupies a central position in current research and theory. The primary moderator variables identified in the literature are sex, biological inheritance, socio-cultural background and personality. In the first chapter of this edition, a careful distinction is made between three sets of variables that make up the antecedents of aggression: the provoking situations, the background moderators which temper the reaction to these situations and the means of aggressing that are available to the aggrieved individual. Understanding the causes of human aggression requires that we keep these three classes of variables conceptually separated, that we recognize the ways in which they interact and that we recognize the ways in which they are embedded in a theory of aggression. Popular accounts of spectacular violent events, like mass murders in schools and restaurants, frequently confound these separate contributors, with some observers blaming social conditions, others citing individual differences or the mental instability of aggressors and still others concentrating on the easy availability of guns. There is no question that all of these factors are involved, but an accurate analysis of the event requires that each must be seen in terms of its proper function and not as an alternative 'cause' that explains everything.

The study of the relation of theories of aggression to the solution of practical problems represents another major emphasis in current work. Increasing attention is now being devoted to the careful study of such everyday concerns as spouse abuse, sexual violence against women and bullying in school. Interest also remains high in the extent to which the mass entertainment media purvey the symbols of violence to the public and in whether these symbols evoke aggression in observers. In the past this problem has been construed as involving only the effects of violence in motion pictures and television, but in the past decade public concern has focused upon two related phenomena: the rapidly expanding market for video games, many of which present violent content to the player, and the rising tide of violence among spectators at rough and aggressive sporting events. In all these areas of applied research, we now see explanations of the findings presented in terms of the theories and conceptual models that have been developed through more basic research. In fact, one of the more promising developments in the study of aggression is the degree to which sophisticated theoretical models are now invoked in discussions of such practical matters as the role of temperature in aggression, the causes of domestic violence and what happens to people when they watch mayhem on their TV screens.

This second edition of *Human Aggression* consists of eight chapters. In the first ('Introduction to the study of aggression'), certain matters of general importance are discussed, e.g. the meaning of aggression, the methods by which it is studied and the background provided by biological inheritance and social learning. The second chapter ('The provocation of aggression') goes into the situational circumstances that provoke affective aggressive behaviour. These circumstances include frustration, painful stimulation, interpersonal attack and such environmental conditions as intense heat or cold and uncontrollable noise. A new conceptual model that links all these antecedents to changes in negative affect is described in detail.

Chapter 3 ('Intervening processes in aggression') describes the intervening processes that mediate the connection between the provocation and the aggressive response. It is divided into two sections, the first dealing with anger and the second with cognitive processing. Included are such topics as excitation transfer, anger as a social construct, the attributional processes in aggression, the social information processing model and the role of social scripts in aggression. Background variables are discussed in Chapter 4 ('Moderator variables in aggression'). Because the genetic-biological inheritance of the person is discussed in Chapter 1, the treatment of moderators in Chapter 4 covers sex, personality and socio-cultural background.

Chapters 5, 6 and 7 are devoted to a discussion of some of the ways in which the theories and concepts reviewed in the first four chapters have been applied to aggressive behaviour in natural settings. In Chapter 5 ('Aggression in life and society'), four topics are reviewed. The first is violence in intimate relationships, with an emphasis on the violence of men towards female partners. The second is sexual violence against women. The third is the effect of aggression within the family, including the intergenerational 'cycle of violence', the effects of parental fighting on children and some of the roots of delinquency in early family experiences. The fourth is bullying among schoolchildren, including some of the social aspects of bullying and certain of the long-range outcomes.

Chapter 6 ('Aggression in Entertainment') organizes the evidence from laboratory and non-laboratory research regarding the effects of observing violence in the cinema and on television according to a number of variables and processes that mediate these effects. The chapter also includes summaries of evidence on the effects of violent video games on game players and a discussion of some of the effects of observing rough and aggressive sporting events. Chapter 7 ('Hostility, health and adjustment') examines two issues. One is the effect of anger and hostility upon physical health, including such questions as whether the expression or repression of aggressive emotions can have adverse effects on the cardio-vascular system. The second issue is that of whether aggressing when angry is followed by a period of less aggression, according to the familiar catharsis hypothesis.

The final chapter ('Postscript') is a short summary of some of the main themes of the book and a suggestion of where the study of aggression appears to be headed.

This book was written for classroom use. It is addressed primarily to undergraduate students who have had at least an introductory course in psychology and are therefore acquainted with the fundamentals of the field. At the undergraduate level it could serve as the basic textbook for a course. Because of the general orientation of the book to basic research on aggression, it may also be useful for graduate students who desire an overview of that research. At the graduate level it will probably best serve the function of a primer used in connection with primary source mater-ials. Students using the book as either a textbook or a secondary sourcebook may find useful the annotated references listed as suggestions for further reading at the end of each chapter. It should also be noted that, although the major focus of the book is on a social psychological approach to human aggression, it also contains material of relevance for the areas of physiological, developmental and personality psychology.

No concerted attempt is made in this book to recommend strategies for the control or elimination of aggression. The book is intended only for purposes of introducing the reader to what is known about human aggression at the present time from research that has been conducted on the problem. Thus, there is extensive discussion of the results of studies but no chapter on public policy. My intention is to inform the reader. It is hoped that any decisions that are eventually made with respect to the problem of human aggression, and what can be done about it, will be based on the information that research has given us.

Russell G. Geen
Columbia, Missouri, USA

ONE

INTRODUCTION TO THE STUDY OF AGGRESSION

Few people would deny that 'aggression' is commonplace in contemporary society. For some, such as those living in the Middle East, the Balkans, parts of central Africa and any maximum security prison in the United States, aggression and **violence** are experienced daily and in intensely personal ways. For others the phenomenon is known mainly in indirect ways, such as through motion pictures and television. However, even those fortunate enough to have been spared the direct experience of lethal violence may occasionally encounter something perceived to be aggression in a less harmful form, like verbal insult, rough physical contact or hostile rejection. Aggression, whether harmful to life and limb or merely painful to the ego, seems to be a real and important part of the human condition.

The broad and inclusive way in which the word has been used, however, makes the systematic study of aggression difficult. To put the matter simply: does it make sense to use the same word to refer to such dissimilar events as a gangland murder, the bombing of a restaurant, a fight at a football match and a cutting remark at a cocktail party? Even if the term is used only in casual everyday speech, its usefulness is obviously limited by the numerous motives and forms of expression that characterize 'aggressive' behaviour. When we attempt to use that word in scientific discourse, the problem becomes even more serious. Science depends on precision and clarity of definitions. From that standpoint, we might do well to forget about a unitary concept of 'aggression' and to search instead for functional relationships between specific acts and their equally specific causes. The various behaviours now subsumed by the word 'aggression' could undoubtedly be studied as individual phenomena defined in terms of their own antecedent conditions, intervening processes, and outcomes. Nevertheless, such studies would obscure the possibility that the aggressive behaviours noted above, however different they may seem, possess some common features. If we are to make any sense of the whole idea of aggression, it is these features that we must seek. We must therefore begin by defining our term.

DEFINITION OF AGGRESSION

Problems of definition

One might think that people would be in substantial agreement on defining something as important and pervasive as aggression, but such is not the case. Probably most people, including psychologists, would agree in general with the definition give by Buss (1961: 1): aggression is 'a response that delivers noxious stimuli to another organism'. Certainly what we ordinarily call aggression does involve aversive stimulation of some sort and intensity, whether it be in the form of a bullet, a bomb fragment, a physical blow, or some more subtle act like an insult or an undeserved criticism. We do not encounter the real problem of stating what aggression is until we attempt to formulate a definition that goes beyond simple harmdoing behaviour. Aggression is not as simple as a purely behavioural definition would indicate. Other elements must be added, and these elements create certain complexities.

Intent to harm

One construct that most people would probably consider necessary to an adequate definition of aggression is *intent* to harm the victim. The notion of intention is explicit in the definition of aggression given by one influential group of psychologists: 'Aggression is . . . an act whose goal-response is injury to an organism' (Dollard *et al.* 1939: 11). Use of the term 'goal-response' indicates motivation and striving, so that aggression becomes the end result in a deliberate series of actions. Dollard and his colleagues specifically rule out the possibility that aggression can be the accidental consequence of behaviour lacking intent to harm: 'One person may injure another by sheer accident. Such acts are not aggression, because they are not goal-responses' (Dollard *et al.* 1939: 11). The idea that intent is required in aggression has been dismissed by some on the grounds that it is a mental concept that lacks objectivity and defies rigorous analysis (e.g. Buss 1961). However, despite the problems that it raises, the concept of intent seems unavoidable. For example, a team of firefighters attempting to rescue someone trapped in a burning building may cause the person pain, but the harm done is hardly deliberate and may even be necessary to save the person's life. The firefighters' behaviour would therefore not be considered aggressive by most observers.

Motivation of the victim

A second characteristic of aggression that should go into a definition has been stated by Baron and Richardson: 'Aggression is any form of behavior directed toward the goal of harming or injuring another living being who is motivated to avoid such treatment' (Baron and Richardson 1994: 7). The unwilling participation of the victim is often overlooked in discussions of aggression, perhaps because it is difficult to imagine situations in which a person does not make at least some effort to escape or avoid being attacked. Still, situations do arise in which a person may tolerate, and even seek out, punishment to atone for guilt. In such a case the willing recipient would probably not accuse the punishing agent of being an aggressor. Baron and Richardson (1994) also consider suicide to be harmful behaviour that is obviously not resisted by the victim, and they therefore conclude that suicide cannot be classified as aggression.

A working definition of aggression

With all of the foregoing in mind, we can now suggest a working definition of human aggression: aggression is the delivery of an aversive stimulus from one person to another, with intent to harm and with an expectation of causing such harm, when the other person is motivated to escape or avoid the stimulus. It is admitted that this definition may not cover all examples and that it can be attacked on several points. Nor does it even begin to deal with many of the variables involved in aggression. For instance, it does not mention the role played by emotions in many aggressive actions. It does not account for the complex cognitive judgements that often precede aggression. It does not take into account the fact that aggression is often reciprocal, or that it may sometimes serve as a valuable 'safety valve' for a person experiencing extreme levels of anger. These and many other such problems all impinge upon a basic definition of aggression, yet they go beyond a simple one and in fact comprise the many variables that constitute much of the material of this book.

The form of aggression

When they hear the word 'aggression' most people probably tend first to think of physical force – a fist-fight, an assault with a weapon, a loud verbal retort or some other form of intense and punitive action enacted in the course of conflict between two people. Actually, according to the definition we have adopted, aggression may be carried out in *any* behaviour actuated by an intent to harm another person against that person's wishes. Spreading vicious gossip about someone in hopes of ruining that person's reputation would be considered aggression. Likewise, damaging or destroying another's property can be a highly effective way of aggressing against that person. Even something as subtle and controlled as a social snub can be a powerful source of harm to the victim, a harm that is clearly intended by the person delivering it.

AFFECTIVE AND INSTRUMENTAL AGGRESSION

The examples of aggression that have been given so far suggest many different kinds of aggressive behaviour inasmuch as they reveal varying causes and motives. It is common in the study of aggression to identify such varieties of assaultive behaviour on the basis of antecedents and intervening processes. Thus we discriminate among such actions as 'angry aggression', 'instrumental aggression' and 'learned', 'imitative' or 'biogenic' aggression because these behaviours differ from each other in important ways regarding their underlying motives. In the animal kingdom, several kinds of aggression are routinely observed, such as maternal, territorial and predatory. Among humans we may also note certain distinctions, such as angry retaliation, self-defence, calm and cold-blooded retribution and violence carried out for purposes of coercion, punishment and profit. Nevertheless, it is customary among those who study human aggression to classify aggressive behaviour into two categories: angry or **affective aggression**, in which harming the victim is the main motive for the act; and **instrumental aggression**, which may or may not involve strong emotions but is motivated by concerns more important to the aggressor than the harmdoing itself.

Affective aggression

Aggression is often accompanied by strong negative emotional states. The emotion that we call anger is usually aroused by some **provocation**. Anger is most often thought of as an intervening condition that instigates, and then guides, **affective aggressive** behaviour aimed primarily at injuring the provoking person. It is accompanied by distinctive patterns of activity in the central and autonomic nervous systems, including activation of the hypothalamus, increased blood flow to the musculature, heightened blood pressure and pulse rate, pupillary dilation and decreased flow of blood to the viscera (Johansson 1981).

The idea that a flash of anger can inspire retaliatory aggression is easy enough to grasp. Sometimes, however, retaliation comes so long after provocation that we find it difficult to attribute the action to anger, an emotion that is relatively short-lived for most people, even though the retaliatory aspect of the anger is still apparent. Frijda (1994) has commented on the possible emotional state involved in this sort of 'delayed-response' affective aggression. It has many of the properties of anger: it is a state of impulse, it disposes the person to action, it is often accompanied by bodily **arousal**, it can become a preoccupation that takes attention away from other matters. But it differs from anger in other ways, one of which is the often extended duration between provocation and response. Frijda suggests that this condition is not an emotion, *per se*, but a complex cognitive state having close links to emotion, that has grown out some purer emotional state. Such a state may be labelled a 'sentiment': the emotion of anger towards the other person becomes in time transformed into the sentiment of *hatred*, which outlives the original anger. Long-term feuds and grudges represent cases in which people are aggressed against because they are hated, not because they have done anything in particular to elicit anger in the aggressor. Frijda's suggestions add an important and usually overlooked dimension to the analysis of affective aggression and indicate that future study of motives for retaliation is in order.

Instrumental aggression

Behaviour need not have a strong emotional basis to be aggressive, however. People often attack others with intent to harm but without necessarily feeling any malice towards them; the aggression is simply a means to some other end. One such end is self-defence, which most courts of law recognize as a valid justification for acts of violence. Aggressive military action is usually carried out for control of territory or to dissuade the enemy from attacking one's own troops. Another type of instrumental aggression is the attempt to establish **coercive power** over others through violence or the threat of violence (Tedeschi and Felson 1994), Finally, in one of the most widely cited research studies in recent times, Milgram (1963) showed that people were capable of committing acts of violence against other human beings simply in obedience to commands from a person with authority. It must be noted that the distinction between affective and instrumental aggression is not a rigorous one. The two kinds of aggression are not mutually exclusive, and some acts of aggression have both affective and instrumental properties. For example, a mother who becomes exasperated at her child's behaviour and uses corporal punishment may be motivated to modify the child's behaviour (an instrumental use of aggression) while still reacting to that behaviour with anger. For purposes of understanding her behaviour, one must determine which of the two categories describes her *principal* motivational state and analyse the relevant variables accordingly.

Proactive and reactive aggression

A number of recent studies of aggression draw a distinction between **reactive** and **proactive aggression** (e.g. Crick and Dodge 1996). The first of these terms refers to aggressive behaviour that is enacted in response to provocation, such as an attack or an insult, and it is manifested in both self-defensive and angry actions. The latter term refers to aggression that is initiated without apparent provocation, such as we see in bullying behaviour. Such behaviour is not evoked by anger, **hostility** or the need to defend oneself, but by other motives that relate to obtaining goods, asserting power, assuring the approval of reference groups and other such goals. Reactive and proactive aggression are the equivalent of what earlier theorists called affective and instrumental aggression. The affective–instrumental (or reactive–proactive) differentiation will come up in certain specific contexts in this book, and the reader should bear in mind the differences between the two kinds of aggression.

The remainder of this book is devoted primarily to a discussion of the processes involved in affective aggression. This emphasis is in no way intended to imply that instrumental aggression is unimportant. However, it has not been studied in nearly the same depth as has affective aggression. There is, for example, no large body of literature analysing the variables involved when one person hurts another for money, nor do we have extensive data from controlled studies on the mediators of self-defence. Some studies have begun to inquire into the antecedents of each type of aggression, and they will be cited. On the other hand, we have a great deal of information on affective aggression and the processes that contribute to it.

The two factors in affective aggression

Eventually, all discussions of aggression get around to causes. Why do some people hurt, cripple or kill others in contexts that in one way or another involve angry reactions to real or imagined provocations? The alleged causes of human aggression tend to be varied and complex, and discussions of them are most often inconclusive. Consider an example. On 20 April 1999, at 11:25 in the morning, two male students entered their high school in Littleton, Colorado, armed with sawn-off shotguns, semi-automatic weapons and homemade pipe bombs. After firing an estimated 900 rounds at fellow students, staff members and an armed security guard, and tossing numerous bombs, the two ended the ordeal by killing themselves. In all, twelve students and one teacher died in the attack, in addition to the killers.

Almost immediately, the news media began reporting opinions on the causes of the mass murder expressed by citizens' groups, newspaper and television commentators, professional psychologists and political figures. The imputed causes were predictably variable. Groups that promote legislation for control of guns cited the easy availability of weapons in the United States. Some psychologists noted that the killers were part of a student subculture that was rejected and ridiculed by their more popular schoolmates, and that they had on occasion expressed hatred for such class 'stars'. It was also noted that the two harboured racist and neo-Nazi sentiments, and that they had taunted one of their victims, an African-American, with a racial epithet before shooting him. Conservative religious groups traced the killing to a breakdown in traditional values and family structure. This social breakdown was attributed not only to a decline in parental supervision but also to such mass cultural effects as violent song lyrics, motion pictures, television and video games. It was also noted that one of the students had obtained detailed information on the manufacture of bombs over the Internet. Many people tended to emphasize one or the other of these 'causes' to the relative exclusion of the others, and to generalize their conclusions far beyond the details of the case.

As we review these antecedents of the Littleton massacre, note that they can be grouped into three categories. Only one of the them is recognizable as a true *provocation* capable in itself of evoking an aggressive response – the insulting and ridiculing behaviour of some of the killers' classmates. Two other explanations are actually related more to *methods* of aggression than to causes – the easy procurement of guns and access to the information necessary to manufacture bombs. The third category pertains to certain variables that may have increased the likelihood that the two killers would behave aggressively under provoking conditions, i.e. what we might call *background* variables: their history of exposure to symbols of violence in the mass media and electronic games, their family situations, their attitudes towards violence, their general values, their personalities. None of these latter variables in itself guarantees the commission of overt aggression, but, by the same token, no provocation is likely to make a person a murderer unless that person is disposed by these background conditions to become one. And, finally, it is obvious that the likelihood of aggressive behaviour is reduced if the means of aggressing are not readily available.

Theorizing on the nature and causes of human aggression must begin with the recognition of the distinction among the three classes of variable: provocation, method and background or disposition. Society will not solve any of its problems with violence by treating the three as if they were equivalent. For one thing, the three relate to different time-frames for the control of violent behaviour. It is probable that the best long-range strategy for controlling and reducing violence would be the creation of a national culture in which aggression does not enter to such a large degree into social and personal value systems and in which impressionable children are not bombarded with violent amusements and entertainments. It is also probable that greater efforts to promote tolerance and mutual respect across racial, ethnic and social class boundaries might decrease the prevalence of the sort of rage that motivated the young men in Colorado. Few people will argue with such propositions for long-range reforms. However, it seems inarguable that the simplest *immediate* strategy for prevention of such violence is to reduce drastically the number of guns in the hands of the general population. It is legitimate to argue for changes in the value system of the country and to advocate greater mutual love and respect, but it is also disingenuous to set up these goals as alternatives to gun control when we are talking about the practical reduction of violence.

Psychologists are, however, more concerned with isolating the causes of aggression than with engineering the means of control. When we speak of the causes of aggression, independent of the relative ease with which it is carried out, we are dealing with two of the classes of variable mentioned above – those pertaining to the social and personal background of the individual, and those pertaining to provocative and anger-inducing situations. This book is organized along lines of such a two-process approach. Such an approach is admittedly only a preliminary statement about affective aggression. It is, furthermore, simple to the point of triviality. However, we gain something by using such a framework for aggression. One sometimes hears that because aggression is part of 'human nature' there is little that can be done about it. Therefore, the argument goes, society should forget social reform and other ameliorative measures that are addressed, among other things, to the control and reduction of violence. We do not deny that the potential for aggression is present in the constitution of human beings. However, by defining aggression as a reaction to situations, we can have some reason for hope that proper social action may at least limit, if not remove altogether, the likelihood of violence. In addition, we can seek to create social conditions that promote behaviour that is incompatible with aggression.

On the other hand, one sometimes hears that all aggression is the result of bad social conditions, cultural deprivations, unhappy childhood experiences and so on. Such arguments tend to remove all responsibility for violence from the perpetrators and to lay the blame entirely on others.

Such arguments do not explain why most people who experience the various conditions thought to be the sole causes of violence are not highly aggressive. We would argue that such people, though instigated to aggress as much as others, do not possess the background characteristics of aggressors. If such is the case, society's task is to discover the conditions under which such relatively unaggressive tendencies are fostered and to seek to implement them more widely.

ORIGINS AND ANTECEDENTS OF AGGRESSION

Considerable controversy exists over the origins of aggression in humans. In this controversy we see repeated the old issue of nature versus nurture in psychology, with many of the old questions raised again. Is human behaviour the result of genetically inherited biological drives and impulses or is it acquired through experience and learning? Is aggression a normal part of human behaviour carried over from our primate ancestors or is it an aberration of human nature originating in social and environmental conditions? Does belief in a biological basis for aggression preclude attempts at social control of violence? Are conflict and war inevitable? Evidence can be adduced for both the biological and the behaviouristic explanations of aggression. There is little doubt that much of human aggression is learned. Behavioural biologists do not deny this. However, neither can it be denied that humans share with lower animals certain dispositions to aggress that are transmitted genetically. In the following two sections we review some of the evidence bearing on these viewpoints.

Biological bases of aggression

Behaviour genetics

The possibility that some human aggression may be attributable to hereditary factors is supported by a growing number of studies. At one time, especially in the United States when behaviourism dominated psychology, few psychologists believed that human behaviour had hereditary origins. It was practically a truism that all behaviour is learned. Nowadays this premise is not as widely accepted. Hereditary aggression in lower animals has never been seriously questioned, and in recent years the idea that at least some part of human aggressiveness is inherited has been gaining increasingly in acceptance.

An obvious problem that arises in the study of the genetic bases of aggression in humans is methodological. Human reproduction cannot be controlled through selective breeding in the same way as that of lower organisms, so alternative means of analysing genetic influence must be found. One such method involves comparison between pairs of twins. Twin studies analyse similarities between members of identical (**monozygotic**) and non-identical, or fraternal (**dizygotic**), pairs. The method rests on the fact that whereas dizygotic twins share a common

Table 1.1 Correlations of twin type (mono- or dizygotic) with personality variables

Scale	Monozygotic	Dizygotic
Altruism	0.53	0.25
Empathy	0.54	0.20
Nurturance	0.49	0.14
Aggressiveness	0.40	0.04
Assertiveness	0.52	0.20

Source: Rushton *et al.* (1986).

environment but are not identical in genetic make-up, monozygotic twins share a common environment and are also identical in heredity. If a trait has some hereditary basis, therefore, it should be shared by monozygotic twins to a greater extent than by members of dizygotic pairs. Correlations of the trait between pairs of twins of each type are compared, and evidence of higher correlations among monozygotics is taken as evidence of some heritability associated with the trait.

The evidence from twin studies on the role of inherited biological factors in human aggression is mixed and inconclusive. The most convincing studies have been those in which comparisons have been made on the basis of self-reports of aggressiveness on personality inventories (e.g. McGue *et al.* 1993). In one such investigation, Rushton *et al.* (1986) administered questionnaires assessing five personality traits to more than 500 pairs of adult twins. Three of the traits (altruism, empathy and nurturance) were assumed to be negatively related, and two (aggressiveness and assertiveness) positively related, to aggressive behaviour. The results (Table 1.1) showed that correlations were higher among monozygotic twins than among dizygotic pairs for each of the five traits. Similar findings of heritability have been reported in studies involving methods other than personality inventories. In one such study, mothers' descriptions of the behaviour of their twin children revealed a significant heritability factor for aggressiveness (Ghodsian-Carpey and Baker 1987).

On the negative side, several studies involving self-report inventories have yielded either small heritability effects or no such effects at all (e.g. Carmelli *et al.* 1990). In most such cases, inventories different from the ones showing positive effects were used, raising the possibility that heritability effects may depend to some extent on the way on which aggressiveness is defined and measured. Nor is the twin study method the only one available for assessment of heritability. Another method that has been used involves assessment of similarities in aggressive behaviour between adopted children and their biological parents compared to similarities between such children and their adoptive parents. Mednick *et al.* (1984) compared the criminal behaviours of adopted persons with similar behaviours in their biological parents and found a high level of concordance between the two for non-violent crimes but not for violent ones.

The picture that we get from research on heritability of aggression is therefore not clear. In a review of 24 studies covering a wide range of methods, Miles and Carey (1997) found that evidence for heritability of aggression depends on several variables, such as the age of the sample and whether aggression is quantified in terms of parent- and self-report or observation of behaviour. Outcomes also seem to depend on how aggression is defined. We still do not have sufficient evidence from any type of study to draw strong conclusions. Replications across samples and research programmes, using similar operations and methods, are badly needed. For the time being, however, the behaviour genetic method has shown that heritability undoubtedly plays *some* part in human aggression (Plomin *et al.* 1990).

Ethology and evolutionary biology

Explanations of human aggression based on the science of behavioural biology, or **ethology**, can be traced back at least to Konrad Lorenz's 1966 book *On Aggression*. Emphasizing the place of human beings within the animal kingdom, Lorenz explained aggression as behaviour triggered by specific external stimuli following a progressive accumulation of aggression-specific energy within the person. Aggression is followed by a cathartic decrease in such energy and the beginning of a new build-up. Although direct evidence for such processes had been obtained through the observation of aggressive behaviour in non-human species, some ethologists have argued that similar processes form the basis for aggression in humans. Evidence adduced in support of this claim is usually based on the method of analogy, i.e. the demonstration that certain patterns of behaviour in one species are similar to patterns in the actions of another because both have evolved under similar environmental demands (Rajecki 1983).

More recently, students of animal behaviour have argued that inferences about human aggression can be drawn from the study of animals that are closely related to humans in terms of genetic endowment, specifically primates. For example, studies of primate organization have shown that social competence is closely tied to an animal's development of the capacity for using aggression appropriately (Higley *et al.* 1994). To be socially competent, the animal must learn sometimes to inhibit aggression, such as when the young male is encountered by a powerful and dominant adult, but at other times to express aggression rather than to withdraw from challenges. The conditions under which the young primate is reared play an important role in determining whether such discriminations are learned. Monkeys that are reared either in isolation or among peers only, without maternal contact, generally show deficits in this sort of learning and, as a consequence, often manifest socially inappropriate aggression. The upshot of this behaviour is that they tend to be socially rejected. Similar rejection of offspring because of either aggressiveness or victimization by others has also been shown among humans (e.g. Dishion *et al.* 1994).

Another biological approach to human aggression emphasizes the evolutionary history of the human species (Geary 1998). The case for this approach has been made primarily in a series of studies by Daly and his associates. For example, these investigators identify male sexual jealousy as a major factor in homicidal violence among young men. Such jealousy is a consequence of the evolution of certain psychological tendencies that enhance the male's confidence in his paternity of offspring borne by the woman or women with whom he has sexual relations. The need to have confidence that alien males have not fathered the offspring motivates the male not only to dominate and control the female (as noted below) but also to compete aggressively with other males for available resources that furnish reproductive opportunities. In modern society such resources are manifested not in nesting sites or feeding territories, as they are in lower animals, but in intangibles such as status and social power. The displays of aggressive *machismo* shown, for example, in youth gangs represent manifestations of status- and power-driven behaviour. Daly and Wilson (1988a) apply this rationale to explaining the commonly observed finding of high rates of homicide among urban men in their twenties. Given an evolved propensity for combative competition, which should be at maximum strength in the years of greatest reproductive power, even minor provocations may elicit violence from such men. The same theoretical reasoning is also used to explain why men kill women more frequently than women kill men. 'Male sexual proprietariness', Daly and Wilson (1988b: 521) conclude, 'is the dominant issue in marital violence. In studies of "motives" of spousal homicide, the leading identified substantive issue is invariably "jealousy" . . . the husband's proprietary concern with his wife's fidelity or her intention to quit the marriage led him to initiate the violence in an overwhelming majority of cases.'

Arguments from evolutionary biology have generally been ignored or dismissed by social psychologists. One reason is that social psychologists traditionally have considered socio-cultural variables to be more powerful determinants of aggression in humans than psycho-evolutionary ones. In response to this objection, some evolutionary biologists insist that the development of human culture is itself shaped by evolved constraints. Culture, according to these observers, is the product of 'the psychology of the culture-bearing organism' (Daly and Wilson 1989: 108), and this psychology is shaped by evolutionary history. Another source of social psychologists' resistance to evolutionary proposals is the impression that acceptance of aggression and violence as 'natural' behaviours necessitates acceptance or endorsement of such actions, an allegation specifically denied by evolutionists (see Thornhill and Thornhill 1992 for a detailed discussion of this issue). Some social psychologists are also sceptical of the evidence that has been adduced for the evolutionary argument to date (e.g. Baron and Richardson 1994: 19–20). It is too soon to tell whether psycho-evolutionists and social psychologists will eventually find much common ground.

Hormones and aggression

The importance of androgenic **hormones – testosterone** being perhaps the best known – in aggression among non-human animals has long been recognized. These hormones have two effects on animals that may influence aggression. First, they can influence the bodily development and the structure and function of the nervous system in the fetus prior to birth.

Such influences are called *organizing* effects. Second, they can cause changes in the moods and behaviours of animals after birth, outcomes that are called *activating* effects. Despite evidence that testosterone activity has been shown to facilitate aggression between males of several vertebrate species and figures, especially at the time of reproductive activity (Archer 1988), whether similar effects occur in human males is still being debated. Some investigators deny that testosterone has any important function in human aggression, insisting that the dominance of social and cognitive factors in human behaviour outweigh any influence that hormones may have (e.g. Campbell *et al.* 1997).

Despite such disclaimers, there is evidence that the aggression of humans shows some hormonal effects similar to those seen in animals. Only a few studies with humans have investigated the effects of prenatal administration of androgens on aggression in childhood and the scant evidence that is available is mixed. Given such ambiguous findings, Archer (1991) concluded that we have little evidence pointing to a possible organizing role of prenatal androgens on aggression. Evidence of an activating function for testosterone in aggressive in humans has been somewhat more impressive (J. Archer 1994). For example, research by Dabbs and his associates has tended to show a reliable positive relationship between testosterone level and aggression in varying samples of males, such as prison inmates (Dabbs *et al.* 1987) and combat veterans (Dabbs and Morris 1990). Hormonal activity in males has also been shown to be correlated with ratings of aggressiveness made by observers or by the aggressors themselves. Susman *et al.* (1987) found that in a sample of adolescent boys the levels of several hormones were positively correlated with descriptions of the boys, made by their mothers, as 'delinquent', 'nasty' and 'rebellious', while Gladue (1991) found that men with relatively high levels of testosterone activity were more likely to describe themselves in aggressive terms than men showing lower levels.

One question that is implicit in all this research is whether hormones raise levels of general aggressiveness or instead create a higher level of readiness to aggress in response to sufficient provocation. For instance, does a high level of testosterone activity make a person more likely to pick fights with others or to seek opportunities for behaving violently, or does it merely increase the likelihood that the person will aggress when attacked? Several studies have shown that levels of testosterone may predispose a person to behave aggressively in provoking situations. For example, Olweus *et al.* (1980) found a significant association between testosterone and self-reported physical and verbal aggression in a sample of adolescent boys, and noted that the relationship was more characteristic for scale items that described aggression as a response to provocation than for those items in which aggression was described in other ways. A series of studies carried out in Holland by Van Goozen and her associates has provided clear evidence that testosterone activity is related to reactive aggression but not to overall aggressive behaviour. In these studies, testosterone level was experimentally manipulated among persons undergoing sex-change treatments. Administration of testosterone to a sample of female-to-male (FM) transsexuals was accompanied by no change in general self-reported aggressive behaviour, but by significant increases in self-reported proneness to respond aggressively to a series of hypothetical conflict situations (Van Goozen *et al.* 1994). Corresponding relations between anger proneness and testosterone were found by Van Goozen *et al.* (1995a) in a study comparing FM transsexuals undergoing androgen therapy with a sample of male-to-female (MF) transsexuals that was being given anti-androgenic agents. The clearest finding of the investigation was an increase in anger proneness among FM transsexuals following treatments, and a corresponding decrease in anger proneness among MFs, with anger proneness again defined in terms of reactions to specific hypothetical situations. Hormone activity has been shown to influence anger even in situations where provocation is not experienced but is merely imagined. Evidence of greater anger in FM transsexuals than in MF and female comparison groups was found in an experiment in which subjects' feelings were assessed after they had role-played a hypothetical frustrating situation (Van Goozen *et al.* 1995b).

Correlations between hormone activity and aggression are usually interpreted as showing that hormone level is the antecedent variable and aggression the outcome. However, some studies indicate that cause and effect may work in the opposite direction, and that testosterone level may sometimes be increased by experiences related to aggression, specifically those in which competitive and assertive behaviour occurs. Research with primates has shown that the level of male testosterone changes as an animal's status changes, rising when the male achieves or defends a dominant position in the group and falling when he is dominated by another male. In a study designed to extend this phenomenon to humans, Mazur and Lamb (1980) found that the winners in tennis matches showed increased levels of testosterone during the hour just after victory, whereas the losers showed decreased levels, provided that the victory had been clear and convincing. Winners of closer matches did not show a similar increase in testosterone. Comparable findings reported by Salvador *et al.* (1987) showed that young male judo competitors who had recently been members of a winning team displayed higher testosterone levels than did non-competing controls, whereas members of a team that had lost showed lower levels than controls.

Furthermore, the chief cause of increased hormonal activity in such athletic settings may not be the high level of activity that they contain, but the inter-male competition that they engender. Gladue *et al.* (1989) found that even winners of a sedentary and relatively non-physical laboratory reaction-time task showed higher testosterone levels following competition than losers. Gladue and his colleagues therefore showed that the effect found by Mazur and Lamb and by Salvador *et al.* is not restricted to strenuous athletic competition and, moreover, that the mere perception of victory is sometimes sufficient to influence testosterone level.

It should be clear from this brief survey that no simple causal relationship exists between levels of androgens and aggression in human males. Testosterone activity appears to be related to competitiveness, striving for mastery and achievement of a dominant status, and all these activities are often associated with conflict and aggression. However, hormonal activity also appears to predict aggression and related actions best when situational conditions make interpersonal conflict and provocation most likely. Thus, hormonal activity would seem to be best regarded as a disposing or 'background' variable in aggression elicited by aversive situational conditions.

Brain mechanisms

The role of certain brain structures in aggression among lower animals has long been known to researchers, leading to the supposition that similar brain mechanisms may contribute to aggression in humans. Two structures have been particularly implicated – the **limbic system** and the cerebral cortex. The limbic system is a collection of interrelated neural ganglia that have direct links to both higher and lower centres of the nervous system. It is a phylogenetically 'old' part of the brain, and it is closely related to emotional experience. In the case of anger, for instance, centres in the limbic system receive inputs from the sensory systems regarding provocations, and these inputs immediately initiate primitive anger reactions. Subsequent interactions between the limbic system and higher centres may refine and direct the emotional state, possibly leading to aggression, but the origin of the emotion is at a lower level. Panksepp (1998: 42) makes this point in the context of a general model of emotion:

> Although it is self-evident that external events provoke our feelings, emotions actually arise from the activities of ancient brain processes that we have inherited from ancestral species. External stimuli only trigger prepared states of the nervous system. The function of ancient emotional systems is to energize and guide organisms in their interactions with the world, but their power arises from their intrinsic nature in the brain.

One approach to studying the involvement of the limbic system in aggression considers the activity of the central neurotransmitter serotonin, or 5-hydroxytryptamine (5-HT). Diminished levels of serotonin have been found to be correlates of reactive aggressiveness in humans (Coccaro 1992). The apparent reason for this is that impoverished levels of 5-HT activity in the nervous system lead to both a heightened tendency to react actively to aversive stimuli – such as by fleeing or attacking another organism – and a decreased ability to control activity under such conditions. Eichelman (1995) has identified the first of these outcomes as the basis for the finding that physical pain can induce aggression towards a bystander (e.g. Berkowitz *et al.* 1981). The latter outcome underlies the ability to respond to a threat or provocation with passive avoidance, i.e. by avoiding any activity that could lead to punishment. Eichelman (1995) regards these two tendencies, both related to serotonin depletion, as the physiological bases for 'impulsive' aggression. Rats that have undergone lesions to the septal nuclei, a part of the limbic system located in the forebrain, reveal marked increases in shock-induced aggression (Eichelman 1971), a finding which suggests that the limbic system is involved in serotonin regulation and that reactive aggression is activated by alterations in serotonin-mediated impulse control. Any lesions in the septal region would therefore interfere with serotonin regulation and predispose an animal (or person) to become

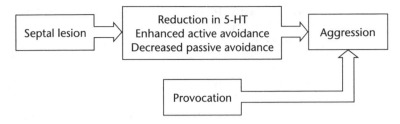

Figure 1.1 Hypothetical model of effects of septal lesions on affective aggression.
Source: based on Eichelman (1995).

more aggressively reactive to provocation (Figure 1.1). In addition, treatments with drugs that enhance or inhibit serotonin activity have been shown to produce effects on aggressiveness that are consistent with the general model described here. One such treatment involves manipulation of the person's level of plasma tryptophan, a precursor of 5-HT. Restriction or limitation of tryptophan will result in a relatively low level of 5-HT activity and should therefore be associated with subsequent high levels of aggressiveness. In a study showing this effect, Finn *et al.* (1998) fed a mixture of amino acids to fasting male subjects, with some of the subjects receiving a nutritionally balanced mixture and the others receiving a mixture devoid of tryptophan. Among subjects who had shown a high level of pre-treatment hostility, the exclusion of tryptophan from the diet led to levels of hostility higher than those shown by subjects who had taken the balanced mixture. No effects of tryptophan manipulation were found among normally less hostile subjects.

The activity of the cerebral cortex also plays an important part in human aggression. As is discussed more fully in the next chapter, increasing attention has been paid in recent years to the importance of cognitive processes in the relation of provocation to aggression. These cognitive processes are mediated by the activity of the cortex. They involve awareness of the provocation and the meaning attributed to it, the judgements that are made concerning the motives of the person responsible, the recall of strategies used in the past for dealing with such situations and executive strategies for the enactment of suitable behaviours. The end result of this complicated processing is that the person does not simply react to provocation at the primitive 'old brain' level but instead controls, modulates and elaborates the response in such a way that it is more suitable to the social situation in which it occurs.

Now, it should follow from this that any damage or dysfunction occurring in the cerebral cortex could, by disrupting the normal flow of cognitive activity, interrupt these controlling and modulating effects and leave the outcome of provocation to the lower and more primitive centres. A growing body of evidence supports this conclusion. Two types of evidence may be cited. The first comes from studies of brain imaging by means of computer-assisted **tomography** and positron emission tomography (PET), a technique that produces images of the brain from which functions such as cerebral blood flow and glucose metabolism can be inferred. In one study involving the PET-scan methodology with four psychiatric patients with histories of violent behaviour, Volkow and Tancredi (1987) found evidence of abnormal blood flow and metabolic problems in the left temporal lobes of all four patients. Similar findings have been reported by Miller *et al.* (1997) from a larger patient sample. Twenty-two patients who showed reduced blood flow to the frontal-temporal region of the brain were compared with 22 who showed a parallel reduction to the temporal-parietal region on a number of aggressive anti-social behaviours. Whereas ten of the 22 showing frontal-temporal anomalies revealed such behaviours, only one of those in the temporal-parietal group did so.

The other body of evidence connecting aggression to cortical dysfunction comes from investigations in which correlations have been shown between various indicators of aggressiveness and less direct measures of deficits in cognitive processing. The latter, called 'soft signs' of frontal-lobe disorder, include such shortcomings as involuntary movements, difficulties in the performance of rapid alternating movements and difficulties in detecting simultaneous stimulation from two sources (Stein *et al.* 1995). These signs can be detected in a neurological assessment. Another technique of assessing soft signs involves the use of standard tests of ability to process information, such as to determine and carry out an organized sequence of responses (e.g. Petrides 1985; Petrides and Milner 1982). One such test that has been used extensively in research is the Spatial Conditional Associative-Learning Task (SCALT), which assesses the ability to learn associations among newly presented stimuli (Petrides 1985). Performance on the SCALT has been shown to predict adult aggressive behaviour in a laboratory setting (Giancola and Zeichner 1994) and to be associated with fighting in young boys (Séguin *et al.* 1995).

Evidence from both imaging studies and investigations using soft signs of frontal lobe dysfunction therefore shows that such dysfunction is associated with relatively high levels of aggressiveness. This conclusion is consistent with the hypothesis that a breakdown in inhibitory cortical control over lower emotional centres is the intervening process. Support for this hypothesis has been reported by Lau and Pihl (1996), who found that subjects in the lower quartile of a large sample given the SCALT – thereby manifesting relatively high frontal lobe impairment – showed higher levels of aggression when provoked than those in the upper quartile even when they were given money for behaving non-aggressively. These aggressive subjects apparently were relatively unable to process cues for the inhibition of aggression.

Social learning

The antecedents of aggression that we have considered so far in this section have all been grounded in the human being's biological system. At one time, during the ascendancy of behaviourism, such variables would not have been assigned much of a place in aggression; such behaviour would have been explained almost entirely as something acquired through conditioning and learning. Today, of course, we recognize that the roles of learned and innate factors in human aggression cannot be described in an either/or way. Virtually every psychologist who investigates the problem recognizes that both are involved and that differences in viewpoint involve the relative emphasis placed on each. To set 'nature' against 'nurture' in discussing human aggression is to create a false dichotomy. Elsewhere in this book it is suggested that both learning and heredity are best understood as background variables that create a level of potential for aggression without being direct antecedents. Aggressive behaviour is a response to conditions in the situation that provoke the person; even when one is disposed to aggress and capable of behaving aggressively, a specific situation must elicit the act. The probability that such behaviour will occur, and also the intensity of the behaviour, will vary according to both the nature of the provocation and the level of potential for aggression set by the several background variables. Certainly people born with dispositions to be violent will be more aggressive when attacked than those lacking such dispositions, and people who have acquired strong aggressive tendencies through **social learning** will react more aggressively than those who have not. Heredity and social learning are complementary factors in human aggression.

The social learning theory of aggression emerged in the 1960s, largely as a result of the theorizing of Albert Bandura and his associates. The approach has undergone several elaborations since its was first presented and it continues to exert a strong influence. It emphasizes the acquisition and maintenance of aggressive response tendencies. Although it does not rule out provocations as important contributors to aggression, the social learning approach treats such events as conditions under which learned aggressive behaviours may be enacted. Likewise, the theory includes a recognition of biological factors in aggression without regarding such factors as direct causes of aggressive behaviour. Instead, the theory assumes that a person's genetic and biological endowment creates a potential for aggression, while the specifics of aggressive behaviour – its forms and frequency, the situations that evoke it and the targets towards which it is directed – are acquired through experience (Bandura 1983).

Social learning consists of the acquisition of responses through observation and the maintenance of behaviours through reinforcement. The normal child observes numerous instances of aggression both in real life situations at home, in school and on the streets, and in the fantasy world of television and motion pictures. By observing the consequences of aggression for the actors, the child gradually acquires a rudimentary knowledge of certain rules of conduct (e.g. that one may sometimes obtain something desirable by using force). In this way a repertoire of aggressive behaviours is built. Whether these behaviours are acted out depends on the contingencies that the child perceives for his or her behaviour. If suitable incentives for aggression are present, the probability of aggression is likely to be high. In addition, the child experiences rewarding and punishing consequences following aggression; aggressive behaviours acquired through observation are likely to be carried out only if the child has been rewarded for such actions.

Bandura (1986) has stated that the processes of social learning depend on the child's forming mental representations of events in the social environment. Rewards and punishments for aggression are represented in the form of *expectancies* of future outcomes of aggression and the utility or *value* that aggression has for the individual. For instance, a child with a history of attaining valuable ends through bullying other children at school soon comes to believe that further bullying in the same settings will continue to deliver worthwhile rewards. As a result, aggression acquires a high degree of value and is likely to be repeated when appropriate situational cues are present. Furthermore, in addition to forming expectancies of the likelihood that aggression will be rewarded, called *outcome* expectancies, the reinforced child also develops a sense of confidence in his or her ability to execute the necessary aggressive behaviours, called *self-efficacy* expectancies. Evidence for both kinds of expectancy was reported by Perry *et al.* (1986), who found that children described as highly aggressive by their peers expressed greater confidence in their ability to carry out aggressive solutions to interpersonal conflicts than less aggressive children, as well as greater confidence that aggression would produce tangible reward and would be successful in forestalling future conflicts.

In a study of the value component of habitual aggressiveness, Boldizar *et al.* (1989) found that peer-rated aggressiveness predicted positive outcomes that children associated with the outcomes of aggression. Children rated as high in aggressiveness attached greater positive value than did less aggressive children to 'control of the victim' resulting from aggression against the latter, and less negative value on such outcomes as the victim's suffering, threat of retaliation, rejection by peers and negative feelings about themselves. In short, children who were highly aggressive saw more good outcomes arising from aggression, and fewer bad ones, than less aggressive children.

A NOTE ON METHODS OF STUDY

Before we go on to a review of studies of human aggression, a word on methodology is in order. Much of the research reviewed in the chapters to follow comes from experimental laboratories. The laboratory study in aggression usually involves a simple two-person interaction in which one person is led to believe that he or she is the victim of a wilful infliction of an aversive treatment by the other. Eventually the first person is allowed to retaliate in some way. Aggression is operationally defined in terms of the overall magnitude of the retaliation. Most often the provocateur is an experimental accomplice playing a well rehearsed role.

The question is often raised as to whether the experimental method is valid for the study of aggression. Does a highly contrived laboratory setting really provide insight into the dynamics of human violence? Or would we be better off to eliminate aggression experiments and to study actual violence in real-life settings? Such questions are not easily answered. The aggression experiment has one advantage over other methods in that it allows a high degree of control, precision and operational definition. It is, therefore, ideally suited to testing causal hypotheses. For this reason, experiments have a high degree of what is called 'internal validity'. On the other hand, conditions and variables that may assume great importance in experimental studies are often less prevalent in the world outside the laboratory. Bushman and Anderson (1998) conducted an extensive meta-analysis of studies of a number of aggression-related variables conducted both inside and outside the laboratory and concluded from their findings that 'when the conceptual variables and processes are the same, parallel results should be obtained in the laboratory and the real world' (Bushman and Anderson 1998: 43). The question of whether or not controlled experiments have external validity, i.e. relevance for 'real world' violence, to go along with their accepted internal validity is therefore a matter of sound theorizing and methodology. Bushman and Anderson (1998: 43) summarize the case well:

> When careful conceptual analyses of both types of situations are conducted and when solid empirical research methods are employed, findings about the relations between conceptual variables will generalize from the laboratory to the real world, and vice versa.

SUMMARY

1 Aggression is defined as the delivery of a noxious stimulus to another person with the intent of harming that person, in the expectation that the aversive stimulus will reach its destination, and without the consent of the victim. In humans, aggression in human beings takes one of two general forms: (a) angry, or affective; and (b) instrumental. Numerous explanations for affective aggression have been formulated. One, based on an evolutionary and biological viewpoint, is that humans share with other animals certain genetically determined tendencies towards aggressive behaviour. Another, based on a behaviourist position, emphasizes the acquisition of aggression through experience, conditioning and learning. The two views are not mutually exclusive. Some aggressive behaviours in humans have biological origins, just as some are learned through observation of other people. Furthermore, aggressive behaviour, once it is part of a person's repertoire, is shaped and developed through learning processes. Both biological inheritance and learned tendencies serve as predisposing background conditions for aggression, which is a response to provoking conditions in the person's environment.

2 Conclusions regarding the role of heredity in aggression based on comparisons of identical and non-identical twins appear to depend on a number of specific variables. These include the characteristics of the samples of people tested, the methods used for measuring aggressiveness and the way in which aggression is defined. Despite these qualifications, however, a growing body of evidence indicates that heritability makes some contribution to individual dispositions to aggression.

3 Certain similarities between aggression in humans and that shown by other animal species, especially primates, have been noted by investigators working in the traditions of behavioural biology and the theory of evolution. Inter-male aggression is attributed to sexual competition driven by naturally selected reproductive pressures and aggression by

males against females to the male's proprietary concern with the latter's sexual fidelity. This approach to human aggression has been criticized by a number of social psychologists who remain sceptical of the evidence adduced by psychoevolutionists.

4 Brain mechanisms and the activity of hormones have also been implicated in human aggression as background factors. Elevated levels of testosterone have been found to covary with aggressiveness in males by creating a heightened disposition to aggress in response to suitable provocation. Some studies have also shown that situations involving competitive and assertive behaviour can lead to elevated testosterone levels, suggesting that the relation between hormone activity and aggression may be in part a reciprocal one. Both the limbic system and the cerebral cortex are linked to aggression, the former as a primitive centre of emotional reactivity to provocation and the latter as a higher centre exercising cognitive controls over emotional responding. In particular, dysfunction in the frontal-lobe region of the cortex is correlated with aggressive behaviour and mood. The activity of the neurotransmitter serotonin is involved in aggression, in that relatively low levels of serotonin activity – such as may be induced through damage to the limbic system or inhibiting drugs – are associated with high levels of aggression.

5 The social learning theory of aggression explains the acquisition, performance and maintenance of aggressive behaviour through principles of observational and instrumental learning. Novel aggressive responses are acquired through observation and converted to dispositional habits by social reinforcement. Consistent with the expectancy-value theory of reinforcement, dispositional aggressiveness is associated with high expectancy of being rewarded for aggressing and with a high subjective value attached to such rewards.

SUGGESTIONS FOR FURTHER READING

Geen, R. G. and Donnerstein, E. (eds) (1998) *Human Aggression: Theories, Research, and Implications for Social Policy*. San Diego: Academic Press. This book is a general introduction to several topics of current interest in aggression research written by authorities in each area.

Hollander, E. and Stein, D. J. (eds) (1995) *Impulsivity and Aggression*. New York: Wiley. Several of the chapters in this volume address the role of physiological mechanisms in human aggression.

Stoff, D. M. and Cairns, R. B. (eds) (1996) *Aggression and Violence: Genetic, Neurobiological, and Biosocial Perspectives*. Mahwah, NJ: Erlbaum.

TWO

THE PROVOCATION OF AGGRESSION

As was noted several times in the previous chapter, aggression is a reaction to some provocation arising in the aggressor's life situation. A person's biological constitution and repertoire of learned behaviours may make that person disposed or not disposed to behave aggressively, but neither guarantees nor necessitates aggression. To account for aggression we must know not only how people become potential aggressors, but also what conditions elicit the aggressive response.

In this chapter some conditions that elicit aggressive reactions in human beings are considered. These conditions are of two kinds. The first consist of **instigations** to aggression that arise out of interpersonal conflicts, such as situations in which people frustrate and interfere with the activities of others, or attack them physically or verbally, or act in ways that threaten their sense of self-esteem, or violate **norms** and values that the person considers important and worth defending. As we have noted, **background variables** are involved in the reactions of the provoked person in such settings; these are noted briefly but discussed in detail in subsequent chapters. The second kind of provoking condition to be considered is that in which the instigation comes from aversive stimulation in the environment, like heat and noise, and from simple physical pain. In such cases a personal agent responsible for the provocation is usually difficult to identify even when such an agent exists. The last section of the chapter is devoted to presentation of an overall model of affective aggression that incorporates the eliciting conditions, the relevant background variables and the intervening psychological processes that mediate the aggressive response.

FRUSTRATION AND AGGRESSION

The frustration–aggression hypothesis

An early attempt to formulate a unitary theory of aggression is represented by the frustration–aggression hypothesis first put forward by Dollard *et al.* (1939). This work was important because it brought to bear on the study of aggression a set of concepts derived from contemporary research in learning and motivation. Moreover, the hypothesis that it offered has led, either directly or indirectly, to a large number of investigations extending to the present time. The frustration–aggression hypothesis as formulated by Dollard *et al.* states that **frustration** produces a condition of readiness or instigation to aggress, and that aggression is always preceded by some form of frustration. Frustration in both the original and revised versions of the hypothesis is defined as 'interference with the occurrence of an instigated goal-response at its proper time in the behavior sequence' (Dollard *et al.* 1939: 7).

The heart of the hypothesis is its statement of a causal relationship between frustration and aggression. No psychologists believe any longer that frustration is the sole cause of aggression, but the other assertion of the hypothesis – that frustration creates an instigation to aggression and ultimately to aggressive behaviour – is more consistent with the evidence. Before we can review some of this evidence, however, it is important that we consider how frustration has been defined *operationally*, i.e. how psychologists have chosen to interpret exactly what constitutes – in the relatively ambiguous terminology of the original hypothesis – an interference with 'an instigated goal-response'. From the beginning, the basis for operationalizing frustration has been broad. Virtually any event that interrupts a relatively effortless flow of activity qualifies as a frustration and a potential antecedent of aggression. Disappointment, irritation, punitive intervention, annoyance, helplessness arising from natural conditions and loss of personal freedom can all, according to this liberal definition, be called frustrations. Indeed, as we look at the literature on ways in which the frustration–aggression hypothesis has been used to account for aggression, we find that this liberal approach characterizes much of the research.

One of the most widely cited studies to be generated by the hypothesis was one by Hovland and Sears (1940), which reported a negative correlation between index values representing the value of cotton and the incidence of lynchings of African-Americans by whites in the American South. In this classic investigation of scapegoating and **displaced aggression**, frustration was defined as the blocking of progress towards the goal of making money from a cotton crop. Over the years, critics pointed out certain artefacts in this classic study that rendered its conclusions problematic, but a more recent study that employs modern statistical analyses not available to the original authors (Hepworth and West 1988) supports its general conclusions.

A few other examples of research in which violence has been attributed to frustration can be mentioned. In a pair of studies carried out in Israel, Landau invoked the frustration–aggression hypothesis to link stressful social changes to aggressive anti-social behaviour. Landau and Raveh (1987) found that certain objective measures of social change – rapid increase in inflation, increased per capita income and car ownership, population density – were positively related to incidences of homicide and robbery. In another study, Landau (1988) found that subjective levels of social stress (defined as expressions of worry or dissatisfaction regarding economics, security or the political situation) were correlated with anti-social

Table 2.1 Correlations of self-reported stress and aggression

	Self-reported aggression	
Stressor	Interpersonal	Sabotage
Role ambiguity	0.28	0.15
Role conflict	0.30	0.14
Interpersonal conflict	0.49	0.34
Situational constraints	0.31	0.10

Note: All correlation coefficients are significantly different from zero at the 0.05 level of confidence.
Source: Chen and Spector (1992).

behaviour. Novaco (1991) used the frustration–aggression relationship to explain the murderous 'road rage' that occasionally occurs on busy and crowded highways in the United States. Certainly, anyone who has experienced one of the traffic jams that now characterize most of the large cities of the world can relate to the frustration felt by the drivers caught in such situations, even though most would probably confine any aggression they might show to horn-honking and shouting. Another application of the liberalized form of the frustration–aggression hypothesis is seen in studies of violence and aggression in stressful occupational settings. In one of these, Chen and Spector (1992) gathered self-report data from 400 white-collar employees sampled from a number of occupations. Among the variables were measures of such work stressors as role ambiguity (feelings of uncertainty about what is expected on the job), situational constraints, conflicts with other persons, the workload and conflicts among various role demands. Included in the behavioural measures were questions regarding instances of interpersonal aggression on the job and sabotage of the work. The four stressors listed were all found to be significantly correlated with measures of both interpersonal aggression and sabotage (Table 2.1). The authors also report that reported feelings of frustration and anger were correlated with interpersonal aggression. Thus, although the study was not designed to test the possible mediation of stress-related behaviours by frustration and anger, the authors discussed their findings in the context of the frustration–aggression hypothesis.

Another common situation that can be construed as frustrating is the loss of employment, especially when job loss is perceived to be undeserved. Under such conditions, being laid off, deemed 'redundant' or forced into unwanted retirement can generate anger and may increase the probability of some form of aggression by the aggrieved party. When such terminations are widespread within a community, overall levels of violence should, according to the hypothesis, show tendencies to increase. In a study addressed to this problem, Catalano and his associates (1993) studied a sample of more than 14,000 people by means of two interviews approximately one year apart. Among the questions asked in the interviews was whether the respondent had, in the two weeks prior to the interview, engaged in physical fighting, used a weapon in a fight, beaten a domestic partner or used excessive force in punishing a child. Catalano and his colleagues found that people who had become unemployed between the two interviews were six times more likely to report any of the aggressive acts prior to the second interview than those who had kept their jobs, even when the initial levels of aggressiveness in the two groups (reported in the first interview) were controlled. However, a part of the difference in violence between the two groups was caused by a *decrease* in aggression among those who did not lose their jobs. This was most likely to happen among workers who kept their jobs in industries that were laying off large numbers of other workers. Those fortunate enough to keep their employment under such volatile conditions probably inhibited any tendencies towards aggressing out of fear of getting into trouble and being fired. Thus, in times of increasing layoffs, aggression among those who lose their jobs appears to be consistent with the prediction of the frustration–aggression hypothesis, whereas the behaviour of those not laid off is a function of both relatively low frustration and high fear of punishment.

Frustration and social conflict

The frustration–aggression hypothesis has attracted some interest as a general model of social and political unrest. Application of the hypothesis to such large-scale matters requires, of course, that the terms 'frustration' and 'aggression' be defined in ways appropriate to the problems being studied. The former is generally inferred from evidence of dissatisfaction over unfulfilled desires and expectations within a society. The latter is often linked to riots, insurrections, civil wars and other such acts of collective violence. In this section two such lines of investigation are described.

Aggression as a response to political instability

Feierabend and Feierabend (1972) have invoked the frustration–aggression hypothesis as an explanation of socio-political violence within a society. Such violence is taken as evidence of political instability. Furthermore, they have linked this social violence to systemic frustration, which is the level of discontent within a society over unsatisfied wants, needs and expectations. If such discontent exists, political aggression and instability constitute a possible outcome, provided that political means for expression of the public will are not available. Furthermore, even when such political options are available, instability can be expected unless these means can provide constructive solutions to the problems of social discontent.

Relative deprivation and political violence

Following a line of reasoning similar to that outlined above, Gurr (1970) has linked political violence to the level of **relative deprivation** in a society. Gurr defines the latter in terms of the extent to which people realize desired standards of material welfare, self-determination, decisional freedom and satisfactory social relationships. If the realization of such outcomes falls short of expectations, a potential for political violence exists within the society. Political violence is defined by Gurr in terms similar to those used by Feierabend and Feierabend. If frustrated people do not blame their problems on the socio-political system, the likelihood of political violence is diminished. It is possible, for example, that a convenient scapegoat may be found, such as a disliked racial or ethnic group, and that frustrations may be taken out on that group rather than on the system. If frustrations are attributed to the political system, however, some form of political violence should be expected. Gurr lists three general types of such violence: turmoil, which is relatively popular, spontaneous and unorganized; conspiracy, which is smaller in scope but more highly organized; and internal war, which is popular, organized and larger in scope.

Whether the potential for political violence actually produces any of the above classes of event depends in part on two antagonistic forces. The first, already noted, is the level of coercive control that the political system possesses. A highly coercive government can, of course, hold down political violence to some extent. However, Gurr proposes that dissident elements within a society also possess some power to coerce, and that if this dissident coercive control exceeds the control exerted by the government, political violence will occur. In recent times we have observed that revolutionary guerrilla armies do appear to have some degree of coercive control over people living within territory controlled by them.

Analyses such as those of Gurr and the Feierabends represent interesting speculative extensions of the frustration–aggression hypothesis to large social phenomena. They show that the hypothesis can be invoked to explain certain social and political changes. However, it should also be noted that such analyses have been seriously criticized by some social theorists who believe that such extensions from experimental psychology are overly simplistic.

Gurr's analysis of relative deprivation has also been criticized on theoretical grounds. Walker and Pettigrew (1984) have argued that in defining the condition in terms of an individual's feelings of being deprived relative to other individuals, Gurr has described what is called *egoistic* relative deprivation. This condition is different from *fraternal* relative deprivation, which is a result of the person's believing that his or her social group is deprived relative to other groups. Walker and Pettigrew propose that collective action such as rioting is a result of this latter condition and not of egoistic relative deprivation. The results of a study conducted in Australia by Walker and Mann (1987) support this hypothesis. In this study, reported feelings of fraternal relative deprivation were positively correlated with expressions of approval for acts of social and political protest. Feelings of egoistic relative deprivation were not correlated with expressions of protest, but were instead related to experiences of physical and psychological stress. Criticisms such as these point out some of the problems that arise in using a concept like frustration, which grew out of individual psychology, in explaining collective aggression. To a certain extent, groups may behave in ways that suggest an analogue of the behaviours of frustrated individuals, but a thorough analysis of collective violence requires the invocation of other principles that better describe strictly social phenomena.

Frustration and arousal

Frustration does not always arise from the actions of others. Sometimes people become frustrated through their own inability to accomplish a desired end and the repeated failure that such inability produces. For example, Geen (1968) found that frustration caused by a subject's inability to complete a task led to as much aggression against another person as did frustration caused by that person's disruptive interference. Why should frustration lead to aggression even against a person who is only an innocent bystander? One possibility is that frustration may serve primarily to elevate the person's level of arousal. A study by Vasta and Copitch (1981) demonstrates the power of frustration to raise arousal levels. In their experiment each adult subject believed that he or she was interacting with a child and was required to present to the child a body of material to be memorized. The job of 'teaching' was presumably to be done through the use of feedback to the learner. A pre-programmed set of responses was given to each subject by the experimenter to simulate the child's performance (no child was actually involved). These responses were such that the child's performance appeared to deteriorate over time due to lack of effort and motivation. The subject was also required to throw a switch every time the child gave an answer, whether the answer was correct or incorrect. The actual purpose of the study was to measure the amount of force which the subject used in making this response. It was reasoned that frustration would be experienced each time the child made an error, and that this frustration would produce increased arousal. The latter would, in turn, be manifested in force applied to the switch. The results bore out this prediction. Even though the response of pressing the switch had no bearing on the alleged performance of the child, subjects made this response more intensely after errors than after correct responses.

Stress, arousal and aggression

If frustration involves heightened arousal in response to changes in the environment, then the frustration–arousal–aggression relationship may be a special case of a more general phenomenon. Investigators of problems other than aggression have pointed out that both major life changes and smaller 'daily hassles' tend to place people under stress (Kanner *et al.* 1981). What we have been calling frustration, i.e. the blocking of progress towards a goal, may be just one event in a larger family of events. What makes frustration in pursuit of a goal aversive and arousing may be the fact that such a condition represents a change from a state to which the person has become adjusted and which the person finds acceptable. Thus we might speculate that the frustration–aggression relationship may be expandable into a more general hypothesis. Such a hypothesis would assert that any significant change for the worse in a person's situation may be sufficiently aversive to cause increased stress and arousal, and that the arousal thus engendered may activate and energize aggressive responses if these responses are highly probable in the situation.

Frustration and coping

Frustration does not always lead to aggression, and one reason for that is that sometimes people have available responses that allow them to cope with the stress of frustration. If people can make responses that lead to instrumentally useful ends instead of aggressing, they may not react to frustration with aggression regardless of how predisposed to aggress they may be. This point is illustrated in a study by Moser and Levy-Leboyer (1985). Persons were observed as they attempted to use a coin-operated telephone that was not functioning. In one condition of the study a set of instructions was posted on the wall of the telephone booth giving information about the location of nearby phones and procedures to follow for recovery of lost money. In the other condition no such information was given. The authors observed that the amount of aggression shown by participants (e.g. hitting, kicking or butting the telephone) was greater among those who had not been given the additional information than among those who had. Possibly the latter group, by possessing specific information about how to proceed, were better able to cope constructively with the frustration than were those who had no such accessible **coping** response.

INTERPERSONAL ATTACK AND AGGRESSION

Comparison of frustration and attack

There can be little doubt that one of the most powerful motivators of aggressive behaviour is the desire or need to retaliate following an attack from another person. Attack may take the form of physical assault or it may be verbal, such as an insult, a harangue or badgering. Some investigators have compared frustration with attack as antecedents of aggression and concluded that attack is by far the more clear-cut of the two (e.g. Geen 1968). Attack has also been described as a more powerful source of arousal than is frustration (Diamond *et al.* 1984). Such comparisons may be misleading, however, in the absence of evidence that the two treatments – frustration and attack – have been manipulated in such a way as to produce comparable outcomes. For example, some frustrations may be extremely intense and some attacks relatively inoffensive. Lacking further knowledge of the subjective effects of each on the person, we cannot simply assume that the attack is more likely to elicit aggression than the frustration.

In addition, the relationship between interpersonal attack and aggression is not a simple one. One does not always lead to the other. One important variable that mediates the connection between an attack and subsequent aggression is the victim's interpretation of the meaning and intent of the attack. If an attack is judged in such a way that it seems justified or if it does not reveal maliciousness or intent to harm on the part of the attacker, retaliation is less likely than if such intent is clearly inferred.

Intent of the aggressor

As noted in Chapter 1, definitions of aggression almost always include the idea of intent to harm. When such intent is lacking, behaviour is generally not considered to be aggressive regardless of how aversive its consequences may be to the victim. Attacks upon oneself are judged in the same way: an attack is probably not considered to be aggressive unless the attacker is thought to be motivated by intentions that are malicious and hurtful. Intent to harm is in fact a more powerful determinant of retaliation than is the absolute intensity of an attack. For example, Epstein and Taylor (1967) showed that subjects who knew that another subject planned to attack them with a highly intense shock were more aggressive in retaliating against this person than when they had no such knowledge, even when the shock was not actually delivered. Furthermore, subjects engage in aggression against a provoking party to the extent that they *perceive* the latter to be acting out of hostile intention, whether or not he or she is actually hostile (Dodge *et al.* 1984).

One question that we must ask in noting the importance of intent in retaliatory aggression is why the absence of malice in the attacker constrains victims not to retaliate. One obvious possibility is that when an attack can be explained by mitigating circumstances, it is not regarded as a stressful event and thus it does not arouse the person. Another way of putting this is to say that an unintentional attack (e.g. being bumped into accidentally by someone) is not upsetting, whereas an intentional act (e.g. being bumped into by someone who deliberately makes contact) causes one to become highly upset. An alternative explanation is that an attack is upsetting and that it disposes the victim to strike back regardless of the intent behind it. However, because people generally do not regard an accidental attack as grounds for retaliation, most people inhibit such dispositions and desires out of a need to behave in a socially correct way.

A study by Zillmann and Cantor (1976) was addressed to this problem, and its results bore out the conclusion that when people believe that an attack is not malicious they do not become as aroused as they would if the attack were regarded as intentional. Subjects in this experiment were verbally provoked by an experimenter either before or after having been told that the experimenter was upset because of unusual pressures and stress. This explanation was found to have a mitigating effect on arousal, as measured by heart rate and systolic blood pressure. When the mitigating information was given before the provocation, assaulted subjects showed no increase in arousal as a function of the attack. When such information was given after the attack, subjects showed increased arousal as a result of the attack, but they became less aroused after the information was given. The data therefore show that when people believe that an attack made upon them can be attributed to extenuating circumstances and is not necessarily malicious, they tend not to become aroused by it.

Violation of norms

An interesting question is when, and under what conditions, malicious intent is attributed to an attacker. To answer this question, we must remind

ourselves that interpersonal aggression takes place in an interactive setting involving two people. Aggression is not an isolated act in most cases.
It arises in the context of an ongoing relationship. Each party to the
relationship has a perspective on the situation, including a set of expectations regarding what is the proper behaviour of the two people involved.
In other words, a certain set of norms exists for behaviour in that setting.
Concepts like 'attack', 'maliciousness' and 'aggression' must be defined with
reference to these norms.

Such an approach to aggression has been defined by DaGloria and
DeRidder (1977, 1979). These investigators discuss aggression as one possible outcome within a situation in which both parties strive for some
goal and each party attempts to prevent the other from attaining that
goal. In the course of this process it is assumed that each party must
deliver some level of aversive stimulation to the other. The norm that is
implicit in such a setting is that participants will deliver such stimulation
only in the amount and degree necessary to attain their goals. Should the
participants exceed that normative level, their behaviour will be judged
by the other to be excessive and motivated by intent to hurt, i.e. it will be
regarded as a malicious attack.

For example, consider two teams engaged in a rough physical sport,
such as American football or ice hockey. Each attempts to score points
and to prevent the other team from scoring. Out of necessity each team
must occasionally attempt to inhibit the progress of the other by making
hard physical contact. As long as the level of contact is normative, i.e. no
more than is required for scoring or defending one's goal, play usually
proceeds without incident. Only when a player hits another with a force
that the recipient considers excessive does the latter regard the behaviour
as malicious. The other is therefore labelled a 'dirty player' or an 'aggressor'.
The response to such a judgement of intent is the delivery of an aversive
stimulus back to the other person at a level that exceeds the level needed
by the victim to attain his goals, i.e. an exact retaliation in kind. (An
interesting analysis of two actual cases of sports violence which illustrate
some of the matters discussed here has been published by Mummendey
and Mummendey 1983.)

DaGloria and DeRidder (1977, 1979) reported evidence supporting this
line of reasoning. In each study, two subjects responded alternately to a
series of signals by making a particular motor response. Each subject
attempted to disrupt the other's commission of the response by delivering
an electric shock precisely at the time of the other person's act. The shock
could be delivered at one of three levels of intensity. Both subjects were
told that shocks at either the highest or the intermediate level would be
sufficient to disrupt the other person's response 100 per cent of the time.
The experimenter manipulated the proceedings so that the subject received
shocks of either the intermediate level or the highest level. Subjects retaliated with shocks of the highest intensity to a greater extent in the latter
condition than in the former. In other words, subjects believed that highly
intense shocks were unnecessary and uncalled for, and that they indicated
malice on the part of the other person. The subject reacted to this belief
by giving intense shocks in return. Along these same lines of reasoning,
DeRidder (1985) has shown that people who observe others engaged in

interpersonal attacks take the normative nature of the attacks into account in judging how malevolent the attacks are. DeRidder found that harmful attacks are labelled as being more aggressive and malicious than are non-harmful ones only when the attack is considered to be in violation of what is normative behaviour in the situation.

To answer the question that was raised at the beginning of this section: malicious intent will be attributed to an attacker by a victim when the level of aversiveness delivered is considered to be inappropriately high, given the norms for the situation. This judgement serves to justify retaliation. In addition, there is some evidence that the victim of aggression considers the attack to be more inappropriate to the situation than does the attacker. A study by Mummendey *et al.* (1984) has shown not only that the attacker tends to regard his or her acts as less aggressive and inappropriate than does the victim, but also that the two persons reverse their perspectives when, at a later time, the tables are turned and the former victim is given the chance to retaliate. The overall conclusion of the study is that 'irrespective of the position in an aggressive interaction sequence, one's own behavior is evaluated as more appropriate and less aggressive than [another's] behavior' (Mummendey *et al.* 1984: 307). Such an egocentric judgement on the part of the attacker reinforces aggressive tendencies within a situation that allows bilateral opportunities for attack. People can always conclude that norms have been violated when they are attacked, but that aggressive behaviour is justified when they are the ones attacking others.

The cognitive–neoassociationist model of affective aggression

We may summarize the foregoing discussion by concluding that aggression is often a reaction to frustration – broadly defined to encompass a range of social, economic and political stressors – and to interpersonal attack that is judged by the victim to be intentional, malicious and in violation of social norms for interpersonal behaviour. Is there any common variable or process that accounts for both of these bodies of evidence? We have already noted one possibility – that both frustration and attack bring about an increased state of arousal that intensifies behaviours made likely by situational circumstances. Another possibility is indicated by a model of affective aggression proposed by Berkowitz (1993), who argues that frustration leads to aggression by initiating *negative affect* which, in turn, is linked to aggression through an associative network. Negative affect is the unpleasant feeling state elicited in a reflexive and automatic way by aversive conditions. This unpleasant experience is linked associatively (i.e. through experience and learning) to a variety of cognitions, emotions and expressive-motor responses which produce two immediate and simultaneous tendencies. One is to aggress and the other is to flee from the situation. If the latter tendency is stronger than the former, the result will be inhibition of aggressive behaviour and the so-called 'anger-in' response (see Chapter 7). If the tendency to aggress is stronger than the flight tendency, the person will be likely eventually to aggress. Thus the initial reaction to frustration is an affective one leading to a simple associative process. However, Berkowitz also points out that higher cognitive processes

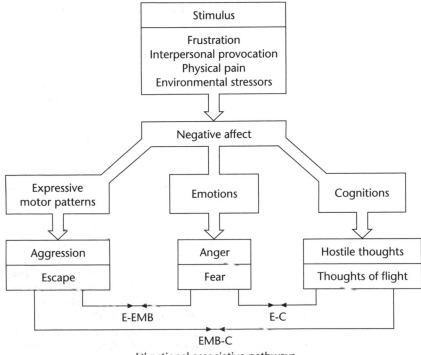

Figure 2.1 Descriptive diagram of process in cognitive–neoassociationist theory of affective aggression.
Note: the directional associative pathways show that thoughts, affective states and expressive motor patterns may evoke each other through association in the absence of other sources of negative affect.
Source: based on Berkowitz (1993).

such as attributions and judgements (see Chapter 3) may intervene to facilitate or inhibit aggression after the initial associative reaction has taken place. The immediate associative affective reaction to provocation is a 'rudimentary' response that eventually becomes refined by higher cognitive activity. Berkowitz's **cognitive–neoassociationist** model of affective aggression is summarized in Figure 2.1.

Berkowitz has tested the model in studies that involve the infliction of moderate physical pain in the laboratory. According to the model, there is no reason to think of physical pain as being essentially different from other classes of stressor, such as interpersonal ones. Pain generates negative affect in much the same way that frustration and attack do, and negative affect is the immediate precursor of aggressive reactions to aversive stimulation in all cases.

Furthermore, pain is a complex experience that includes the physical stimulus responsible for the aversiveness, the person's understanding of the cause of his or her experience and the overall state of unpleasant negative affect that is the consequence. Berkowitz (1983) has reported an experiment in which subjects were required to immerse their hands in painfully cold water (the 'cold pressor' task). Some were specifically told that this experience might be painful, whereas others were not. Those who were warned of the painfulness of the cold pressor later expressed stronger feelings of irritation, annoyance and anger than did those who were not so informed. In addition, subjects in the former condition were also verbally harsher and more critical towards another person than were those in the latter. Thus, when the cold pressor was labelled as painful, more negative affect was elicited than when this labelling did not take place, as well as greater aggressiveness.

Pain may therefore serve as a condition for aggression. However, as noted in Chapter 1, aggression is an act of delivering noxious stimulation to another person with intent to cause discomfort. People may experience negative affect and even strike out at someone when they are in pain, but does this mean that they intend to hurt the other person? The findings of a study by Berkowitz et al. (1981) indicate that it might. Subjects in this study gave rewards and punishments to another person in connection with a task performed by the latter; during this time subjects kept one of their hands immersed in water that was either extremely cold or comfortably tepid. In addition, some of the subjects were told that administration of punishments to the other person would hurt that person's performance, whereas others were told that punishment would facilitate performance and therefore help the other. Overall, subjects gave more rewards than punishments. However, the proportion of rewards given, relative to punishments, was lowest among subjects who were exposed to the cold pressor and also told that punishment would hurt the other person. In other words, the combination of cold-induced pain and the knowledge that punishing the other person would hurt that person led to the highest relative degree of punishment. In addition, subjects who were given the cold pressor treatment described themselves as feeling more tense, irritable and annoyed than those exposed to warmer water.

ENVIRONMENTAL CONDITIONS AND AGGRESSION

The cognitive–neoassociationist model is especially attractive because it supplies an explanation for a wide range of provocations that do not necessarily involve interpersonal activity, situations in which the antecedent of aggression is some change in conditions in the environment that induce a temporary state of stress. Extreme environmental changes, particularly those that are inescapable and uncontrollable, can become highly aversive stressors and may, for that reason, evoke negative affect, feelings of hostility and aggressive behaviours. In this section we examine some of these potentially stressful conditions.

Ambient temperature

Archival evidence

The belief that aggression is more likely in hot weather than in cool weather is a common one. It was expressed in the nineteenth-century 'thermic law of delinquency', proposed by Quetelet in 1833, a sophisticated version of the popular idea that crimes of violence are more likely in the summer months than during colder times of the year. Today we can observe the same principle expressed in the Uniform Crime Reports of the Federal Bureau of Investigation in the United States, which has shown that peak occurrences of common crimes of violence (such as assault, rape and murder) occur in the hottest summer months. In recent years several attempts have been made to determine whether ambient temperature is a reliable antecedent of aggression and what psychological mechanisms might account for such a relationship. The resulting research has involved both laboratory experiments and the analysis of archival data on correlations between seasonal and daily temperature changes and changes in the incidence of violent behaviour. The findings of archival studies are reviewed first.

In an early investigation, Carlsmith and Anderson (1979) studied the incidence of urban riots in several American cities between 1967 and 1971, along with average daily temperatures in the same cities over that period of time. They found that the relationship of riots to temperature was direct and linear, a conclusion consistent with conventional wisdom concerning how 'long, hot summers' promote irritability, anger and the probability of aggressive outbursts. The likelihood of a riot was found to be greatest when the temperature was extremely high and lowest when temperature was extremely low.

A similar direct relationship between ambient temperature and aggression was reported by Anderson and Anderson (1984), who found a direct and linear relationship between temperature and the incidence of murders, assaults and rapes in two large American cities. These researchers also found that daily temperature was related to the ratio of violent to non-violent crimes: the hotter the day, the greater was the proportion of crime that was assaultive in nature.

In another study, Anderson (1987) analysed statistics on crime for the entire United States over the decade from 1971 to 1980, and found the incidence of violent crime to be significantly greater during the third quarters of the years (the months of July, August and September) than in any other quarter. In the United States, these three months are typically the hottest of the year. Incidence of non-violent crime also peaked during the third quarters of the years surveyed, but not to the same extent as violent crime. The direct relationship of temperature to violent crime was found even when a large number of other variables known to contribute to crime (e.g. per capita income, age, education level) were controlled.

Finally, a study by Anderson *et al.* (1997) has shown that the linear temperature–aggression effect holds across much longer periods of time. In two archival investigations, these researchers assessed the relation between year-to-year changes in temperature and two types of crime – those which involved violence to the victim (homicide and aggravated assault) and those which involved threat to the victim's property (burglary and motor vehicle theft) – during the years 1950 to 1995. The results showed that average annual temperature was significantly correlated with incidence of violent crime but not with property crime. A significant positive correlation between the average number of days in which the highest temperature exceeded 90 °F and the incidence of violent crimes carried out in the summer (cf. Anderson 1987) was also found.

Additional evidence that suggests a direct relation between temperature and aggression comes from studies showing a higher rate of violence in geographical regions characterized by hot temperatures than in cooler areas (Anderson 1987; Anderson and Anderson 1996). Taken together, therefore, the data from the archival studies by Anderson and his associates indicate that, across a range of aggressive acts from riots to assaultive crimes, temperature is related to aggression in a direct way. Hotter years, seasons, months and days are more likely than cooler ones to yield such behaviours as murders, rapes, assaults, riots and wife-beatings. Hotter regions of the world have more aggression than cooler regions. The evidence for a direct heat–aggression relationship is therefore consistent.

Ambient temperature, affect and cognition

Anderson and his colleagues have proposed that deviations in ambient temperature from a moderate level elicit affective and cognitive states that underlie and mediate aggressive behaviour. This proposal is part of a General Affective Aggression Model (GAAM) that is described in Chapter 3. These investigators have found support for the proposal of affective–cognitive mediation in experimental studies involving the manipulation of ambient temperature. In two experiments, Anderson *et al.* (1995) created three levels of temperature: comfortable (varying in the two experiments between 72 and 78 °F), warm (between 79 and 87 °F), and hot (between 87 and 95 °F). Subjects were assigned to one of these conditions during a session in which either a video game or a brief period of aerobic physical exercise constituted the main activity. The overall results from the studies showed that as temperature was increased, the subjects' levels of heart rate (arousal) and of self-reported hostile affect and hostile cognitions all increased in a direct and linear way as predicted by the integrated model. A second laboratory study (Anderson *et al.* 1996) extended and refined the Anderson *et al.* (1995) experiments. In one condition of this experiment, subjects were assigned to one of five groups in which the temperature was manipulated to vary between 55 and 95 °F. Thus the range of ambient temperatures in this study ran from hot to uncomfortably cold, and both hostile affect and hostile attitudes were assessed by self-report measures. For both of the measures of aggressive affect, a curvilinear relation to ambient temperature was found, with the least such affect found among subjects who worked under conditions of moderate temperature. Both very high and very low temperatures evoked significantly more negative affect than this intermediate level. Thus, negative affect is produced not just by high heat but by large departures from a moderate 'comfort zone' in both higher and lower directions.

Although the laboratory research reported by Anderson and his associates provides convincing evidence of a direct, linear relationship between temperature and the affective, cognitive and arousal mediators of aggression, the GAAM has not been clearly supported to date by evidence of a similar relationship for aggressive behaviour. The results of other experimental studies have in fact suggested that the relation is not linear but curvilinear, in that under some conditions the induction of high temperatures in the laboratory leads to a *decrease* in aggression from what is shown under conditions of more moderate temperature. In one such experiment, Baron and Bell (1975) found that high temperature inhibited aggressive behaviour in subjects who had previously been angered by the victim of their aggression even though it increased aggression in those who had not been angered. Baron and Bell (1975) explained these findings by proposing that negative affect is an intervening variable linking heat to aggression. Being attacked by another person increases negative affect, as does being subjected to intensely high temperature. Moreover, these two sources of affect are additive, so that the person's overall level of displeasure results from a combination of the two. When negative affect is experienced to a moderate degree, the person is stimulated to behave with aggression towards an available target. However, extremely high levels of negative affect produce only a desire to escape from the unpleasant situation. Subjects in the Baron and Bell experiment who were both attacked and exposed to excessive heat were therefore more highly motivated to get the experiment over with and leave than they were to retaliate against their attacker.

The evidence from the archival studies for a linear relation between temperature and aggression is quite strong. In contrast, the evidence from some laboratory studies, of which that of Baron and Bell (1975) is one example, fails to show an unambiguous positive heat–aggression relationship. This discrepancy in the findings from laboratory and archival data requires some comment. First, it should be noted that Baron and Bell do not argue for a curvilinear relationship between heat and aggression. What they do claim is that heat is one contributor to negative affect, and that this affective state will, if it becomes strong enough, elicit escape responses that interfere with aggression. The analysis of archival data such as those reviewed above does not allow us to make any judgements of whether or not people will choose to escape from heat rather than to riot or commit crimes. Furthermore, it is possible that heat and aggression *are* related in a curvilinear way and that if it were ever possible to observe behaviour under hot enough experimental conditions such a result might be found. Furthermore, it is also possible that, if ambient temperature ever got high enough, crimes of violence might show a decrease. Another possibility is that laboratory settings magnify a person's freedom to escape from hot situations. In the typical experimental laboratory, this option is usually quite salient. In fact, experimental procedures in effect in most American universities (where a large number of the experiments on aggression are carried out) require that subjects be explicitly reminded that they are under no constraints to stay. It is not surprising, therefore, that experimental research should show that the desire to escape conflicts with the motive to retaliate. In real life, however, people can be extremely uncomfortable in hot settings without believing that escape is a realistic choice. Under such conditions, heat and aggression may be more directly related. Obviously, this issue will be settled only by experiments in which aggressive motives and motives to escape the situation are manipulated independently prior to a behavioural assessment of aggression (Anderson and Anderson 1998).

Noise

The stressful effects of noise have been well documented. Urban settings are usually characterized by high levels of noise which are usually variable, unpredictable and uncontrollable by the average person. The harmful effects of noise include loss of hearing, hypertension, stress and decreased efficiency in problem-solving. We might expect that because of its stressful nature intense noise might also be related to aggression. It is, but only under certain conditions. The major role of noise in aggression is that of an *intensifier of ongoing behaviour*. If the behaviour is for some reason aggressive, then the introduction of noise facilitates the expression of aggression. Noise may also contribute to aggression by reducing the individual's ability to withstand and tolerate or cope with frustration.

If we recall that frustration is often an antecedent of aggression, then any condition that reduces frustration tolerance becomes relevant for aggression: frustration may lead to aggression only when people lose their ability to live with it with equanimity. The less capable people are of living with frustrations, the more likely they are to react to them with aggression. This may represent one way in which noise contributes to aggression. A few studies have shown in a more direct way that noise can be an antecedent of aggressive behaviour. The reason in each case appears to be that noise *intensifies* aggression that is elicited by other features of the situation. An example is provided by a study by Geen and O'Neal (1969). In this experiment male subjects were shown a scene from a motion picture – either a brutal prize fight or an exciting but non-hostile athletic competition – and then instructed to deliver electric shocks to another person as punishment for errors on a task. As is shown in Chapter 4, observation of symbolic portrayals of violence frequently predisposes the observer to become aggressive. During delivery of the shocks half the subjects heard a tape recording of moderately loud noise, whereas the other half heard no noise. The noise was not sufficiently loud to be painful to the subjects. Those subjects who were stimulated with loud noise after having seen a violent movie were more aggressive than subjects in any other condition of the experiment. Arousal elicited by noise apparently energized the aggressive reaction of the violent movie that subjects in that condition were disposed to make. The significance of this study is that it shows that arousal can energize aggression in a person who is disposed to aggress (in this case because of seeing a violent film) even though the person presumably has no reason to feel anger or hostility towards the victim.

Sometimes, however, people are angry with others and do have a clear motive to aggress. Under these circumstances, noise energizes and intensifies the anger-driven behaviour. In addition, we might expect that certain features of the noise, such as its controllability or predictability, might influence the amount of arousal that it produces. Thus, in situations involving both noise and provocation, we would expect that aggression would be most intense when the noise is unpredictable and not under the control of the aggressor. Evidence supporting part of this hypothesis has been presented by Donnerstein and Wilson (1976), who found that subjects who had been attacked by an experimental confederate and then exposed

Table 2.2 Average duration of shocks given by subjects (in seconds) as a function of noise, prediction and control

	Treatment	
Arousal condition	Provocation	No provocation
No noise	2.33[b]	2.10[c]
Control	2.41[b]	2.07[c]
Predict	2.74[a]	2.11[c]
No control	2.83[a]	2.15[c]

Note: Cells having common superscripts are not significantly different from each other.
Source: Geen (1978).

to aversive and uncontrollable noise later retaliated more intensely against that person than did subjects who had received controllable noise.

Other studies show that predictability is not as important a factor in mediating noise-induced aggression as is controllability. Geen (1978) carried out a study in which these two variables were manipulated separately. Some subjects in this study were first given a large number of moderately intense electric shocks by a confederate, whereas others were given only a few mild shocks. Later all subjects were allowed to shock the confederate. During this period the subject heard moderately loud noise. In one condition the subjects were free to turn off the noise at any time, and most of them did in fact terminate the noise before the end of the period. In another condition the subjects were told ahead of time exactly when the noise would be turned off, but were also informed that this would be done by the experimenter; these subjects could therefore predict the duration of the noise but lacked control over it. In another condition subjects were not given control or informed about the time of termination of the noise: the noise simply ended at the arranged time. A comparison group of subjects were given no noise at all.

The results of the study are shown in Table 2.2. Among subjects who had been provoked by being given strong shocks, possession of control over the noise had a mitigating effect on the intensity of their retaliation. Subjects who could control the noise were less aggressive than those who could only predict the time of offset and also less aggressive than those who could neither predict nor control the noise. Subjects who had control were, in fact, no more aggressive than those who heard no noise. Control over the noise, therefore, appears to be the single most important variable mediating the influence of noise-induced aggression.

DISPLACED AGGRESSION

Aggression is often a straightforward matter: one person is frustrated or otherwise provoked by another and reacts to this treatment by some act of harmdoing, either outright physical violence or in some other form, with the intent to hurt the other. Sometimes, however, the aggressive response that would rightfully be directed towards the provoking party is deflected on to another target who may have done nothing to provoke the aggressor, or, at most, has committed some minor offence. For example, a man who has been berated by his boss may go home to find that his young son has broken a window in the garage. He then responds to this irritant by exploding in rage against the child and forbidding him to watch television for a month. This behaviour is called **displaced aggression**.

The study of scapegoating described by Hovland and Sears (see above, p. 22) exemplifies displaced aggression. In fact, it was as a corollary to the frustration–aggression hypothesis that such aggression was introduced to social psychology. In that context it was treated as a substitute for the retaliation that a frustrated person would like to exact upon the frustrator but inhibits because of fear of retribution or social ostracism. Such reactions to frustration are fairly common in everyday life, where society does not encourage direct retribution but does permit 'safety-valve' aggression against other targets. Nevertheless, when interest in the frustration–aggression hypothesis began to decline, so did the popularity of the whole idea of displaced aggression. This familiar sort of behaviour was eventually ignored by students of human aggression.

Actually, displaced aggression occurs more often than would be suggested by the narrow conceptualization of the process contained in the frustration–aggression hypothesis. It can be seen, for example, in many of the situations described earlier in this chapter in which aggression is aimed at people who have done nothing to provoke the aggressor and are in fact just innocent bystanders. The irate motorist who is angered by heavy traffic on a motorway and responds by swearing at or threatening another driver is displacing his aggression to a single individual who is not responsible for his irritation. The person who becomes violent when the temperature rises often reacts to his discomfort by harming people who have no control over the weather. The person who is in pain may be driven to lash out at someone nearby who did not cause the pain. All of these are instances of displaced aggression. Noting that further analysis of this concept may yield important insights into human aggression, Marcus-Newhall *et al.* (2000) reviewed 49 studies in which displaced aggression occurred and concluded that evidence for such aggression is reliable. They also found indications of the operation of certain moderator variables that had not previously been suggested.

The greater is the intensity of the initial provocation, the *less* intense will be any displaced aggression caused by it, and this is true whether that provocation is from an identifiable human source or from impersonal conditions like environmental stress. This finding can be explained in terms of a contrast effect: when the initial provocation is very unpleasant, any person who is encountered shortly afterwards will probably be less aversive than the provocation and will evoke positive feelings. The strength of these feelings, which inhibit displaced aggression against the person, should increase as the strength of provocation increases. However, this inhibition can be overridden if the target person does something to irritate the potential aggressor. Such an irritation, even when relatively innocuous, 'triggers' aggressive acts that would ideally be directed against the original frustrator. For this reason, when inhibitions are weakened, the stronger the initial provocation, the stronger the displaced aggression. The more negative the general setting of the interaction, the greater the displaced aggression, even though the target may not have done anything to trigger it. Negative settings prime negative thoughts and reactions, according to the cognitive neoassociationist theory described earlier in this chapter. These negative thoughts and expressions may be sufficiently strong to overcome inhibitions and facilitate displaced aggression. Marcus-Newhall and her associates put displaced aggression in a larger theoretical context by suggesting that it represents a specific instance of a persistent need to carry out a goal-directed act after progress towards the goal has been blocked. After being provoked, the person sets the goal of retaliating against the provocateur but is unable to follow through either because the latter is unavailable or because of fear of punishment for aggressing. The unsatisfied goal-directed tendency leads to rumination over the provocation, which persists until some substitute target is found and aggressed against.

SUMMARY

1 Two common types of provocation that can evoke aggressive behaviour are interpersonal conflicts and aversive stimulation in the environment. One of the first variables to be studied as an antecedent of interpersonal conflict is frustration, defined as interference with an instigated goal response. In practice, frustration has been defined in broad terms as any act that produces irritation by interrupting normal activity. The correlations between aggression and such phenomena as economic disappointment, social and political stress, loss of employment and road rage have all been explained by reference to the frustration–aggression hypothesis.

2 Frustration has been linked to aggression theoretically in terms of its capacity for increasing the person's level of arousal, a conclusion strengthened by the finding that frustration in task performance caused by one's own inability can elicit aggression against an innocent bystander.

3 Interpersonal attack, either physical or verbal, is another important antecedent of aggression. Attributions of the causes of the attacker's behaviour mediate such retaliatory aggression. Judgements of malicious intent on the attacker's part facilitate retaliation, and judgements that the attacker's behaviour has been influenced by mitigating circumstances inhibit retaliation. Violation of social norms that set limits on the conditions of interpersonal attack also influence aggressive retribution: attacks that exceed these normative limits invite greater retribution than those which do not.

4 Berkowitz's theory of cognitive-neoassociationism provides a general model for the relation of frustration and attack to aggression. In the model, any condition that elevates the level of negative affect for the person activates cognitions, related affective states and expressive motor tendencies linked to negative affect in memory. Physical pain and

environmental stressors have similar effects. These effects are immediate and preliminary to any cognitive appraisal of the situation.

5 Examples of environmental stimuli that can be antecedents of aggression are high ambient temperature and noise. Analyses of ambient temperature reveal a generally direct relationship between temperature and aggressive and anti-social behaviour. Anderson explains this relationship by means of a General Affective Aggression Model that postulates cognitive, affective and physiological reactions to high temperature as the mediators. The relation of noise to aggression has been shown to be largely a function of the degree to which a person perceives the noise to be beyond personal control.

6 Displaced aggression, once treated largely as a part of the frustration–aggression hypothesis, has been re-examined and found to be a reliable phenomenon. Preliminary investigation has indicated that the process may be moderated by such variables as the intensity of the original provocation, the behaviour of the target of displaced aggression and the general level of negative affectivity in the situation. A suggested mediating mechanism is ruminative goal-directed thinking that follows interruption or blocking of the primary intent to aggress.

SUGGESTIONS FOR FURTHER READING

Anderson, C. A., Anderson, K. B., Dorr, N., DeNeve, K. M. and Flanagan, M. (2000) Temperature and aggression, in M. Zanna (ed.) *Advances in Experimental Social Psychology, Volume 32*. San Diego: Academic Press, pp. 63–133. This chapter provides the most current review of research on temperature and aggression, interpreted in terms of the General Affective Aggression Model.

Berkowitz, L. (1989) The frustration–aggression hypothesis: an examination and reformulation. *Psychological Bulletin*, 106: 59–73. In this review, Berkowitz interprets the frustration–aggression relationship along the lines of the cognitive neoassociationist model.

THREE

INTERVENING PROCESSES IN AGGRESSION

The next matter that we must consider concerns the immediate effects of being provoked, and how these effects are linked to aggression. Certain psychological processes evoked by provocation mediate the commission of aggressive acts. One such process involves the generation of emotional excitement and feelings, all of which we generally call anger. Actually, as we will see below, anger has been described in many ways and its effects are not as simple and straightforward as popular formulations might suggest (e.g. 'The two men got into a fight because they were angry with each other'). The other intervening processes that follow provocation are cognitive in nature. They consist of ideas about the provoking situation, interpretations of what the situation means and projected plans for dealing with the situation as its meaning takes shape in the mind. A review of these affective and cognitive processes will show that the relation of provocation to aggression is neither automatic nor simple.

ANGER

It is commonplace to say that being provoked makes people angry. Since ancient times, it has been generally assumed not only in everyday thinking but in most philosophy, literature and religion that the emotion of anger is an emotional response to provocation that mediates subsequent aggression. Writing in the fourth century BC, Aristotle summarized the sequence of provocation–anger–aggression in terms that still express everyday wisdom. He perceived that the most common cause of anger is being insulted by another person, and that such insult must be perceived as arbitrary and malicious: people become angry with 'those that laugh at them and jeer and scoff at them (this is insulting) and those who harm them in such ways as are suggestive of insult. And these actions must be of such a kind as are neither in return for anything nor beneficial to those

who do them; for it is then that they seem to be done by way of insult'
(*Rhetoric* VI, 2.2). Although anger has a physiological side, manifested in
what we today call autonomic arousal and experienced as painful feelings,
this is not its most important characteristic. What is most important for
aggression is the person's understanding of how he or she has been treated
by the other and how that treatment has caused the pain being felt. This
understanding is closely tied to the desire for vengeance that animates
subsequent action. The belief that anger somehow leads directly to aggression has been represented in modern times by theories that treat emotions
as 'drives', such as neobehaviourism, and by certain popular concepts of
psychotherapy. In both cases, anger is regarded as having essentially
motivational properties. A number of psychologists have, however, taken
different viewpoints on the relation of anger to aggression, and some of
these viewpoints are reviewed below.

Excitation transfer

The cognitive–neoassociationist theory of aggression (Berkowitz 1993;
see Chapter 2) treats the emotional, cognitive and behavioural consequences of negative affect as parallel processes. None necessarily elicits
either of the others, even though they may manifest considerable influence on each other. One consequence of this independence is that the
theory does not treat anger as a necessary condition for aggression, as
older neobehavioural theories had done. The experience of anger is an
involuntary state that is usually elicited along with the instigation to
attack, but it does not play any causal role in the latter. Other theories
make anger a necessary intervening variable that mediates the relationship of provocation to aggression. One such theory is that of Zillmann
(1988), who defines anger as a conscious experience generated by two
events. The first is an increase in physiological arousal arising from 'social
or environmental conditions that pose a threat to welfare and well-being'
(Zillmann 1988: 52). The second is the recognition of conditions in the
environment by which this arousal state is explained. Arousal elicited by
a threat to one's well-being is labelled as anger on the basis of salient
environmental cues, one of the most salient being the person responsible
for the threat. That person therefore becomes the target of anger and for
any aggression that the anger motivates.

Having defined anger as a joint product of increased arousal and
cognitions by which arousal is labelled and understood, Zillmann has
further proposed that arousal elicited by events other than provocations
may under some conditions become mistakenly associated with the latter.
This phenomenon, called **excitation transfer**, pertains to situations in
which two arousing conditions occur in sequence. Autonomic arousal
does not dissipate immediately upon termination of the condition that
elicits it. Therefore, if two arousing events are separated by a short amount
of time, some of the arousal caused by one may be transferred to the
other and, as a result, increase the intensity of emotion experienced in
response to the latter event. In this way, arousal evoked by conditions

having nothing to do with provocation or instigation to aggression can intensify anger associated with a concurrent provocation.

An experiment by Zillmann *et al.* (1972) is often cited as evidence for the transfer of anger in the way just described. Some of the subjects in this study were first provoked by an experimental confederate, after which half the subjects engaged in strenuous physical exercise by riding an exercise bicycle. The other half performed a sedentary task. When subjects were later allowed to aggress against the confederate, those who had been provoked and then put through strenuous exercise were more aggressive than those who had also been provoked but who had performed the less physically demanding task. The effect of exercise on aggression was minimal among subjects who had not been provoked.

It should be noted that the temporal arrangement of the events involved in excitation transfer is critical to the process. Some time, but not too much, must intervene between the first (irrelevant) source of arousal and the second (emotional) event. If too much time elapses, of course, all excitation from the first source will dissipate. If not enough time expires, the aroused person will still experience salient and obvious symptoms of autonomic arousal (such as shortness of breath and sweating after exercise), which will easily be attributed to their true cause. Such a clear explanation for arousal should forestall any transfer of that arousal to the emotional event. However, once the most obvious signs of activation have abated, the person should be less likely to make a correct **attribution** and transfer of excitation will become more likely (Cantor *et al.* 1975).

The temporal course of events described here is important because it makes possible a comparison of the excitation transfer principle with the response-energization approach described above (p. 42). Arguing from the latter position, one could dismiss excitation transfer as unnecessary and argue that the increased aggression following, let us say, physical exercise is due only to increased drive which activates any response being made in the situation. We would expect that the drive arising from exercise would be at maximum strength immediately after the exercise and that it would decay over time. For that reason, the energization of aggression would be greatest when no time elapses between the two arousing events. According to Zillmann (1978), however, for reasons noted above, this should be the condition under which excitation transfer is *least* likely. There is some evidence bearing on this matter from a study that does not involve aggression and it supports Zillmann's analysis. Cantor *et al.* (1975) found that among subjects who had taken vigorous exercise, sexual arousal in response to erotic materials was greatest after a period of time had elapsed following the exercise. It was established that in this condition subjects were still physiologically aroused but no longer reporting the salient symptoms of arousal. This, of course, is exactly what Zillmann predicted.

The principle of excitation transfer is important for another reason. Once arousal has been labelled as anger, it can influence aggression far beyond the time at which arousal has dissipated. Thus, the misattribution process has implications for long-range behaviour. An experiment by Bryant and Zillmann (1979) illustrates this point. Students in a class were first shown videotapes that were highly arousing, moderately arousing or relatively non-arousing; none of the videotapes portrayed violence or aggression. Subjects were then provoked by a hostile and insulting person described as a guest lecturer. Eight days later, the students were given an opportunity to express negative feelings about the guest lecturer, knowing that negative ratings would hurt that person's chances of obtaining a teaching position. Those students who had seen either the highly arousing or moderately arousing video eight days before were more critical and hostile in their ratings of the target than were those who had seen the non-arousing video. The arousing effects of the videotapes had undoubtedly worn off in eight days. However, when subjects made their hostile ratings of the target they could presumably recall the anger that they had felt, and the amount of anger they experienced seemed to depend on which videotape they had seen. It should be noted that anger was not directly measured, however.

Anger as a socially constructed state

The idea that there is a necessary connection between anger and aggression has been dismissed by Averill (1982), who has discussed anger as an emotional syndrome constructed as a result of appraisals of events and manifested in socially defined roles. For anger to be aroused, a person must not only be provoked in an objective sense but also interpret the provocation in such a way that the anger syndrome is engaged and experienced. Thus, for example, a person who is attacked by another person must appraise the attack for what it is and, in effect, label it: 'I have been attacked by this person.' Once this interpretation of the precipitating event has been made, social rules and standards prescribe how the attacked person should feel; hence the experience of anger. Anger, in Averill's view, also has clear socially defined objectives, such as the rectification of some imagined or perceived wrongdoing, the restoration of lost self-esteem or the upholding of social norms. We become angry with those who have attacked us personally in a wrongful fashion and with those who violate the rules and standards of our society and culture. Aggression is not the only response to anger, however. In an extensive examination of the consequences of self-reported anger, Averill (1982) found that 83 per cent of subjects who reported having been angered by an instigator reported also that they had reacted with some form of aggression, but fully 75 per cent reported that they had responded in a non-aggressive way, such as by talking over their problem either with the instigator or with a neutral party. (Because subjects could endorse both reactions to the incident, it is obvious that many reacted both aggressively and non-aggressively.) Furthermore, when Averill asked his subjects what actions their anger might motivate, angry retaliation against the other person was found to be a less powerful incentive than restoration of self-image, while a number of others reported that 'bringing about a change in the behavior of the instigator' was their main concern. The most commonly reported incentive for anger was 'to reassert . . . authority or independence, and to improve (one's) image' (Averill 1982: 177).

Anger as a risk factor for violence

In the context of clinical psychopathology, anger has been treated as a predictor, or risk factor, for violent behaviour. Developing psychometric instruments to measure anger is therefore a primary concern of clinicians who deal with anger-prone clients. It is important that the scales designed to assess anger be built on a conceptual base that defines the emotion in terms of not only the client's experience but also the conditions that provoke it and the outcomes that it produces. Novaco (1994) has developed a sophisticated theoretical analysis that brings together some of the ideas previously described in this book and also takes into account both the intrapersonal and social dimensions of anger.

On the intrapersonal side, Novaco (1994) begins by defining anger in terms similar to those used by Zillmann (see above): it is an emotional experience consisting of physiological arousal and a cognition that one has been antagonized, i.e. a label that one attaches to the arousal. He points out that this labelling is not a time-consuming, deliberate decision (as we sometimes tend to think of cognitive activity), but an automatic process that emerges immediately in the perceptual process. Thus, a provocative act, provided that it evokes a perceptible increase in arousal, is immediately encoded by the victim as a feeling of anger. Note that for Novaco an immediate state of negative affect, which is a critical step in Berkowitz's cognitive–neoassociationist model, is not necessary. Cognitive appraisal is part of the perceptual process. In another respect, however, Novaco's analysis agrees with that of Berkowitz, because he goes on to say that the cognitive appraisal of anger is associated with 'an inclination to act in an antagonistic or confrontational manner toward the source of the provocation' (Novaco 1994: 32). This linking of cognitive, affective and expressive motor patterns in the initial response to provocation is, of course, at the heart of the cognitive–neoassociationist analysis. Important as it is as an activator of aggression, however, anger is neither a necessary nor a sufficient cause of aggressive behaviour. Aggression need not be prompted by anger (as is the case with instrumental aggression), and anger alone will not lead to aggression if the person lacks a social learning history that makes such behaviour probable.

This brings us to the matter of anger in social contexts. The social environment does more than determine the learning history of the individual. It also sets the conditions for the activation and expression of anger. Reasoning along lines similar to those used by Averill (1982), Novaco (1994) stresses the importance of contextual factors in understanding the generation, experience and outcomes of anger. Anger not only arises in specific social environments; it is largely shaped and given meaning by the latter. The hospitalized patient, for example, learns how to express and act out anger under the conditions of the institution, so that certain aspects of role-playing are involved. The assessment of anger as a risk factor for aggression must involve the construction of scales that tap several experiential and social dimensions. Novaco (1994) has described the construction of such a test (the Novaco Anger Scale: NAS). It first measures the cognitive aspect of anger, with separate scales measuring tendencies to attend to provoking incidents, a general suspiciousness of others, disposition to ruminate over provocation and generally hostile attitudes. The NAS next covers the arousal aspects, with scales measuring self-reports of intensity and duration of angry feelings, irritability and somatic tension. The behavioural aspect is indicated by scales assessing tendencies to respond to anger impulsively, the extent to which verbal aggression is used, the disposition to engage in physical confrontations and the use of indirect aggression. The situational aspect of anger is measured by five scales that provide an indication of anger across a range of provocative circumstances: disrespect from others; feelings of being treated unjustly; frustration; perception of annoying traits in other people; and everyday annoyances and 'hassles'. These scales, which measure persistent tendencies to experience and react to anger (i.e. *trait* anger), are positively and significantly correlated with measures of the experience of anger in real life settings (i.e. *state* anger). Inasmuch as state anger is usually an immediate precursor of aggression, the NAS is therefore a useful indicator of risk for violent behaviour.

The suppression of anger

One final aspect of anger must be considered – the possibility that it may be aroused in a provoking situation yet not be expressed in any overt and observable way. It may simply be held in, suppressed and 'bottled up'. Obviously, no connection between anger and aggression will be seen when this happens. That anger can produce two consequences, one an overt expression of aggression (either directly in the form of attack or displaced to such high-intensity behaviours as slamming doors and kicking furniture) and the other a suppression, has long been recognized in both classic psychoanalytic theory and research on human psychophysiology. These two reactions have come to be called, respectively, the 'anger-out' and 'anger-in' patterns of response. Whether a provocation will elicit one or the other of these responses is a function of several variables. Obviously, situational constraints, such as expectation of being punished for acting out anger, will be most likely to produce the anger-in outcome. In addition, individual differences in tendencies to resort to one or the other of the reactions, possibly reflecting a combination of genetic and acquired dispositions, have been assessed through psychometric means (Spielberger *et al.* 1995). The most important result of the study of anger-in and anger-out patterns, however, has been the demonstration of their connection to stress and physical illness. This matter is discussed in a later chapter.

COGNITIVE PROCESSING

Angry, affect-driven responses to being provoked tend to be impulsive and immediate. This is not to say, however, that cognition plays no role in the course of aggression following provocation. The processes of judgement, interpretation, attribution of cause and response selection all figure into the direction and control of aggressive behaviour, and in this chapter we will survey some of the theory and research that has been addressed to such cognitive mediation.

From impulse to cognition

Berkowitz is explicit in treating anger as a primitive, preconscious reaction to aversive stimulation, defining the anger, hostile thoughts and aggressive motor patterns evoked at this stage as 'rudimentary'. Beyond this point, cognitive processes become important in further aggression. This raises an obvious question: at what point, and for what reason, does aggressive behaviour become subject to the effects of cognitive processes, e.g. judgement, interpretation, decision-making and response selection? Zillmann has suggested that cognitive processing may be involved even *before* the provocation occurs. In the previous chapter we noted, for example, the experiment by Zillmann and Cantor (1976), in which it was shown that if subjects had been given prior information that could lead them to attribute a provocation to mitigating circumstances, subsequent affective arousal was attenuated. Berkowitz has suggested that cognitive control mechanisms are activated when the person begins to pay attention to how bad he or she feels (Berkowitz and Troccoli 1990). Once awareness of the negative affect evoked by the situation comes into play, the person goes on to detect and analyse other features of the immediate situation in which the provocation has occurred.

Attributional mediators of aggression

We have noted that provocations such as attacks or frustrations need not always lead to aggression. Certain interpretations of these events must be made for aggression to follow. The provocation must be regarded as intentional and malicious in intent. It must be viewed as a violation of normative behaviour in social situations. A number of attributes are therefore assigned to the provocative act by the person against whom it is directed. In this section we review in greater detail the nature of the attribution process that intervenes between provocation and aggression. This process has been summarized by Ferguson and Rule (1983), and their conclusions form the outline of the section.

Ferguson and Rule base their attributional analysis on the answers to three questions that a person asks after having been harmed by someone. The questions are:

1 *What was the act of harm that was done?* The answer to this question goes into the intent of the actor and whether or not the actor could foresee the harmful consequences of the act.
2 *What ought to have been done under the circumstances?* The answer to this question is based on consideration of what is normative in the situation and what values are held by the observer.
3 *Does any discrepancy exist between what has been done and what ought to have been done?*

Depending on the answers to these questions the victim of harm will either hold the actor culpable or absolve him or her of blame. Anger will be experienced to the extent that he or she is held responsible for the harm that has been done. Aggression is assumed to be a direct outgrowth of anger.

Understanding the harmful act

The first judgement that the harmed person makes is whether the other person acted intentionally or whether the harm was not intentional. If a judgement is made that the harm was intended, it is further classified as either malevolent or not malevolent in intent. If the act is judged to be unintentional, a further determination is made of whether or not the harmdoer could have foreseen the consequences of his or her actions. Hence the act of harm may be defined as one of four types: (a) intentional and malevolent; (b) intentional but not malevolent; (c) not intended but foreseeable; and (d) unintentional and unforeseeable, this last type of harm being truly accidental. Three separate attributions must be made before an act can be located within this scheme: intent, motive and foreseeability.

Attributions of intent

Judgements of intentionality are made along two general lines. One has to do with the nature of the situation and the other with the character of the harmdoer. In the first case, a judgement is made as to whether the harmdoing was the only act possible, whether any reasons for it (other than infliction of harm) could be imagined and whether the consequences of the act for the actor were mainly harmful or beneficial. For example, a victim, harmed by someone but knowing that the harmful behaviour was the only option that the perpetrator had, is likely to conclude that the act was not intentional but was compelled by circumstances. If, for example, a motorist swerves to avoid hitting a child and in so doing strikes and kills the child's dog, this latter act would usually be considered unintentional. Furthermore, the motorist in this case might show sorrow over killing the child's pet, indicating thereby that his or her outcomes were aversive. This, too, would elicit a judgement of unintentional harm.

Some other judgements of the immediate situation will also serve as keys to the intent of the harmdoer. Intent will often be inferred from judgements about whether the actor enjoys the harmful behaviour or not. When transgressors against others show happy facial expressions during the commission of harmful acts, their acts are usually classified as intentional more than when the perpetrator has a sad countenance. We also infer intent from the amount of effort that the transgressor expends in carrying out the harmful act. A person who overcomes many obstacles en route to doing harm to someone is more likely to be called an intentional aggressor than another person who encounters less difficulty. Planning carefully the act of harm represents such an expenditure of effort, a fact that is reflected in consideration by the legal system of 'premeditation' as a condition for first-degree murder. The second type of appraisal that leads to a judgement of intentionality has to do with characteristics of the harmdoer. If a person is known to have done a lot of harm in the past, any harmful act by that person should have a strong likelihood of being judged intentional. In addition, stereotypes based on membership in categories such as race, sex and physical attractiveness also enter into judgements of intent behind harmdoing.

Attributions of motive

Once a judgement on intentionality has been made, the victim must then decide whether the intent was malicious or not. Harmful behaviour that is seen as instrumental to the attainment of other ends is generally regarded as being less malevolent than harmdoing for its own sake (Rule 1978). If the harmdoing serves some prosocial purpose it also tends to be regarded as not malevolent. Hitting a mugger to restrain him from attacking an elderly woman would be considered a generally benign act by most people. Athletes who are subjected to verbal abuse by a coach who wants them to play with greater intensity also tend not to view the coach's behaviour as malicious in intent. Finally, harm that is seen as retaliation for some prior provocation tends to be regarded as less malevolent than harm inflicted without an apparent desire for retaliation (Harvey and Rule 1978).

Attributions of foreseeability

An act of harmdoing need not be intentional to be regarded as blameworthy. Ferguson and Rule (1983) point out that sometimes the failure to avoid doing unintended harm that can be foreseen is also cause for assigning moral culpability to the actor. Foreseeability can be of two types. One is negligence on the part of the person. If the person knows that something he or she is about to do to another person will cause unintended harm, but is either too lazy or too indifferent to seek an alternative course of action, we attribute negligent foreseeability to that person. The other type of foreseeability is the product of ruthlessness on the part of the actor, who makes no attempt to prevent unintentionally harming another person because some other selfish purpose would be served by the action.

One basis on which judgements of foreseeability are made is the locus of causality of the act. In general, acts of harmdoing that are regarded as due to internal causes (i.e. specific behaviours of the actor) are judged to be more foreseeable by the actor than are those attributed to external causes. For example, a study by Brickman et al. (1975) showed that subjects make a judgement of greater foreseeability in the case of automobile accidents when the accident is due to an internal cause (e.g. the driver was not looking at the road) than when it is due to an external cause (e.g. failure of the steering mechanism). Another basis for judgement is the degree of control that the actor is thought to have over events. In a study that has an indirect bearing on this point, Arkkelin et al. (1979) found that drivers involved in accidents were held more responsible by subjects when the accident was due to a known mechanical fault than when it was due to daydreaming. Daydreaming may be an unforeseeable cause of an accident because the driver has no way of knowing ahead of time whether he or she will daydream while at the wheel of a car. However, driving a car with a known fault is a clear case of negligence, in which the possibility of an accident can be foreseen.

Judging what ought to have happened

Each of the four types of harmful act described above can be compared to some norm that prescribes activity in the situation in question. These norms reflect the basic values of the parties involved and are determined by the culture in which the action is carried out. Most cultures have a norm that condemns the infliction of intentional malevolent harm on another person. Most also have a norm that excuses or justifies the occasional infliction of intentional but non-malevolent harm. The pain caused by a physician in treating a patient or that inflicted by a police officer in the normal course of duties fall into this category. Thus the person who commits harm that is wilfully malevolent is judged to be more culpable for the act than is someone who commits harm that is not.

Another social norm that is probably fairly common is that a socially responsible person should do everything possible to avoid doing unintended harm to others. When a harmful act is seen as unintended but foreseeable, therefore, it should be judged more harshly than when it is not foreseeable, i.e. truly accidental. The latter type of act is usually not judged as one indicating blame or moral culpability. A few studies have attempted to ascertain which of the types of harmdoing elicits the strongest condemnation. The evidence indicates clearly that intentional and malevolent harm is judged to be the most blameworthy and deserving of punishment (Rule and Nesdale 1976). In addition, non-malevolent intended harm is usually rated as no more wrong than accidentally inflicted harm (e.g. Ferguson and Rule, 1980).

Social information processing

Because behaviour in situations of interpersonal conflict is guided by cognitive representations of events, whether aggression occurs is to a large extent a function of how **social information** is processed. A person who is deficient in the ability to process and respond to social cues may manifest reactions to social information that are inappropriate or maladaptive. Such maladaptive behaviour may cause other people to reject the person, and this outcome may in turn have several undesirable consequences, including further rejection by peers, depression, and chronic and characteristic aggressiveness. Dodge and his colleagues have developed a model that identifies several processing stages, at any one of which faulty processing may be predicted by the person's level of maladjustment.

In the most recent version of the model, Crick and Dodge (1994) have described six stages (Figure 3.1): (1) *encoding* of cues arising from both the actions of other persons and one's own acts (e.g. a woman encounters an acquaintance at a meeting, is ignored by that person and feels upset); (2) *interpretation* of those cues (the snubbed woman decides that

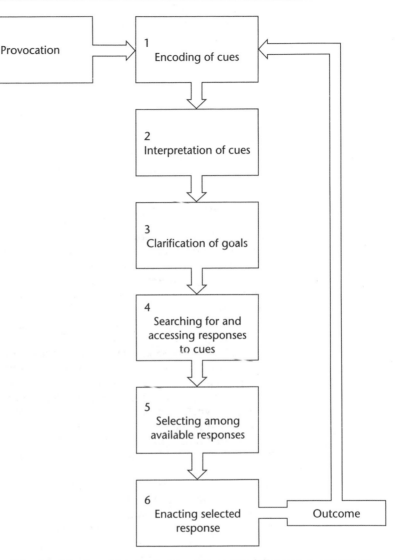

Figure 3.1 Model of social information processing following provocation.
Source: adapted from Crick and Dodge (1994).

her acquaintance has ignored her out of hostility and malevolence and
that her own feeling is anger); (3) clarification of the *goals* of the interaction (the victim of the ostensible snub decides that she will not be friendly
to the other woman if she sees her again); (4) the search for, and gaining
of *access* to, responses to the cues (upon meeting the other woman later,
the first has the option of ignoring her in return or of saying something
unfriendly); (5) the *decision* to select one of the available responses for
the present situation (the woman determines that she will refuse to speak
to the one who snubbed her); and (6) behavioural *enactment* of the chosen

response (the woman, on meeting the other, ignores her). The stages in the model are not precisely linear and unidirectional. For example, encoding and interpretation tend to occur virtually simultaneously, as do response access and response decision. Still, in conceptual and theoretical terms, the model describes an ongoing stage-to-stage sequence in which feedback cues from the person's behaviour at stage 6 contribute to the encoding of a stimulus input at the beginning of a new round of processing (e.g. the woman's decision to retaliate by snubbing the first woman may be met with further hostility from the latter). The process described by Crick and Dodge is therefore embedded in an ongoing series of transactions between people and their social environments.

The hostile attribution bias

When social information is generated by a provocative interpersonal exchange, any tendency that the person may have towards attributing hostility to the other person can influence the cognitive construction of the exchange and the response that one makes to it (i.e. Figure 3.1, stages 1 and 2). For example, Dodge (1980) found that boys who had been described by their peers and teachers as being highly aggressive reacted more aggressively to the frustrating actions of another boy than did their less aggressive peers, even though the intentions of the frustrator were not at all obvious. Dodge concluded that in the absence of clear information about the intent behind the frustration, aggressive boys attribute hostile motives to the frustrator. In another early study, Nasby *et al.* (1979) found that aggressive boys made attributions of hostility towards a peer even when that person's intentions were clearly benign. The authors described this tendency to see hostility in the acts of others as a **hostile attribution bias**. This bias may be the product of some of the processing deficiencies described by Dodge and his associates, such as inefficient encoding and interpretation of social cues. Actions that are not hostile may simply be misread by the victim because of some deficit in cognitive processing. In support of this idea, Dodge and Newman (1981) found that aggressive boys pay less attention to available social cues than their less aggressive counterparts, react to situations more quickly and, when responding quickly, are more likely to commit the hostile attribution bias. Other evidence suggests that aggressive boys may not be less attentive overall than less aggressive peers, but more likely to attend selectively to aggressive cues in the social situation (Gouze 1987). Still another possibility is indicated by the finding of Dodge and Tomlin (1987) that aggressive boys are more likely than non-aggressive ones to reach a conclusion regarding the intent of others on the basis of personal beliefs and schemata rather than information about the situation.

Generation of solutions to conflict

The hostile attribution bias exemplifies the deficits in encoding and interpretation of social cues described by Crick and Dodge (1994). Other studies have provided evidence that aggressiveness is related to deficits elsewhere in the information-processing cycle as well, such as in the ability to generate a wide range of possible solutions to conflict (i.e. Figure 3.1, stages 4 and 5). Deluty (1985a) assessed children's suggested solutions to a set of hypothetical interpersonal conflicts, and found that aggressive boys and girls both tended to generate large numbers of aggressive solutions but relatively small numbers of assertive ones, suggesting that individual aggressiveness may limit the number of responses available to access. A similar finding was reported by Slaby and Guerra (1988): highly aggressive adolescent students generated fewer solutions to hypothetical interpersonal problems than did less aggressive students. This same pattern of findings was also shown in terms of other dependent variables. The more aggressive the students, the fewer additional facts they requested before responding, the more they showed the hostile attribution bias, the more likely they were to generate hostile goals in the interaction and the fewer consequences of aggression they were able to foretell. Aggressive subjects also tended to generate less effective solutions.

One question that arises from the finding that aggressive children tend to generate predominantly aggressive solutions to conflicts is whether such children truly lack the ability to conceptualize non-aggressive alternatives or whether they have such responses available but simply do not access them. The evidence tends to support the latter alternative. Highly aggressive children seem to be capable of articulating socially constructive solutions, but they react to problem situations rapidly and impulsively, and without taking the time necessary to process all available information (Lochman *et al.* 1989). When methods are used that require subjects to respond to conflicts with greater deliberation, such as multiple-choice formats that describe a number of alternatives from which the subject must choose, the large processing deficits normally found in aggressive subjects relative to non-aggressive ones are attenuated (Lochman *et al.* 1989).

Reciprocality of aggression and social competence

It is clear from the studies reviewed here that the relationship between aggressiveness and social competence is a reciprocal and cyclical one, as Crick and Dodge (1994) have stated. Aggressive children and adolescents interpret cues in potentially provocative situations in such a way that they attribute hostile motives to others and, in general, react in aggressive ways. Such aggressive reactions may not be the most effective under the circumstances. Such behaviour invites social rejection (Dishion *et al.* 1994; Dodge 1983) that may, for various reasons, make the child even more aggressive (Huesmann 1988). For instance, rejection by one's peers or teachers may promote a continued deficiency in the processing of relevant social information. Studies have shown, for example, that rejection by peers leads to processing problems similar to those observed elsewhere in highly aggressive children (e.g. Crick and Ladd 1990). It has also been found that depressed children show the hostile attribution bias more than non-depressed children, a finding that may be significant in the present context to the extent that depression tends to be associated with social rejection (Quiggle *et al.* 1992).

Social scripts

Script construction and retrieval

As children gain experience with aggression and its consequences, they develop a more elaborate sense of the rules of conduct prescribed by society and also tend to take on these rules as guides for behaviour. In this way, aggression comes under the control of internalized standards and norms. Over time the person's behaviour and the social context in which it normally occurs may become routinized. Huesmann (1988) has proposed that persistent aggressive behaviour is to be understood in terms of the internal cognitive representations, or *schemata*, that people form of their environments. The child who uses aggression successfully as a means of settling interpersonal conflicts exposes himself or herself, by virtue of this behaviour, to a large number of aggressive scenarios. These scenarios are the units out of which more complicated behavioural **scripts** are constructed. Scripts become encoded in memory and are later retrieved as guides for behaviour. Each time this happens the script becomes more firmly established and maintained, through rehearsal, as a director of behaviour. In addition, subsequent aggressive experiences may lead the child to elaborate on available scripts and, as a result, develop more abstract and generalized aggressive strategies for dealing with conflicts. The result is a high probability that the child will retrieve an aggressive script when future conflicts arise and that aggressive behaviour will be the consequence. The recall of an aggressive script is especially likely in situations that resemble the ones in which the scripted scenarios were acquired. Aggression, in turn, adds new aggressive scenarios to memory. The bully, for example, may generalize his offensive behaviour from the school to other social settings in the neighbourhood. In this way aggression can become self-perpetuating in ongoing and ever-mounting cycles.

The process of script construction involves not only exposure to scenarios but also a selection among the many scenarios that are available. This latter process follows from certain normative beliefs that the person holds (Guerra *et al.* 1994b). Normative beliefs are 'abstracted general knowledge about acceptable and unacceptable behaviors' (Guerra *et al.* 1994a) that is acquired by the child through the socialization process. The formation of a script for aggression requires not only that a certain course of action be seen as efficacious for solving a conflict, but also that it be consistent with normative beliefs. These beliefs enter into the process of script formation in three ways: (a) by affecting the relative salience of situational cues and ways that they are evaluated; (b) as cues for retrieval of scripts consistent with the beliefs; (c) as 'filters for behaviour' to reduce the likelihood of enacting scripts inconsistent with beliefs. For example, a father who holds the normative belief that children must show unquestioning obedience may react initially to a rebellious child by focusing on her or his acts of independence and by labelling these acts disapprovingly. Guided still further by his belief in parental dominance, he will then be likely to retrieve behavioural scripts that call for asserting power over the child, by force if necessary. Finally, this same belief will make it likely that the father rejects any responses to the child's independence that are likely to make him look 'permissive'. The likelihood of aggression and physical abuse thereby becomes increased as an alternative to the rejected behaviours. Some of the processes of script retrieval and enactment are automatic, although certain complex scripts may include intent and conscious reflection.

Aggression and cognitive activity

The acquisition of aggressive scripts may also reflect some underlying cognitive processes that emerge during socialization. The research reported by Huesmann and his associates has revealed a positive correlation between early aggressiveness and subsequent cognitive processing. As part of a **longitudinal study** of a large sample of children conducted over a 22-year period, Huesmann *et al.* (1987) found that high levels of aggressiveness at age eight were a good predictor of poor adult intellectual functioning, whereas early cognitive functioning – while being closely related to aggressiveness at age eight – was not a reliable correlate of aggression at later ages. As a result of these findings, Huesmann (1988) formulated a dual-process model of aggressiveness and intellectual activity. The first of the two processes operates early in the life of the child and explains the positive relationship between aggressiveness and intellectual functioning at age eight. Poor intellectual processing may produce aggression at first by causing frustration in the normal problem-solving settings, such as those encountered by children at school. Several consequences may follow. The 'slow' child may react to the frustration with aggression. Because of his or her intellectual deficit, the child is relatively unable to understand the inappropriateness of aggression or to formulate alternative reactions. At the same time the child's aggressive behaviour brings about a low rate of reinforcement for non-aggressive responses. The child therefore encodes mainly aggressive strategies for frustrating situations.

The second process begins at this point. Once an aggressive strategy has been encoded, it tends to persist and to exert a reciprocating effect on intellectual processes. By hindering good relationships between the child and both teachers and peers, aggressive behaviour interferes with the child's chances at intellectual opportunities and advancement. The aggressive child is not popular and is not afforded many chances for growth through positive social interactions. The child therefore continues to do poorly in school, the low level of intellectual functioning is maintained and the cycle is repeated. Whereas poor intellectual functioning led originally to aggression, aggression now becomes the source of continued intellectual deficits. From this process arises the correlation between aggressiveness at age eight and poor intellectual functioning later in life.

The General Affective Aggression Model

As noted above, Anderson and his associates have developed a model of intervening processes in aggression that bears some resemblance to Berkowitz's cognitive–neoassociationist approach. This **General Affective Aggression Model** (GAAM) evolved from the research on temperature

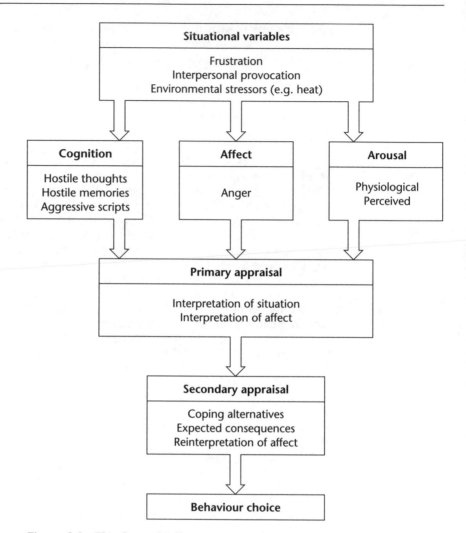

Figure 3.2 The General Affective Aggression Model.
Source: based on Anderson *et al.* (1995).

and aggression carried out by this group, which was reviewed in the preceding chapter, but it applies equally well to all affective aggression. It is represented in Figure 3.2. Like Berkowitz, Anderson considers negative affect to be a consequence of any aversive antecedent condition. Whether or not negative affect mediates the activation of hostile thoughts, memories and associations – as Berkowitz has argued (Chapter 2) – or whether it is a concomitant of the latter effects – as Anderson's model clearly shows – is not a matter of practical concern. Anderson has written:

> Affect may well indeed be a prime source of organization of such networks, although such a claim is not central to our theory. What is central is the idea that activation of one element in a network tends

to increase automatically the accessibility of other elements in that network, as a function of the strength of the linkage and strength of the initial activation.

(Anderson *et al.* 1995: 436)

The latter point, as we have seen, is also a critical element in Berkowitz's cognitive–neoassociatonist hypothesis. For Anderson, however, affect, cognition and arousal are all parallel processes engendered by provoking conditions. Discussion of the cognitive effects of provocation, and of the role of 'aggression scripts' in behaviour, has been taken up earlier in this chapter. These scripts are situation-specific patterns of aggressive behaviour that are acquired either directly or by observation in the social learning process. Anderson is therefore proposing that aversive conditions evoke not only hostile thoughts and memories, but also dispositions and motives to carry out aggressive acts. In other words, through the activation of affective and cognitive pathways, the person is 'primed' to behave aggressively if he or she is sufficiently provoked.

Note that in addition to recognizing the cognitive and affective consequences of aversive conditions, Anderson identifies physiological arousal as a third consequence. We have already seen (Chapter 2) how actual physiological arousal can contribute to aggression by intensifying any response considered appropriate to the situation, e.g. attacking when provoked. Arousal may also have other effects on aggression involving certain cognitive processes that are discussed below. For now, we need only recognize that Anderson incorporates arousal into the model as an important mediator of the effects of aversive stimulation.

This model incorporates the higher-level cognitive processing that, in Berkowitz's approach, comes after the initial affective and associative response to the stimulus. For Anderson, therefore, the immediate outcome of the affective, cognitive and arousal reactions is a cognitive appraisal of the situation, whereby the person makes a quick judgement of what happened, why it happened (e.g. was the provocation, if personal, deliberate or malicious?) and how angry he or she feels. This rapid appraisal will be influenced by the hostile thoughts, the negative affect and the arousal level that characterizes the person at this time. The person may then make a second appraisal, one requiring more time and cognitive resources, and which involves consideration of, for example, ways in which the person can cope with the situation, the likely consequences of various courses of action and circumstances which might alter the intensity of the state of anger.

As we saw in Chapter 2, Anderson and his colleagues carried out a programme of experimental research aimed at uncovering the underlying process variables in the temperature–aggression relationship, and their findings were explainable in terms of the GAAM. The model has since been extended to account for other findings, such as the cognitive and affective effects of exposure to violent movies and television (Anderson 1997), video games (Anderson and Dill 2000) and lyrics in rock music (Anderson and Haynes 1996). These types of stimuli increase aggressive feelings and cognition relative to non-violent control stimuli. A more complete discussion of such effects is given in Chapter 6.

Alcohol, cognitive processing and aggression

The figure of the belligerent drunk is a common one in folklore. Certainly a correlation between alcohol intoxication and aggressive behaviour has been accepted implicitly throughout much of human experience. The reasons for that correlation, however, have not been obvious. The effects of alcohol intoxication on aggression have been documented in a number of studies (Bushman and Cooper 1990), but a detailed analysis of the mechanisms whereby it interacts with other proximal variables has not been made. However, considerable evidence from experimental studies by Taylor and his associates suggests that ingestion of alcohol may interfere with cognitive processing, so that the intoxicated individual is less able than a sober one to interpret accurately the more subtle social cues that can arise in interpersonal conflicts (Taylor and Leonard 1983). This relative insensitivity may dispose the inebriated person to respond more to gross aggression-related cues in the situation than to information about the other person's motives or to situational constraints (Gantner and Taylor 1992). It may also render the inebriated person less able to utilize stimuli in the situation that call for inhibition and restraint in aggressing, like the threat of social disapproval or retaliation from others.

An analysis of studies on alcohol ingestion and aggression carried out by Ito *et al.* (1996) isolated certain situational factors pertinent to aggression to which intoxicated and sober people react with different levels of attention. Consider the presence or absence of provocation. Normally, people are more likely to attack another person when they have been provoked by that person than when they have not. It is a characteristic of the normally socialized person that he or she does not hurt another person without a reason, and there are plenty of cues in the social situation reminding us of this fact, cues ranging from the likelihood of social ostracism to the possibility of legal action. When a person becomes intoxicated, attention to these cues may be diminished, and the person should become, relative to a sober one, more likely to behave aggressively despite the lack of provocation. Steele and Josephs (1990) have discussed this sort of reduction in cue utilization during intoxication, which they have labelled 'alcohol myopia'. When provocation is clearly present in the situation, the sober person will become more aggressive by losing inhibitions. Thus, the tendency of the inebriated person to be more aggressive than the sober person (which we will call the 'alcohol effect') should be greater in situations where there is no obvious provocation than in those where provocation is manifest. Ito and her colleagues found this to be true in their review of pertinent studies. They also found, however, that the general tendency of intoxicated people to pay less attention to situational inhibitors of aggression relative to sober people can be overcome by other cues in the situation that increase attention to the self. When inebriated people are led to become more self-conscious (as, for example, when they know that their behaviour is being observed via a video camera) the alcohol effect is reduced, i.e. self-consciousness has a greater inhibitory effect on intoxicated persons than on sober ones. Persons under the influence of alcohol under these conditions appear to overcompensate in the extent to which they bring their behaviour under inhibitory control.

SUMMARY

1 The connection between provocation and aggression involves the mediation of cognitive, affective and arousal processes. These mediators interact with others in various ways specified in several current theories.

2 Arousal from a source that is not related to a provocation may summate with arousal elicited by a provocation. For this misattribution, called 'excitation transfer', to occur, a short period of time must elapse between the provocation and the stimulus that produces the irrelevant arousal so that the most salient symptoms of the latter will have time to dissipate. In addition, misattribution is more likely when the source of the extraneous arousal is ambiguous. Any activity that increases arousal can, when combined with sufficient provocation, serve as an antecedent of aggression. Because of the anger-labelling that follows excitation transfer, an arousing condition may lead to aggression far beyond the time at which the arousal itself has dissipated. Thus, the misattribution process has implications for long-term behaviour.

3 Anger may also be defined as a social construction. Like other emotions, it may be a socially defined and constructed syndrome of affective, cognitive and physiological processes. Social variables must also be taken into account in defining the conditions under which anger occurs, the way in which it is acted out and the means used to assess it as a risk factor for violence.

4 Cognitive processing is a second source of intervening processes in aggression. The victim of harm appraises the situation and attributes certain characteristics to the harm that has been done. Harmdoing may be classified as one of four types: (a) intentional and malevolent; (b) intentional but not malevolent; (c) not intended but foreseeable; and (d) unintentional and unforeseeable, this last type of harm being truly accidental. Three separate attributions must be made before an act can be located within this scheme: intent, foreseeability and motive. Judgements of intentionality are made along two general lines. One has to do with the nature of the situation and the other with the character of the harmdoer.

5 The attribution process is part of a larger one involving the processing of all social information in a provocative interchange. Processing begins with the encoding and interpretation of the provocation, after which judgements are made about the goals of the interaction and the availability of alternative behaviours to carry out those goals. The choice and enactment of a response completes the processing cycle. Highly aggressive people have been shown to manifest a relative tendency to place hostile interpretations on interpersonal exchanges that are ambiguous in nature and to choose aggressive actions from among the available responses.

6 The selection of aggressive responses to provocation is also guided by the individual's store of aggressive scripts acquired in the course of

socialization. Retrieval of aggressive scripts is a function of the strength and generality of the script, the degree of similarity between the conditions under which the script was acquired and the conditions of the current provocation, and the normative beliefs about aggression that the person holds.

7 The General Affective Aggression Model is an overall scheme that brings together both the affective and cognitive mediators of aggression, along with physiological arousal, treating the three as independent, but mutually interacting, paths from provocation to aggression.

8 Current approaches to the study of the role played by alcohol intoxication in aggression stress the effects that inebriation has on cognitive processing. Intoxication influences aggression mainly by restricting the range of informational stimuli in the environment that might otherwise provide cues for the inhibition of the behaviour.

SUGGESTIONS FOR FURTHER READING

Crick, N. R. and Dodge, K. A. (1994) A review and reformulation of social information-processing mechanisms in children's social adjustment. *Psychological Bulletin*, 115, 74–101. A concise summary of cognitive processes involved in utilizing and acting upon social information, which has specific application to aggressive interchanges.

Huesmann, L. R. (1998) The role of social information processing and cognitive schema in the acquisition and maintenance of habitual aggressive behavior, in R. G. Geen and E. Donnerstein (eds) *Human Aggression: Theories, Research, and Implications for Social Policy*. San Diego: Academic Press, pp. 73–109. An extensive and in-depth review of the author's studies of social information processing.

Kassinove, H. (ed.) (1995) *Anger Disorders: Definition, Diagnosis, and Treatment*. Washington, DC: Taylor & Francis. This book contains essays by leading authorities who describe anger as a clinical problem.

FOUR

MODERATOR VARIABLES IN AGGRESSION

The basic model that we have been following in this book treats aggression as a joint result of provoking, stress-inducing conditions and certain background variables that increase the likelihood aggression as a response to those conditions, as well as the intensity of that aggression. Two important background, or moderator, variables have already been discussed: biological inheritance and social learning history. Both may predispose a person to respond with aggression to acts of provocation (Chapter 1). They are, however, only two of many such background variables. In this chapter we review three others that have figured prominently in the literature on aggression. They are: (a) sex; (b) personality; and (c) socio-cultural variables that encourage or facilitate aggressiveness. All these variables interact with situational provocations, i.e. they *moderate* the effects of such provocations, to produce varying amounts and levels of aggressive behaviour.

SEX DIFFERENCES IN AGGRESSION

Although it is commonly believed in our society that men are more aggressive than women, the evidence from research on the subject reveals effects that are far from simple. Most investigators would probably agree that men are typically more physically aggressive than women (e.g. Reinisch and Sanders 1986), but differences of opinion exist regarding the basis for this effect, the conditions under which it is found and the nature of the cognitive and affective processes that mediate it.

Biology or culture?

One of the longest-standing theories of sex differences in aggression attributes these differences to inherent physical differences between men and women. This idea has been discussed above (Chapter 1) in the general discussion of the biological basis for aggression. The possibility that sex differences may have a genetic basis has been pointed out by Maccoby and Jacklin (1974). These authors base their conclusion on the findings of four lines of evidence: (a) that men are generally more aggressive than women in virtually all human cultures; (b) that males are more aggressive than females early in life, at a time prior to the shaping of individuals by differential socialization pressures; (c) that greater aggressiveness in males relative to females is found in non-human primates as well as in humans; and (d) that aggression is related to sex hormones and can be influenced by administration of these substances. This viewpoint has been challenged by critics who have cited studies that fail to support the assertions listed here and who emphasize instead the importance of differential socialization practices as the basis for male–female differences in aggression. It should be noted that Maccoby and Jacklin do not attribute *all* sex differences to biological differences, but insist only that the latter provide the background within which situational variables operate. Archer and McDaniel (1995) reported findings from a cross-national study that are consistent with the assumption that both biological and cultural factors are involved in sex differences in aggression. Stories written by subjects in response to hypothetical interpersonal conflicts revealed that in each of 12 national samples males wrote a higher proportion of violent themes than females, suggesting possible underlying biological causation. However, the degree of male–female differences in the proportion of violent themes written varied widely across national samples, suggesting social and cultural causation as well.

Norms, expectations and beliefs

Sex differences in aggression have been the subject of several major reviews. Frodi *et al.* (1977) found that sex differences were associated with several variables. One is the sex of the instigator and the victim: the majority of studies reviewed in 1977 showed that both sexes were less likely to aggress against a woman than against a man. In addition, women were more likely than men to consider aggression inappropriate, to repress aggression and to experience guilt or anxiety in connection with aggressive actions. These findings indicate that the two sexes respond to normative prescriptions in judging aggression and in the affective states that accompany it. Women and men were also found to differ in terms of their appraisals of, and reactions to, situational conditions.

Provoking conditions

Conditions that evoke anger in women tend to be different from those that elicit anger in men. For example, Harris (1993) found that women are more angered than men by insensitive or condescending behaviour from a man and by verbal abuse and condescending behaviour from another woman, whereas men are more angered than women by a physical attack from another man. Sexual infidelity by a partner has also been shown to excite greater feelings of anger and desire for punitive action in women than in men. Paul *et al.* (1993) found that women reported greater anger than men towards both their unfaithful partners and their rivals for the partner's affections. Women also were more likely than men to react to infidelity by assertive behaviour towards both partner and rival. In a subsequent study, Paul and Galloway (1994) observed that women expressed stronger approval than men of such actions as 'badmouthing' and harassing their rivals.

In a comprehensive review of studies on sex differences, Bettencourt and Miller (1996) reported that sex and provocation interact in predicting aggression: men were more aggressive than women under neutral conditions, whereas provocation attenuated sex differences. In addition, Bettencourt and Miller found that although provocation reduced sex differences in general, specific types of provocation differentially affected the degree to which this attenuation occurred. For example, threats to self-esteem had little effect on women's aggression, whereas insults or physical attacks led to relatively high aggressiveness. Among men, threat to self-esteem was as provocative as physical attack and more provocative than insult. Bettencourt and Miller also found that men were more aggressive than women when physical aggression was the method made available to subjects, but no more aggressive than women when verbal or written aggression was involved.

Beliefs about consequences

The conclusion of Frodi *et al.* (1977) that the aggressive behaviour of men and women is controlled in part by social norms and expectations is consistent with a similar conclusion by Eagly and Steffen (1986). In a meta-analysis these investigators found that a large amount of the sex difference in aggression can be traced to beliefs about the negative consequences of aggression. Women are less aggressive than men when they believe that acting aggressively will harm the victim, pose a danger to themselves (e.g. by leading to retaliation) or evoke intense feelings of guilt or anxiety. This set of affective and cognitive processes may conspire to inhibit expression of aggressive behaviour. The findings of a study by Harris (1991) show how norms regarding male–female aggression tend to discourage aggression against women, especially by men. Harris asked male and female subjects to respond to two fictitious scenarios involving provocation and retaliation in which the sex of the aggressor and the retaliating victim were systematically manipulated. Harris found that subjects of both sexes thought that aggression against a female victim is inappropriate, that women are more justified than men in retaliating for aggression against them and that retaliation against a woman is less justified than retaliation against a man.

Eagly and Steffen (1986) concluded that the beliefs of men and women regarding the consequences of aggression become especially divergent under conditions that involve physical aggression. This may explain why most studies find that men are especially likely to be more aggressive than

women when the aggression is physical and assaultive, and why male–
female differences are attenuated when aggression is more psychological
(e.g. verbal abuse). Such findings indicate that men and women differ in
terms of the mode of aggression that they typically prefer to use.

Mode of aggressing

Relational aggression

As noted above, there is evidence for sex-linked preferences for specific
aggressive behaviours, with adult males tending to prefer using physical
aggression more than women, and women opting for other, less physical
acts. Whereas some reviewers have pointed out that such preferences do
not entirely explain sex differences in aggression (e.g. White 1983), it
seems clear that they are important contributors. Moreover, such sex differences in the type of aggression employed appear long before adulthood,
as recent research by Crick and her associates has shown. This work indicates that girls engage in what has been termed **relational aggression** to a
greater extent than boys (Crick and Grotepeter 1995). This aggression
consists of activity that 'harms others through damage to their peer relationships or to the threat of such damage' (Crick 1995), such as excluding
the victim from one's playgroup or threatening withdrawal of friendship
and acceptance. In many respects, relational aggression is functionally
similar to physical aggression. Children who typically use relational aggression to control or hurt others are more prone to form hostile attribution biases in situations involving relational conflicts than children who
are not usually aggressive in this way, and are also more emotionally
distressed by such conflicts (Crick 1995). Children also label relationally
manipulative behaviours as 'aggressive', i.e. as an appropriate accompani-
ment to feelings of anger and intent to harm (Crick *et al*. 1996).

Sex and developmental trends

The results of recent studies conducted in Finland and in Great Britain
add further support to the idea that differences in method of aggressing
contribute to sex differences in aggressive behaviour. The Finnish studies,
conducted by Lagerspetz, Björkqvist, and their colleagues, involved young
children, adolescents and adults. Some clear developmental trends were
found, as well as sex differences. From a cohort of eight-year-olds, Björkqvist
et al. (1992) gathered peer- and self-reports of what children in a class do
when angry. A factor analysis of the several behaviours listed by the
children yielded factors of direct and indirect aggression and a third factor
of non-aggressive withdrawal behaviours. Direct aggression included such
behaviours as physical assaults and verbal abuse carried out by the aggressor
against the target. Indirect aggression involved either using other people
to carry out aggressive intentions against the target or other manipula-
tions of the social network designed to exclude and isolate the target.
Boys showed significantly more direct aggression than girls, whereas girls
were slightly, but not significantly, more prone to use indirect aggression
and to withdraw peacefully than boys from anger-inducing settings. In

the 11-year-old cohort, boys were higher on the direct aggression factor than girls and girls were higher on both the indirect aggression and the non-aggression factors. In addition, girls were found to be organized into smaller, tighter friendship groupings than boys, a condition that might facilitate the manipulation of the social environment for purposes of indirect aggression (Lagerspetz et al. 1988); a similar difference in organization of friendship groupings had not been found in the study of eight-year-olds. Thus, whereas sex differences in the use of direct aggression were found in young children, the emergence of parallel sex differences in indirect aggression came later. Indirect (e.g. relational) aggression obviously involves the learning of tactics and strategies that can come only after a certain level of gender-role socialization has been attained. In a study of adult subjects, Björkqvist et al. (1994) found that men and women also tend to report being the *victims* of different kinds of indirect aggression. Men report a high level of aggression against them that is indirect, but is also personal in that it is disguised to seem rational and non-malicious (like having their work evaluated unjustly), whereas women report high levels of socially manipulated aggression, such as having false rumours spread about them.

The factor analysis of reported behaviours in the 15-year-old cohort yielded four factors: direct physical aggression, direct verbal aggression, indirect aggression and non-aggressive withdrawal. Boys showed greater use of direct physical aggression than girls and girls manifested more indirect aggression and withdrawal than boys. No sex differences in direct verbal aggression were found. Again, friendship units tended to be smaller among girls than among boys, with a larger number of pair friendships. The 18-year-old subjects revealed significant sex differences for both indirect and direct verbal aggression and for non-aggressive acts, with girls showing higher levels than boys in each case (Lagerspetz and Björkqvist 1994). No sex differences in direct physical aggression were found, mainly because the levels of such aggression among both boys and girls were very low. In fact, one of the most striking findings to emerge from the studies involving adolescents was the dramatic decline in physical aggression among boys from the ages of 15 to 18. The decreased use of physical aggression among boys was accompanied by an increased use of verbal and indirect aggression. This raises the possibility that aggression does not change as a function of age as much as it merely changes in the way in which it is expressed. If men become less directly and more indirectly aggressive with age while women remain more prone to use indirect than direct aggression, this could account for the finding that sex differences decrease with age (Hyde 1984; Eagly and Steffen 1986). The major findings of the Finnish studies are summarized in Table 4.1.

Cognitive constructions

The findings from the Scandinavian studies reviewed above show sex differences in preferred modes of aggressing for boys and girls, with these differences tending to become attenuated with age. Among adults, sex differences appear to be manifested more in the cognitive constructions that people place on provoking events, in the affect elicited by these

Table 4.1 Summary of Finnish studies of sex and development differences

Cohort	Aggression-related measures			
	Direct	Indirect	Non-aggressive	Small groups[a]
Eight-year-olds	B > G	(G > B)[b]	(G > B)[b]	
Eleven-year-olds	B > G	G > B	G > B	G > B
Fifteen-year-olds	B > G[c]	G > B	G > B	G > B
Eighteen-year-olds	G > B[d]	G > B[e]	G > B	

[a] Refers to tendency to form small and potentially exclusive friendship groups.
[b] Non-significant tendency only.
[c] Direct *physical* aggression only; no sex differences in direct verbal aggression.
[d] Direct *verbal* aggression only.
[e] Indirect *verbal* aggression only.

events and in the anticipated consequences of aggression. As has been noted in earlier parts of this review, the cognitive constructions that are placed on provocation and aggression mediate to a large extent the degree of aggression that such events evoke. A similar conclusion may be drawn with respect to the findings of Campbell and her associates in Britain (Campbell and Muncer 1987; Campbell 1993) that men and women interpret their own aggressiveness in different ways. Whereas men tend to define their aggression as instrumental behaviour that allows them to control other people, women tend to regard theirs as emotionally uncontrolled behaviour. Thus, while men characteristically see aggression as a useful and satisfying activity, women tend to react to it with guilt and repression. Campbell *et al.* (1992) have developed a self-report scale by means of which subjects can describe their aggressive behaviour in either instrumental or expressive (i.e. emotional) terms. Instrumentality versus expressivity is reflected in several dimensions, such as the form that aggression takes, the social value of aggression and the specific cognitions and emotions that accompany conflict and aggression. Campbell *et al.* (1992) found that of the 20 items that comprised the scale, 12 showed significant sex difference effects, with men choosing the instrumental alternative and women the expressive. In a subsequent study, Campbell and Muncer (1994) administered the same scale to samples of respondents that varied in terms of sex as well as occupation (soldiers or nurses), and found that both variables were related to beliefs in expressivity versus instrumentality of aggression. As in the earlier study, women were more expressive in their self-descriptions and men less expressive. In addition, nurses, whether male or female, were more expressive than male and female soldiers. Thus, sex role identity influences the social construction that is placed on aggression in much the same way as sex identity. The findings of Campbell and her associates all involve adults. Archer and Parker (1994) have extended the findings of differential social construction of aggression by showing that the same sex difference is found in pre-adolescent youngsters, indicating thereby that the socialization process that underlies the typical male–female difference begins early in life. Archer and Parker have also shown the same boy–girl difference in the case of indirect, verbal aggression. The tendencies of males to regard aggression as instrumental behaviour and of females to regard it as undesirable emotionality therefore appear to emerge fairly early.

A subsequent study reported by Archer and Haigh (1997) indicates that the effects predicted from the theory may be moderated by other characteristics of the subject, characteristics possibly linked to education and social class. This study was different from most investigations into the social psychology of aggression, in that the subjects were not highly socialized middle-class students but incarcerated criminals. Male and female inmates were given two scales: the Buss–Perry Aggression Questionnaire (which is described in the following section), by which they indicated their aggressive behaviours and feelings, and a scale developed by Archer and Haigh to measure tendencies towards both expressive and instrumental beliefs about aggression in each respondent. In many respects the correlations between the scales reaffirmed the earlier findings by Campbell, Archer and others. For the entire sample of men and women, instrumental beliefs were positively correlated, as expected, with self-reported aggression on all four of the subscales of the Aggression Questionnaire (physical, verbal, anger and hostility). Expressive beliefs were negatively correlated, again as predicted, with physical and verbal aggression. In addition, expressive beliefs were stronger among women than among men. Archer and Haigh's findings differed from those of previous studies, however, by showing that beliefs in the instrumental value of aggression were as strongly held by women as by men. In addition, no sex differences were found in ratings of physical aggression. Prison inmates therefore seem to represent a population within which women develop what would otherwise be considered 'male' beliefs in the value of aggression and also reveal aggressive tendencies consistent with those beliefs. Archer and Haigh did not present data revealing the underlying causes of this lack of sex differences in instrumental beliefs, but their findings do indicate that such beliefs are a function of more than just sex differences.

PERSONALITY AND AGGRESSION

Stability of aggressive behaviour

For many years social psychologists did not study the role played by personality variables in aggression. This indifference to personality was the result of two characteristics of the study of human aggression. First, a relative scarcity of reliable and valid personality scales to measure aggressive tendencies – for many years the Buss–Durkee Hostility Inventory was a lone exception to this generalization – has discouraged researchers who might otherwise have included personality variables in their research designs. Second, much of the research that has shown an effect of personality on aggression has been addressed to the practical clinical problem of identifying personality traits that signify pathological states, not to the testing of theories of person–situation interactions. For that reason, they have not clarified the status of personality traits as moderator variables. In addition, social psychologists tend to explain behaviour in terms of situational demands and to relegate individual differences to a secondary explanatory status, if indeed they use such explanations at all.

Arguments against studying the role of personality in aggression are usually based on the contention that aggressive behaviour is unstable across time and conditions. However, evidence for the consistency of aggression has been reported by a number of investigators in several countries (e.g. Deluty 1985b; Stattin and Magnusson 1989; Eron and Huesmann 1990). In a major investigation, Olweus (1979) reviewed a large number of longitudinal studies of aggressive behaviour and patterns of responding in children, noting in each study the coefficient of stability in aggressive behaviour from one assessment period to another. The lengths of time intervening between measurements varied from study to study, as did the ages of the children at the outset of each study. Measures of aggressiveness included direct observation, teacher ratings, clinical ratings and judgements made by other children.

Olweus found considerable evidence for stability of aggressive behaviour. Clear individual differences in level of aggressiveness emerged as early as the age of three, with such stability lasting for as long as 12–18 months. School-age children aged eight to nine showed aggressive behaviour patterns that were correlated with aggressiveness as long as 10–14 years later. In some instances, the magnitude of correlation was sufficient to account for 25 per cent of the variance at the later age. Aggressive behaviour at ages 12–13 also showed a high degree of stability for periods of one to five years, with between 50 and 90 per cent of the variance accounted for. Such findings indicate that aggressive behaviour is to some degree a function of generalized aggressiveness.

The postulation of stability in aggressive behaviour does not necessarily mean that certain people behave aggressively most of the time. Olweus suggests instead that individual differences contribute to aggression in concert with cognitive appraisals of the situation, emotional reactions and tendencies to inhibit aggression. Personal aggressiveness interacts with situational variables to predict aggressive behaviour. An interactional approach is also the basis for a two-factor theory of anti-social behaviour proposed by Moffitt (1993), who notes that whereas most anti-social behaviour begins and ends during adolescence, a small number of people manifest some sort of anti-social activity over the entire lifespan, beginning in early childhood. This latter group is the one that is most relevant to the present discussion. The origins of lifecourse-persistent anti-social behaviour lie in neuropsychological deficits that may be prenatal or perinatal in nature. These deficits may involve verbal deficits as well as deficits in 'executive' function, such as inattention and impulsivity; they may be the result of a host of factors, among them genetic inheritance, maternal drug abuse, poor prenatal nutrition and postnatal understimulation. The product of these conditions is an infant who is cognitively, affectively and behaviourally 'difficult'.

If the difficult child is placed in an environment that is nurturant and supportive, the problems are often overcome. However, if the child is reared in a more adverse environment, his or her behaviour may become progressively anti-social. At the same time, prosocial skills do not develop. Thus, through an interaction between neuropsychological deficits and early experiences with the environment, the beginnings of an anti-social personality are formed. This personality is maintained past childhood through two subsequent interactions with the environment. One is the tendency of anti-social people to construct a functional environment that is consistent with their personality by means of the hostile attribution bias. The other is the tendency to select or create environments that conform to anti-social behaviour patterns (e.g. Patterson *et al.* 1992). As a result of these ongoing reciprocal person–situation interactions, anti-social behaviour becomes stable and consistent (see Caspi *et al.* 1987).

Assessment of aggressiveness

Attempts to assess stable individual differences in aggressiveness with tests and inventories have yielded mixed results. Several inventories for the assessment of hostility and manifest aggressiveness have been published, but solid evidence of reliable and valid personal moderators of situational causes of aggression is not commonplace (see Edmunds and Kendrick 1980 for a review). Of the many scales published, some have generated a fair amount of attention among researchers. The Cook–Medley Hostility Scale (Cook and Medley 1954) has been used widely, but mainly in connection with measuring the implications of hostility for health, so that it is outside the scope of this review (Smith 1992). The same is true of the State-Trait Anger Scale and the Anger Expression Scale developed by Spielberger and his associates (1985). Of the personality measures that have been used in research on aggression *per se*, the most popular has been the Buss–Durkee Hostility Inventory (BDHI: Buss and Durkee 1957). Factor analytic studies of the seven subscales that comprise the Buss–Durkee inventory have typically yielded two factors, one described usually as 'aggressiveness' (i.e. revealing tendencies towards aggressive physical and/or verbal behaviour) and the other as 'hostility' (i.e. revealing tendencies towards attitudes of suspiciousness and resentment and towards wishing to see others come to harm). In a meta-analysis of several large factor analyses of the BDHI, Bushman *et al.* (1991) identified these same factors, and labelled them, respectively, *overt* and *covert* hostility.

Citing several psychometric weaknesses in the BDHI as the reason, Buss and Perry (1992) developed a new inventory built on a factorial structure similar to that of the original. Instead of the seven subscales of the original inventory, the new Aggression Questionnaire consists of four: physical aggression, verbal aggression, hostility and anger. The four scales are positively correlated with each other to a moderate degree, with the highest correlations reflecting the relation of anger to both physical and verbal aggression and hostility. Thus, as was the case with the BDHI, aggressiveness and hostility emerge as factors in the new scale, with anger serving as a 'psychological bridge' between the two components. Scale scores were also positively correlated with peer ratings of physical and verbal aggression, anger and hostility in a sample of male college students, with correlations ranging from $r = 0.20$ for verbal aggression to $r = 0.45$ for physical aggression. The Aggression Questionnaire therefore holds some promise as a predictor of aggressiveness and hostility. However, it is still a new scale that requires considerably more construct validation.

Personality variables as moderators of aggression

Irritability and general aggressiveness

A major programme of research into individual difference variables in human aggression has been reported by Caprara and his associates, who have conceptualized a number of personality variables as antecedents of aggressive behaviour and developed scales to assess these variables. Intercorrelations among the several variables have yielded a preliminary factorial structure of the aggressive personality, and the factors of the system have been shown to articulate with measures from other systems and theories, such as the five-factor model of personality (Caprara *et al.* 1994). The three scales most consistently related to aggressive dispositions have been **irritability**, emotional susceptibility and **dissipation–rumination**. The first of these scales is defined as a 'readiness to explode at the slightest provocation, including quick temper, grouchiness, exasperation, and rude-ness' and the second as 'the tendency to experience feelings of discomfort, helplessness, inadequacy, and vulnerability' (Caprara *et al.* 1985: 667). Dissipation–rumination refers to a tendency to retain or augment feelings of anger over time following provocation, as opposed to a tendency to dissipate such feelings and become less angry (Caprara 1986). In several studies in laboratory settings, Caprara and his colleagues have shown main effects on aggression for each of these variables, often paralleling main effects of frustrating or provoking treatments, such as task failure or insults (e.g. Caprara 1982; Caprara *et al.* 1983, 1987).

The study of how the various personality scales relate to aggressive beha-viour raises the question of their status as moderator variables. As noted, several experimental studies have shown main effects for the personality variables. However, for personality to moderate situational effects, it is necessary to show an interaction between these variables and experimen-tal treatments. Caprara's research has shown that such interactions are specific to certain combinations of treatment and personality variable. The variable shown most often to moderate the effects of provocation on aggression is irritability, provided that the provocation is operationalized in terms of failure at a task. In studies in which subjects have been given false feedback about task performance, those who are high in Irritability have reacted to negative feedback with more intense aggression against a target than those who score low on that variable (Caprara *et al.* 1983). Emotional Susceptibility has been shown not to interact with the feed-back treatment variable, and when interpersonal insult is used as a means of provoking the subject, neither Irritability nor Emotional Susceptibility serves as a moderator variable, but Dissipation–Rumination does, with persons classified as high ruminators–low dissipators showing greater retaliatory aggression than low ruminators–high dissipators (Caprara 1986).

In three studies, Bushman has reported a moderator effect of the trait of physical aggressiveness on both aggressive behaviour and cognitive processing. Bushman and Geen (1990) found that male subjects who had scored high on the Irritability scale of the BDHI listed a greater number of hostile and aggressive thoughts after seeing a moderately violent videotape than did those who had scored low on Irritability. The authors invoked Berkowitz's theory of cognitive neoassociationism in concluding that a high level of personal irritability may reflect a large and highly articulated network of aggressive associations that is likely to be primed by stimuli related to violence. Bushman (1996) confirmed this supposition by showing that highly aggressive subjects made more aggressive verbal associations to ambiguous words than did less aggressive subjects. Finally, Bushman (1995) demonstrated a link between personal aggressiveness and aggressive behaviour in response to provocation following the observation of televised violence. Provoked subjects who were shown a violent videotape were more aggressive in their level of retaliation than those shown a less violent tape only if they were also high in physical aggressiveness as assessed by the Buss–Perry Aggression Questionnaire (see p. 69). Bushman's findings are especially significant because they show clear situation–person interactions and do so within the context of a well developed theory.

Self-esteem and narcissism

The research described above stipulates some fairly straightforward effects of personality variables that are closely related conceptually to aggressive behaviour. Personality may also enter into aggression in more subtle ways through processes related to maintenance and enhancement of self-esteem. To the extent that being provoked threatens or weakens self-esteem and retaliation helps to restore it, such behaviour might be expected to vary as a function of existing levels of the variable. Protection or restoration of self-esteem has been cited as a cause of aggression by numerous reviewers (e.g. Averill 1982), but whether high or low self-esteem is most seriously affected by threats has not been clear. In a review on the subject, Baumeister *et al.* (1996) have concluded that aggression is usually an outcome of threats to highly favourable views of the self, i.e. high self-esteem. They suggest that the person with high self-esteem may direct anger towards others as a means of avoiding a downward revision of the self-concept. This is especially true of people whose high self-esteem is fragile, unstable and susceptible to challenge (Kernis *et al.* 1989). A related finding has been reported by Tangney *et al.* (1992): that people who are relatively prone to experience *shame* are also more likely to express anger and hostility and to blame others for bad things that happen to them. Shame is an aversive emotion that brings about a negative evaluation of the self and a temporary breakdown in self-esteem. The corresponding tendency to blame others shown by shame-prone people may cause them to become angry and hostile towards those they see as the cause of their poor self-esteem. Thus shame may be an intervening variable that moderates the effects of provocation on self-esteem.

Bushman and Baumeister (1998) have drawn a distinction between self-esteem and the related variable of **narcissism**, and have argued that it is the latter, not the former, that is closely related to aggression. Their distinction is made on the grounds that while self-esteem is a cognition about oneself – the cognition that the self is valuable and worth respect – narcissism is more a matter of emotion and motivation – the emotion of self-love and the motive to be superior to others. Thus, Bushman and Baumeister conclude that narcissists 'care passionately about being superior to others, even if they are not yet convinced that they have achieved this superiority' (p. 220). It is because insults and other attacks upon the self interfere with the motive for superiority that narcissists become furious at such attacks. To test this hypothesis, these investigators conducted an experiment in which male and female subjects wrote short essays that were presumably evaluated by another person. Feedback to the subject, which consisted of experimentally controlled information, either praised or criticized the subject's essay. The subject was later given an opportunity to aggress against the evaluator in the course of another task. Both narcissism and self-esteem levels of the subject had been assessed before the experiment. As expected, Bushman and Baumeister found that narcissism interacted with ego-threat. Only among subjects who were high in narcissism did ego-threat provoke more aggression than praise. Self-esteem, by contrast, was not related to aggressive behaviour.

Impulsivity

The provocative conditions described in Chapter 2 do not guarantee that aggressive reactions will follow. In general, humans are capable of controlling their aggressive impulses and suppressing their desires to strike back at people who offend them. This control is part of a larger biological organization in which the tendency to activate expressive behaviours and the counter-tendency to inhibit them are usually maintained in a sort of balance. In one detailed description of this balance, Jeffrey Gray and his associates have shown that mutually antagonistic 'behaviour activation' and 'behaviour inhibition' systems are organized within the central nervous system (Gray 1982). Within such a balanced excitation–inhibition system, certain variables predispose the person's behaviour to tilt in one direction or the other. One such variable is the relative strength of the person's tendencies to express and act out emotional impulses compared to the strength of inhibitions. A person who typically expresses such impulses is said to have an 'impulsive' personality.

Individual differences in impulsiveness, sometimes called 'impulsivity', have been studied in connection with aggressive behaviour, particularly that of persons who have been diagnosed as manifesting personality disorders. After reviewing the evidence for a relationship between personality disorders and aggression, Widiger and Trull (1994) concluded that it is the impulsivity component of such disorders that is related to aggression, not an active disposition to become aggressive. Simply stated, people who are highly impulsive lack sufficient control over their expressive behaviours to suppress them to the extent that less impulsive people do. Other studies, however, indicate that impulsivity, while being an important contributor to reactive aggression, is not sufficient in itself to bring about such behaviour. On the basis of research on impulsivity extending over thirty years, Barratt concluded that a combination of high impulsivity and high anger creates the most powerful antecedent of aggression. Certain stimuli readily evoke powerful anger in some people. When these same people are predisposed to react to all emotional situations impulsively, aggression is a likely consequence (Barratt 1994).

As noted above, Gray has described a neuroanatomical organization that underlies the behavioural activating and inhibiting systems. Recall that in Chapter 1 we noted that low levels of seratonergic activity have been shown to be correlated with impulsive aggression. Siever and Davis (1991) have developed a psychobiological model that expresses this relationship. Noting that both **serotonin** activity and impulsiveness in behaviour are a result of underlying inherited biological factors, they conclude that the first of these mediates the second, i.e. that the disinhibition of impulsive aggression is a function of associated serotonin depletion. Others have noted that impulsiveness, while being to some extent an inherited tendency, is nevertheless not entirely determined by biology and is in fact due in part also to socialization experiences in childhood (Barratt 1994).

Attachment style

The concept of **attachment style** was introduced to the literature on personality a generation ago by the British psychiatrist John Bowlby. Reasoning from an evolutionary standpoint, Bowlby argued that attachment behaviour between a child and a nurturing adult is organized and regulated by a control system in the central nervous system. The action of this regulatory system serves the evolutionary functions of protection and survival. When an infant is alarmed, anxious, ill or tired, the system becomes activated and the child seeks comfort and protection from its mother, father or other care-giving agent. Infants are less likely to feel fear or distress when they are confident that the care-giver is available and will be responsive to its expressions of discomfort. (Bowlby's theory is described in his classic multi-volume work *Attachment and Loss* (1969, 1973, 1980), but a concise summary may be found in his book *A Secure Base* (1988)).

The parent–child attachment develops within the child's first year of life, and it takes one of several forms depending on the ways in which the parent reacts to the child's overtures for nurturing. If the typical reaction is one of consistent and reliable accessibility, care and helpfulness, the child will develop a *secure* attachment to the parent, an attachment based on confidence that the parent will be available when needed. Such a child will not be overly distressed when the parent is absent for a brief period and will, when the parent is present, feel comfortable interacting with his or her surroundings, being content to make only occasional contact with the parent. Quite different is the attachment behaviour of children whose parents do not give them consistent or reliable nurturing. These children develop insecure attachments. Some become anxious over the possible loss of parental love and manifest this anxiety in a clinging, overly dependent style of behaviour that includes both fear of separation and anger prompted by this fear. Their attachment style has been characterized as *anxious-ambivalent*. Others become dismissive, distant and avoidant, revealing a

Table 4.2   Adult attachment styles

Concept of others	Self-concept	
	Positive (self as worthy of love)	Negative (self as unworthy of love)
Positive (trustworthy, accessible, caring)	Secure	Proccupied
Negative (rejecting, uncaring)	Dismissing	Fearful

Source: adapted from Bartholomew (1990).

rejection of intimate attachment to the parent. This sort of insecure attachment is also founded on fear of rejection and abandonment and is called the *anxious-avoidant* style.

The particular attachment style that develops early in life becomes a prototype for relations between the child and the parents in later childhood. Eventually it generalizes to other people as well in the form of an *adult attachment style* that closely resembles the style formed in the first year of life. The growing child develops a 'working model' of expected relations between himself or herself and those with whom close relations are maintained, such as spouses, sweethearts and friends. The working model, which can be thought of as a sort of 'picture in the mind' of oneself and certain important others, is founded on two core beliefs (Bowlby 1973: 204). One is the person's belief that these others are caring and loving individuals who can be trusted to be available for help when the going gets bad, and the other is the person's conviction that he or she is someone who deserves such love and care. Both of these beliefs are forged in parent–child interactions early in life.

The two dimensions in the working model form the basis for a taxonomy of adult attachment developed by Bartholomew and Horowitz (1991), in which four styles are defined (Table 4.2). Persons with secure attachment styles are those who combine trust in the love that is forthcoming from others with a belief that they are themselves lovable people. Those who accept the caring propensities of others but deny that they are worthy of such (i.e. those with a preoccupied style) spend much of their time actively seeking the affection that they crave. Persons with a dismissing style – by which intimacy is rejected – also wish for caring attachments but have come to believe that people do not wish to establish them. In general, these three styles are comparable to the secure, the anxious-ambivalent, and the anxious-avoidant ones described above. The fourth category – the fearful attachment style – is typical of people who neither expect intimacy from others nor think themselves worthy of such treatment. Such people are socially inhibited and non-assertive, and they tend to be exploited by others.

The relationship of attachment style to aggression is found most clearly among people who manifest one of the insecure styles. This was noted by Bowlby (1973), who observed that anger was often produced by the fear of abandonment and neglect that characterizes the insecurely attached child. Such anger can build in children as the indifferent parental behaviour continues. 'The most violently angry and dysfunctional responses of all', Bowlby (1973: 249) wrote, 'are elicited in children and adolescents who not only experience repeated separations but are constantly subjected to the threat of being abandoned.' Given that adult attachment style is a generalization of that formed in childhood, we would expect that people who form attachments to spouses and close friends, i.e. those who have entered intimate relationships with others, will manifest more violence within those relationships if they are also insecurely attached than if they are more secure in the relationship.

In a study that reported evidence for this hypothesis, Dutton and his associates (1994) obtained self-reports of attachment style from a large sample of men with a history of abusive treatment of their wives, using a scale that identifies the four styles outlined by Bartholomew and Horowitz. This scale yields four scores for each respondent, reflecting the degree to which the person is secure, dismissing, fearful and preoccupied. The subscale that yielded the highest positive correlations with self-described anger, jealousy and verbal abuse of partners was the one measuring fearful attachment. The relation of anger to the fearful style appears to be counter-intuitive, but possible reasons can be imagined. Dutton (1998), for example, has suggested that people who live in fear of rejection may develop anger as a defensive reaction (much as cornered animals often attack their feared antagonists). The attachment style score that showed the next highest correlation with anger, jealousy and verbal abuse was the preoccupied. High scores on the measure of secure attachment were negatively related to all three of the latter variables. Overall, then, anger, jealousy and abusiveness were closely related to insecure attachment within the intimate relationship. Insecure attachment has also been linked to anger, jealousy and hostility in other studies (e.g. Simpson 1990; Cooper *et al.* 1998; Mikulincer 1998). As we note in the following chapter, jealousy is an important contributor to spousal abuse.

CULTURAL INFLUENCES ON AGGRESSION

National culture

The analysis of social and cultural influences on aggression and violence has been based on studies that compare indices of aggression across social and cultural groups. Two types of study are described in this section: those that make comparisons among national cultures and those that make comparisons among subcultures within a single nation. An example of the first type is the research programme reported by Archer and Gartner (1984), which involved the creation of a Comparative Crime Data File (CCDF) out of statistics from 110 nations and 44 major cities over the period from 1900–70. From this file comparative rates of several crimes, including homicide, rape and criminal assault, were calculated and cross-national comparisons were made. One comparison revealed that the United States has the highest rate of homicides among the industrial nations of the world. Further analysis of cross-national data suggests that one cause of this high rate is the relatively easy availability of firearms in the United States (D. Archer 1994), a conclusion supported by other findings showing that countries that enacted major controls over access to firearms showed overall decreases in rates of violent crime following implementation of those controls (Podell and Archer 1994). Another possible explanation for the relatively high incidence of violence in the United States is a tendency for Americans to generate aggressive solutions to interpersonal conflicts to a greater degree than people from some other nations. Archer and McDaniel (1995) have reported findings from a cross-national study that support this conclusion. Subjects in 12 countries – ten Western countries, Japan and Korea – were asked to write stories describing the resolution of a number of hypothetical interpersonal conflicts; these stories were later analysed for violent and non-violent themes. Slightly more than 30 per cent of the themes written by American subjects contained some type of violence, which was the fourth highest among the 12 nations, after New Zealand, Australia and Northern Ireland. This finding indicates that Americans may be more likely to think of violent solutions to problems than persons from most other industrial nations.

Another finding reported by Archer and Gartner (1984) suggests that nations may come to be characterized by different levels of aggressiveness to the extent that they participate in collective violence through war. Participation in wars, especially as major combatants, can cause countries to bestow some legitimacy on violence, with an increase in post-war violence, relative to pre-war levels, as a consequence. From data in the CCDF, Archer and Gartner found that countries that participated in the First and Second World Wars were more likely than neutral nations to experience a post-war increase in homicide rates. Participation in smaller wars, such as the Vietnam War, produced a similar, though less pronounced, outcome. The effect of war on subsequent social violence was also greater in countries that had suffered large combat losses than in those that had been less heavily involved, and greater in the victorious countries than in the losers. A nation that engages in intensely violent activity and is rewarded for such behaviour with victory may be providing a strong message regarding the instrumental value of violence to its people. It would not be surprising, therefore, if attitudes towards conflict resolution were affected to some degree by this lesson.

Subcultures of violence

Violence may therefore become embedded in social norms that prescribe the conditions under which aggression is an acceptable, and even socially desirable, behaviour. Such a prescriptive process is manifested not only in national cultures, but also in what Wolfgang and Ferracuti (1982) have called **subcultures of violence** within larger national societies. The presence of such subcultures is not restricted to any one society or nation. In many societies we may observe such practices as the vendetta, the blood feud and the practice of stereotyped masculinity seen in the familiar *machismo* syndrome. The origins of the various subcultures of violence depend on the history and circumstances of the society, but regardless of origins, the subculture mandates the values, beliefs and attitudes of its members. As such, it forms part of what we have been calling the background variables in aggression.

Some recent studies indicate the existence of regional subcultural differences in aggression within the United States associated with differential norms for aggressive behaviour (Cohen and Nisbett 1994; Nisbett and Cohen 1996). Nisbett and his colleagues have found that homicide rates among white non-Hispanic males living in rural or small town environments in the southern part of the country are higher than corresponding rates in similar settings in other regions. Southern white males do not endorse violence in general to a greater degree than non-Southerners, but they are more likely to favour aggressive behaviour in defence of human life and property and in response to insults. Defence of property, loved ones and personal respect forms the basis for a 'culture of honour' in the rural American South (Nisbett and Cohen 1996). Attitudes favouring punitive discipline of children also tend to be more strongly held in the South than elsewhere. Furthermore, white male homicide rates are higher in those parts of the rural South in which the herding and tending of animals is the main basis for agriculture than in those regions characterized by crop farming. Nisbett and Cohen (1996) have explained the latter finding by observing that herding economies have historically emphasized physical aggression as a means of protecting animals. Violent behaviour is therefore ingrained in the social fabric of such subcultures and is a readily accessible response to the person who feels that his honour has been impugned.

The concept of subcultures of violence has been criticized on grounds that certain of its central assumptions are open to question. Tedeschi and Felson (1994) have argued that the concept rests on two sequential relationships: demographic factors must be closely linked to certain values, and these values must in turn mediate aggressive and violent behaviour. After surveying a number of relevant studies, Tedeschi and Felson concluded that the evidence for these assumed relationships is weak at best. In a variant of Nisbett's original hypothesis, Baumeister and Heatherton (1996) have proposed that subcultures do not promote or encourage aggressive behaviour as much as they define the conditions under which such behaviour is acceptable, i.e. they disinhibit aggressive reactions to situations that in other subcultures would be restrained. The regional effects documented by Nisbett may therefore reflect the influence of culture on the rules by which anger is expressed and displayed behaviourally.

SUMMARY

1 Male–female differences in aggression have been explained in terms of both genetic inheritance and the individual's history of socialization. Men tend to be more aggressive than women in most human cultures, especially when physical aggression is the criterion. Probably at the very

least, innate biological differences between men and women provide a background against which cultural influences operate in shaping the specifics of human aggression.

2 Certain cultural norms influence the differential commission of aggression by men and women. The proscription of aggressing against women is generally observed by both sexes, while women are more likely than men to consider physical aggression inappropriate, to repress such behaviour and to experience guilt or anxiety over aggressing. Whereas men and women react aggressively to provocations, women are less aggressive than men in the absence of provocation. The two sexes also perceive different situations to be provocative, with women reacting most strongly to condescending behaviour from others and to sexual infidelity by a partner, whereas men are more angered by physical attack.

3 Men and women also differ in their preferred means of aggressing. Physical aggression is more common among men than women, but there is evidence that women are at least as likely to use verbal aggression as men. Women also learn at an early age the uses of 'relational aggression' – the harming of others by threatening to disrupt or damage a person's social acceptance within the peer culture. Longitudinal studies of male–female differences in aggression have shown that: (a) boys use direct physical and verbal aggression more than girls until late adolescence, when both sexes show a decrease to equal low levels of physical aggressiveness and girls become more verbally aggressive than boys; (b) in early adolescence, boys are more physically aggressive than girls; and (c) from childhood to late adolescence, girls use indirect and relational aggression more than boys.

4 Another dimension of male–female differences in aggression is shown in the finding that men interpret their own aggressiveness as instrumental behaviour that enables them to get ahead in life, whereas women regard their aggression as emotionally uncontrolled expressive behaviour. This difference reveals underlying differences in socialization of boys and girls that begins at an early age and is closely connected to the differential teaching of specific sex roles. This difference is not found in male and female prison inmates, among whom women hold instrumental beliefs as strongly as men. The holding of typically male instrumental beliefs about aggression predicts aggressive behaviour, whereas the holding of typically female expressive beliefs is associated with inhibition of aggression.

5 The stability of aggressiveness over time shown in longitudinal studies indicates that stable individual differences in personality are involved in aggressive behaviour. Such individual differences moderate the effects of provocation. Irritability, high and unstable self-esteem, narcissism, impulsivity and an insecure, fearful attachment style towards others are predictors of aggression.

6 Both national culture and subcultures within the larger society may contribute to aggression through the fostering of certain attitudes and beliefs that support aggressive behaviour. Among the national beliefs that contribute to aggression are those that prompt thoughts of violence as effective means of problem-solving and those shaped by successful aggression in war. Subcultures of violence can affect aggression

by promoting beliefs of stereotyped masculinity and instrumental aggression, as well as by creating a culture that emphasizes the defence of possessions and personal honour.

SUGGESTIONS FOR FURTHER READING

Campbell, A. (1993) *Men, Women, and Aggression*. New York: Basic Books. A description of the theoretical rationale for the concepts of sex differences in instrumental and expressive aggression.

Caprara, G. V., Barbaranelli, C., Pastorelli, C. and Perugini, M. (1994) Individual differences in the study of aggression. *Aggressive Behavior*, 20, 291–303.

Österman, K., Björkqvist, K., Lagerspetz, K. M. J. *et al.* (1998) Cross-cultural evidence of female indirect aggression. *Aggressive Behavior*, 24, 1–8. A study replicated in several countries showing certain consistencies in the use of indirect aggression by women.

FIVE

AGGRESSION IN LIFE AND SOCIETY

In the first four chapters, the main emphasis has been upon the processes in human aggression that have been established through research, much of which has taken the form of controlled experiments. Over the past several years, a new body of research evidence has emerged, one in which the main aim is not to discover psychological processes but to find answers to specific practical problems of aggression in everyday life and society. In this chapter we turn our attention to some of this research by examining studies of: (a) violence in intimate relationships; (b) sexual aggression; (c) aggression in family settings; and (d) bullying among children. As we shall see, much of this research involves the application of processes discussed in Chapters 1–4 to the specific problems being investigated.

VIOLENCE IN INTIMATE RELATIONSHIPS

The experimental study of aggression almost always involves a situation in which a single subject interacts with a stranger under conditions that are carefully controlled by the experimenter. In some cases the 'other person' is in fact a confederate of the experimenter acting out a prepared script and in some the behaviour of that 'person' is merely a simulation produced by the experimenter. Regardless of what method is used – one involving a real second subject, a confederate posing as one or a simulation – aggression does not occur in the context of an ongoing relationship that contributes variables of its own to the hostile relations. However, a number of observers have pointed out that much, if not most, human aggression of the affective, non-instrumental sort is between people who do know each other, who are often members of a family and who sometimes live in intimate relationships.

Violence within close relationships is a fairly common occurrence, and it is male aggression against the female that constitutes the major problem for society. Although some studies have shown that acts of aggression by women against male partners are numerically as common as those of men against women, the aggression of males is typically more severe and dangerous than that of women (Straus 1993). In this section of the chapter, therefore, we concentrate on acts of violence committed by men against their female partners. Several variables have been identified as correlates of such aggression. In general, these variables fall into two classes: those pertaining to the immediate and proximal elicitors of abuse, and those that function as background, dispositional and contextual contributors, with the background variables serving as moderators of the effects of the more immediate causes (see Chapter 4).

Proximal variables

The alleged provocation

The immediate activator of spouse beating is some event that irritates the aggressor. It is important to note that much of the time this irritation is not related to any normally provocative act on the part of the partner; it is sufficient that the male merely *thinks* that his mate has done something offensive. As noted below, such thoughts often arise from misperceptions of the situation by the abusive male. This event may incorporate any of a number of specific provocations and may arise within the family context or outside of it. A common example of the latter is the case of the man who is berated by his boss at his work, and who then takes his anger home with him and blows up and attacks his wife over some trivial disagreement. Such behaviour would be a case of the larger class of acts called displaced aggression, discussed above in Chapter 2. A common provocation that arises inside the relationship is any behaviour on the part of the wife that the husband takes as a challenge to his power and dominant status (Claes and Rosenthal 1990). These immediate irritators derive much of their potency from some of the background or dispositional variables to be discussed later. A woman's independent and self-assertive acts, for example, may have little effect on some males, whereas they may evoke rage and a violent attack from a man who needs to dominate and control women. Aggression in such settings may also be regarded as the expressive-motor counterpart of immediate negative affect arising from the imagined provocation, according to the principles of cognitive–neossociationism described by Berkowitz (Chapter 3). Higher order cognitive processing may also be involved. In unions marked by strife and discord, poor communication between the spouses is an important mediator of aggression (e.g. O'Leary and Vivian 1990). The male appraises some act by the woman – such as a verbal statement – in a hostile and defensive way. This appraisal is a consequence of both the man's immediate affective state and more long-standing variables. When the background conditions are such that the union is stressful and unsatisfactory, when antagonism towards the woman is already felt by the man, when he adheres to beliefs that men should exercise power and control over women and when his personality disposes him to be aggressive, he is likely to attribute malicious intent to his partner's behaviour.

The escalation of violence

The process described above is recognizable, of course, as a manifestation of the hostile attribution bias described in Chapter 3 (see also Holtzworth-Munroe and Hutchinson 1993): men who attribute hostility to the behaviour of their wives are likely to respond to that behaviour in an angry, hostile and verbally abusive manner. Such reactions may engender genuine negative affect and hostility from the woman in return. An escalating cycle of animosity may be initiated, culminating in a physical attack. In addition, over the course of such a stormy relationship the intensity of aggression can escalate. Verbal abuse early in a relationship has been shown to be a reliable predictor of physical violence later on. Murphy and O'Leary (1989) found that incidence of verbal and **passive aggression** (labelled as 'psychological aggression') measured prior to marriage was significantly correlated with physical aggression during the first six months of marriage, and that later acts of psychological aggression were also correlated with physical violence in subsequent assessment periods up to 30 months into the marriage. After reporting similar findings, O'Leary and his associates concluded that 'The origin of spouse abuse and a concomitant weakening of marital bonds appear to be rooted in the formative stages of a marriage' (O'Leary *et al.* 1989: 267).

Alcohol abuse

Another proximal contributor to spousal aggression is alcohol abuse. Numerous studies have shown that alcohol use is a major contributor to marital violence (e.g. Hamberger and Hastings 1991; Stith and Farley 1993), but a detailed analysis of the mechanisms whereby it interacts with other proximal causal variables has not been made. However, as noted above (Chapter 3), evidence from experimental studies indicates that ingestion of alcohol may lead to aggression by interfering with normal cognitive processing. An intoxicated male with a tendency to be abusive towards his mate may perceive only that she has done something which, in his imagination, is offensive and provocative, and may simply not attend to other cues that could mitigate these hostile perceptions.

Dispositional and contextual variables

Dispositional and contextual background variables in spouse abuse can be divided into three broadly defined categories: (a) those pertaining to aggression and violence in the abuser's family during the abuser's childhood; (b) the immediate state of the relationship between the abuser and the victim (e.g. dissatisfaction with the relationship and/or a large imbalance in power between the man and the woman); and (c) the personality of the abuser.

The childhood history of the abuser

A history of witnessing parental aggression as a child, or of being the victim of parental abuse, has been shown to be correlated with spouse abuse in adulthood (e.g. Hotaling and Sugarman 1990). A history of having been abused in childhood has also been identified as a correlate of spouse abuse (MacEwen and Barling 1988). The more general question of the harmful effects of these two background factors on children is discussed more fully later in this chapter.

Differential power between partners

Spouse abuse is correlated with a number of other contextual variables related to the current state of the relationship. One of the most potent of such variables is stress arising from general dissatisfaction with the marriage (e.g. O'Leary and Vivian 1990). Such stress alone is not a sufficient condition for spouse battering, however. While it may provide the negative affect that motivates the behaviour, the aggressive act itself is guided by the cognitions and beliefs held by the abuser. Attitudes and beliefs that support spousal aggression are reliable predictors of such abuse. For example, Stith and Farley (1993) found that approval of marital violence by husbands was directly linked to wife battering. These investigators also found that battering was correlated with denial of equality of the sexes by the male, which contributed to the belief that wife abuse is acceptable behaviour. Such behaviour could possibly be enhanced by the existence of an actual power differential in the relationship.

Recognition of such a power differential is one of the bases for a **resource exchange theory** of general domestic violence formulated by Gelles and Cornell (1990). This theory holds that aggression in the home will occur when the perceived rewards for aggressing are high and the costs low. This theory may help to explain spousal aggression. Beating the female partner is rewarding to the man who has a high need for control and the exercise of power. In general, the costs of wife beating are low relative to the costs that aggressive behaviour may entail in contexts outside the home. The domestic setting is private, and society tends to regard abuse within that setting as a 'family matter' that does not concern the community at large. This reward–cost difference provides an incentive for aggression that will probably become manifest if the other conditions noted above are present.

Personality of the abuser

The personality of the abuser has been the object of considerable study, and several individual difference variables have been shown to play a role in spouse abuse. Depressive symptoms have been found in abusers more than in other males (e.g. Julian and McKenry 1993). In addition, impulsivity (Bersani *et al.* 1992), aggressiveness (Hamberger and Hastings 1991) and hostility (Barnett *et al.* 1991) have all been shown to correlate with incidence of spouse abuse. The extent to which psychopathology is involved in wife battering is open to debate. O'Leary (1993) has found that some, but not most, physically abusive men show psychopathic personality disorders. He concluded that whereas psychopathology may be involved in cases of extreme physical violence, at more intermediate levels impulsiveness and defensive tendencies are better predictors.

To date, theoretical integration of the variables involved in spouse abuse is still rudimentary, although several sophisticated multivariate analyses have been reported. A theoretical approach that has been suggested above would treat spousal abuse as a pathological consequence of the communications that transpire between partners, mediated by the formation of cognitive appraisals and judgements that increase the probability of aggression. We know that pre-existing levels of hostility and anger dispose people to attribute hostile intent to the actions of others. We also know that depression can contribute to such attributions. Thus, to the man who has these characteristics, acts by his spouse that may be completely neutral in an objective sense will often be defined as malicious and will invite an angry counterattack. Furthermore, if the man is highly dependent on his spouse and also holds stereotypical beliefs about male dominance, any act of independence on the woman's part could easily be regarded as betrayal and a threat to his emotional security. Incorrect attributions of this sort might well be enhanced in a mind so fogged by drugs or alcohol that it is incapable of integrating all relevant information. Given the angry and hostile state thus engendered in the man, any tendency towards impulsivity could easily translate into battering activity directed against the wife. Any further perceptions by the male that his wife is weaker than he, that she commands fewer resources and that she has less social support can exacerbate the violence (e.g. Claes and Rosenthal 1990).

The single most informative programme of research on the role of personality in spousal abuse has been one conducted by Dutton and his colleagues (Dutton 1998). Three types of spouse abuser have been described in this work. One is the **overcontrolled** abuser, a man who on the surface looks like anything but a violent person. He tends instead to deny and hold in his rage, which is considerable because he also tends to feel chronic resentment for what he considers to be frustrations and provocations in his everyday life. This rage builds until it erupts in an act of violence against an available target – like his partner. A second kind is the **psychopathic** abuser, a man who not only abuses his partner but also fights and brawls with other men. His aggression, moreover, is usually aimed at controlling and intimidating others, i.e. it is more instrumental than affective. Interesting as these two types are, however, it is the third variety, the *borderline* abuser, that has been the object of most of Dutton's research.

The borderline abuser manifests a number of specific characteristics. First, his abusive behaviour towards his partner is intermittent but regular, and it is more frequent than that of the overcontrolled abuser. It is confined to the family and does not spill over into more general aggressiveness like that of the psychopathic type. Also unlike the psychopathic type, the borderline abuser does not appear to those outside the family to be a violent person. Only his spouse, and possibly his children, ever see his darker side. Finally, as Dutton has pointed out, his abusive behaviour follows a regular and cyclical pattern. It is a three-stage pattern that has become familiar through descriptions in the popular media. It begins with feelings of hostility and resentment towards the partner that build in intensity. The source of these feelings is explained below. This stage is marked by growing anger as well as by increasing anxiety and depression.

This smouldering affect finally reaches the point at which some act on the part of the spouse, perceived against the backdrop of the man's hostile attribution bias, is felt to be a provocation. The second stage follows: an outburst of aggressive behaviour that can result in serious physical injury or, in some cases, even murder. This stage then gives way to the third, in which the abuser becomes contrite, asks the battered partner to forgive him and expresses exceptional tenderness and love. Eventually, however, the old resentments begin to build again, and the cycle is repeated.

This third type of abuser has been called 'borderline' because he reveals a **borderline personality organization** (BPO) that supplies the key to why he acts in the way that he does. Much has been written about the defining characteristics of the BPO (see Millon 1996 for a discussion and review), but Dutton has focused on three in his investigation into the personality structure of abusive males. These three features of the BPO have been indicated by previous research: disturbances in identity, a tendency to use primitive defence mechanisms and an experience of transient states of uncertainty over what is real. By disturbances in identity is meant, in general terms, an inconsistent and uncertain self-concept, including feelings of being 'empty inside' and of being an impostor. Primitive defences include tendencies to categorize people as 'all good' or 'all bad' and to project upon other people faults that the individual refuses to admit in himself. An inventory assessing these three components of the BPO has been developed by Oldham and his colleagues (1985).

Dutton hypothesized that the cyclical type of abuser described above would manifest all three of these characteristics; hence the designation of such a person as borderline. In a study testing this idea, Dutton and Starzomski (1993) administered the Oldham inventory to groups of men known to be spouse abusers and investigated the degree to which scores on the three scales measuring self-concept, primitive defences and sense of reality correlated with the degree of abusiveness reported by the wives of the men, i.e. the victims of the male violence. Dutton and Starzomski found significant positive correlations between each of the measures of the BPO and several indicators of abusiveness: physical aggression, as well as psychological abuse such as dominance and intimidation, restrictions on freedom, ridicule and humiliation. They concluded that the borderline personality underlies the cyclical and episodic spousal aggression shown by this familiar type of abuser.

Other studies have shown that an important antecedent of the behaviour of cyclical male abusers is a childhood history of abuse or neglect by his parents. Such experiences early in life appear to contribute to the borderline personality disorder. Dutton (1998) has indicated that the early experiences most commonly reported in retrospect by male adult abusers are those involving alienation from, and abuse or neglect by, their fathers and mothers, especially the fathers. Included among the punitive behaviours of the parents is a disposition to humiliate the growing boy and subject him to feelings of shame. Recall the finding reported by Tangney and her colleagues, cited in Chapter 4, that shame-prone people are especially likely to express anger and hostility and to blame others when things go wrong (Tangney *et al.* 1992).

If we now put together the several strands of evidence that have been cited so far, a general picture begins to emerge. A history of parental neglect and abuse in childhood produces a sense of shame and feelings of personal inadequacy that culminate in a relatively incomplete sense of self, accompanied by feelings of depression and anger, and a tendency to blame others for one's problems. It will be recalled also that fear of abandonment by the parents – which can be a consequence of neglect and abuse – fosters the development of an insecure and fearful attachment style that generalizes to subsequent adult relationships. This attachment style contains a factor of anger towards others, as noted in Chapter 4. For the male with such a history, an intimate relation with another person brings out the pattern of aggressive behaviour seen in the borderline abuser. The uncertain sense of self that characterizes the fearfully attached, borderline male motivates him to seek, in an intimate relation with a woman, reassurance and comfort as his negative feelings about himself begin to mount. Dutton has summarized the process:

> As the tension and dysphoria build, the BPO men unconsciously require their partners to take it away, to soothe them, to make them feel whole, to make them feel good. But they do not express this – indeed, are unaware of it and so cannot express it . . . Instead, they begin to act counterproductively, uttering hurtful words and generating actions that distance their partners. These build to a crescendo with the acute abusiveness episode.
>
> (Dutton 1998: 89)

SEXUAL VIOLENCE

Arousal and inhibition

Although it is usually treated as a separate topic, male sexual aggression shares certain features with general violence against women. The most obvious difference between the two is that rape and sexual degradation, in addition to being motivated in large part by anger and animosity towards women, also involve sexual arousal. Most analyses of the causes of sexual aggression include sexual excitement, but the extent and meaning of that variable are not clearly understood. Some investigators have hypothesized that rapists are more sexually aroused by forcible sex than by mutually voluntary intimacy, and that they prefer rape to normal sex as a consequence. This **'preferred sexuality' hypothesis** has been supported by some studies (e.g. Quinsey *et al*. 1984), but not by others (e.g. Hall *et al*. 1993). The results of extensive research by Barbaree and his associates have consistently failed to show that sexually aggressive men are more aroused by verbal descriptions of rape than by similar descriptions of consenting sex, even though they are more aroused by rape descriptions than non-rapists (e.g. Baxter *et al*. 1986). To account for these findings, Barbaree and Marshall (1991) have proposed that the major difference between rapists and non-rapists has to do with the extent to which the suffering of the rape victim inhibits sexual arousal. In non-sexually aggressive men, the violent aspects of rape tend to cancel out the sexual arousal evoked by its erotic side; in rapists this mitigating effect on sexual arousal is not present. Consistent with this inhibition hypothesis, rapists have been found to be generally less empathic than non-rapists (Rice *et al.* 1994). In addition, in a study by Porter and Critelli (1994), males who described themselves as highly sexually aggressive focused mainly on the sexually arousing cues in a description of a date rape, whereas less sexually aggressive men focused on inhibiting cues, such as the moral wrongness of the act.

The relationship between sexual arousal and sexual aggression is therefore neither simple nor direct. Malamuth and his colleagues (e.g. Malamuth 1986) have shown in several studies that sexual arousal influences sexual violence only through interaction with other cognitive, affective and attitudinal variables. For example, Malamuth and Check (1983) found that sexual arousal to verbal descriptions of rape was determined by an interaction between the victim's ostensible feelings following the attack and the self-admitted likelihood of the male subject that he would commit rape if he thought that he would go unpunished for it. In a subsequent study, Malamuth *et al.* (1986) found that subjects who were highly aroused by description of forcible sex scored higher than those who were less aroused on a number of attitudinal variables. Males who were greatly aroused by thoughts of forced sex attributed responsibility for rape to the victim, believed that rape victims enjoy being abused, held highly stereotyped opinions of male and female roles and attitudes supporting aggression against women and considered the act of forcing a woman to have sex to be attractive.

Personality variables as moderators

Sexual callousness

The variable *likelihood of raping* (LR) moderates sexual aggression and attitudes towards women as well as arousal. Men who manifest a high level of LR are more likely than low scorers to report that they have used force against women for sexual reasons and that they will do so again. Under controlled laboratory conditions, men high in LR are more aggressive towards women than men low in LR, but not towards other men (Malamuth 1984). Likelihood of raping is similar to a characteristic of callousness towards women that has been observed by several investigators to be related to sexual violence. For example, male subjects in an experiment by Check and Guloien (1989) reported that they were more likely to use sexual coercion after seeing a videotape showing either violent pornography or non-violent pornography in which the woman was degraded than they were after seeing a videotape of non-violent sexual activity. The emergence of attitudes favouring sexual violence against women may therefore be facilitated by the cultivation of a callous and dehumanizing view of women as objects of sexual manipulation. The adverse effects of pornography may lie not so much in its power to excite

men to commit rape as in its slow and cumulative contribution to attitudes and values that reduce a woman to the status of a sexual reward for
the conquering male. Prolonged exposure to pornography appears to have
such an outcome. For example, Linz *et al.* (1984) exposed male viewers to
films of predominantly sexual violence once a day for five days. They
found that anxiety in response to the films declined over the five days, as
did perceptions that the material was violent and degrading to women.
Enjoyment of the films increased over the same period.

The power motive

Several observers of male sexual violence have concluded that such behaviour is motivated by male needs to dominate, humiliate and generally
exercise coercive power over women. This approach constitutes a major
emphasis among many feminist writers, who tend to regard the power
differentials that underlie sexual assault as inherent in the institutional
structure of modern society. From a social psychological standpoint, however, the basis of these dominance-related needs is to be sought more in
the motive dispositions of the individual, with social institutions playing
a role through their influence on the person's history of socialization.
From this perspective, it would be expected that men who have been
socialized in ways that dispose them to seek relationships in which they
may dominate others would be likely to enter into coercive sexual relations with women, at the expense of affectionate ones, to a greater degree
than men who have not been trained in this way. According to this
argument, an important predictor of male sexual violence would be a high
need for power, coupled with a low need for intimacy and affiliation.

Zurbriggen (2000) has reported evidence supporting this conclusion.
She gathered self-reports from male subjects on two scales, measuring the
respondents' past experience in, respectively, seducing and coercing women
into sexual relations. Measures of need for power and need for affiliation
were also obtained. Finally, Zurbriggen assessed the readiness with which
her male subjects associated words conveying sexual meaning (e.g. 'inter-
course', 'undress') with words having mainly connotations of power (e.g.
'master', 'abuse'). Obviously, if such a tendency to associate sex with
power is strong, then situations of intimacy with women should prime
access to thoughts of power and dominance that could eventuate in sexual
assault. Both the need for power and the tendency to associate power
with sex should therefore be good predictors of sexual aggression.

The results of the study bear out this analysis. Zurbriggen found that
among male subjects a high level of power motivation was linked with
self-reported seductive and coercive sexual behaviour. Likewise, the tendency to associate sexual words with power words predicted coercive, but
not seductive, sexual activity. Finally, the two variables interacted, such
that the positive relationship between power motivation and coercive
sexual behaviour was found in men who had strong tendencies to associate power with sex, but not among those who had weak tendencies to
make this association (Figure 5.1). The need for intimacy/affiliation was
not involved in male sexual aggression.

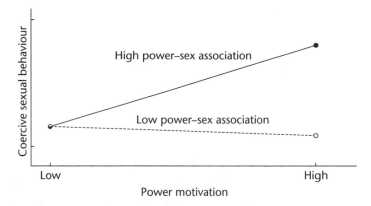

Figure 5.1 Interaction of power motive and power–sex association tendencies as predictor of male sexual violence.
Source: modified from Zurbriggen (2000).

The confluence model: hostility and impersonal sexuality

Another personality variable that embraces a wide range of affective, emotional and cognitive processes is hostile masculinity (HM), a constellation of tendencies assessed and described by Malamuth and his colleagues. In his initial study, Malamuth (1986) showed that a degree of self-reported sexual aggression was positively correlated with the motive to dominate women sexually, with attitudes of hostility towards women and with acceptance of violence against women. Subsequently, Malamuth and his associates developed a comprehensive model of male sexual aggression which states that such aggression in early adulthood is the result of a confluence of two broadly defined factors, of which hostile masculinity is one. This disposition is the product of an insecure, defensive, overly sensitive and distrustful attitude, especially in interactions with women, along with a tendency to desire control and domination of women (Malamuth *et al.* 1991). It may also include an element of uncertainty over one's ability to carry out the stereotyped male sex role as a powerful and commanding figure (Malamuth *et al.* 1995).

The other factor that predicts sexual aggression in the model is disposition to treat sexual relations as casual, uncommitted, promiscuous and playful. This attitude of *promiscuous–impersonal sexuality* leads the man to consider women merely as objects to be used rather than as sexual equals. When it combines with masculine hostility, the confluence of the two tendencies creates a set of beliefs and motives prompting sexual aggression as a means of building a more positive self-image. The woman who is sexually dominated and used poses less of a threat to the hostile and insecure male than one who is free and autonomous. Malamuth *et al.* (1991) discovered that HM interacted with sexual promiscuity to predict sexual aggression. Males who were both sexually promiscuous and high in HM were more sexually aggressive than promiscuous, but non-hostile, men. In addition, non-sexual aggression was related to HM but not to promiscuity. The relevance of HM for non-sexual aggression is shown

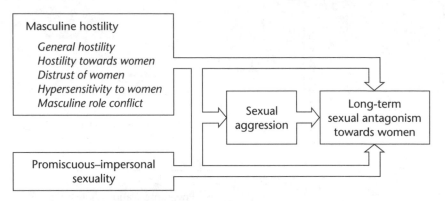

Figure 5.2 Relationship of predictor variables to early likelihood of sexual aggression and long-term antagonism towards women.
Source: based on Malamuth *et al.* (1995).

further in the experimental finding of Malamuth and Thornhill (1994) that male subjects conversing with a woman showed a positive correlation between HM and tendencies to be domineering and condescending in the interaction; when the conversational partner was another man, no such correlation was found. Malamuth *et al.* (1995) subsequently extended the confluence model to predict that the conditions that determine a likelihood of becoming sexually aggressive in early adulthood also contribute to a general tendency to be antagonistic in relations with women later in life (Figure 5.2).

Cognitive processing

In addition to sexual arousal and personality variables, cognitive processes play an important role in sexual aggression. Several investigators have reported that men who hold rape-supportive beliefs and attitudes also tend to be less accurate than men who do not hold such beliefs in interpreting women's feelings and motives in normal interaction. A study by Murphy *et al.* (1986) showed that relative inability to distinguish between friendliness and seductiveness, and between assertiveness and hostility, in a woman's behaviour was associated with rape-supportive attitudes in men. The tendency to misread assertiveness as hostility was also correlated with sexually aggressive behaviour. A related finding was reported by McDonel and McFall (1991): deficiency in detecting negative cues from a woman (i.e. unwillingness to engage in sexual behaviours) in the context of hypothetical dating scenarios was related to rape-supportive attitudes and to self-confessed likelihood of committing rape. Both studies suggest some type of perceptual error or inadequacy in social information processing as likely reasons for the observed correlations. Another way in which cognitive processing may mediate sexual violence has been suggested by Malamuth and Brown (1994). These investigators hypothesized that male sexual aggressors may have a suspicious schema about women that influences their perceptions of women's behaviour and judgements of what it signifies. In general, such men believe that women do not reveal their true feelings in interacting with men and that, regardless of what they say and do, they are typically hostile or seductive. Thus, acts of friendliness are taken as sexual invitations and assertiveness is judged to be hostile and aggressive. The findings linking sexual aggression to information processing in interactions between men and women are interesting because they indicate certain basic processes that underlie both sexual and non-sexual violence against women.

To summarize, research on male sexual aggression has identified several types of antecedent: physiological arousal, cognitive–affective processes and personality variables. In a general model that organizes all these factors, Hall and Hirschman (1991) have proposed that sexual violence is a product of four different antecedents that may or may not function jointly: physiological sexual excitement, cognitions that justify sexual violence, poor affective control and personality disorders. Whereas the four components in combination increase the probability of sexual aggression, each may serve as a motivator independent of the others. It is assumed that one of the four is usually the primary motivator in any given situation. Furthermore, each of the factors underlies and explains a specific subtype of sexually aggressive person. Males who become sexually excited by rape fantasies, who associate sex with aggression and who are relatively uninhibited by aggressive contextual cues tend to form one subtype. Those who are motivated primarily by cognitions that justify sexual aggression tend to select situations for their deviant sexual activity in which such justifications can be argued (e.g. the victim provoked the attack, or she enjoyed it despite her protests). Acquaintance rape may be a common manifestation of this latter subtype (Koss *et al.* 1987). The third subtype is characterized by episodic and poorly controlled outbursts of anger towards women. It is relatively unplanned and violent, and it may be part of a larger problem of impulse control that makes the person aggressive in more general ways (Hall and Proctor 1987). The fourth subtype is distinguished mainly by the chronicity of his sexual aggression, arising from some developmentally-related personality disorder. Such a pattern characterizes the serial rapist.

VIOLENCE IN THE FAMILY

The cycle of violence

In a preceding section of this chapter, a connection was noted between spousal abuse and the childhood experiences of the abuser. The correlation between childhood experiences of being aggressed against and later manifestations of aggressive behaviour has led some investigators to propose that 'aggression breeds aggression' in what has been termed a **cycle of violence**. Despite the attractive simplicity of this idea and its implication of a cause–effect relationship, it has been disputed by a number of investigators who have pointed out that the effects of childhood abuse are not as obvious as the 'cycle' theory implies. Widom (1989a) identified seven categories of research to which the cycle hypothesis has been broadly relevant. These include the effects of being abused or neglected as a child on: (a) becoming an abuser of one's own children; (b) committing murder as an adult; (c) delinquency in adolescence; (d) manifesting generally violent behaviour in adulthood; (e) showing high levels of aggressiveness in childhood; and (f) engaging in subsequent aggression against the self. A seventh category involved the effects of early exposure to violence by others, whether directly in family settings or indirectly through the mass media. Widom concluded that although some evidence for the cycle of violence can be adduced, the body of evidence as a whole suffers from numerous methodological difficulties that raise doubts about the cycle hypothesis.

In a study designed to avoid some of the methodological pitfalls that had characterized some of the earlier research, Widom (1989b) compared a group of children that had been physically or sexually abused or ne-glected with another cohort of children that had not suffered these experiences. The groups were matched for age, sex, race and social class backgrounds. Overall, 905 cases were analysed according to a prospective design in which adolescent delinquency and adult criminal violence were predicted from childhood records. Both physical abuse and neglect in childhood were found to be strong predictors of adult criminal viol-ence, with physical abuse the stronger. This study therefore supports the concept of a cycle of violence in one of the six categories identified earlier by Widom (1989a): the relationship of abuse to violent adult behaviour. Some recent investigations have been addressed to discovering the nature of the psychological processes involved in the cycle of violence. One variable that predicts the effect is the severity of physical abuse received by the person during childhood. Persons who have been subjected to harsh physical discipline by their parents should be more likely to be physically abusive than others whose childhoods were not as severe. In a study that lends indirect support to this idea, Zaidi et al. (1989) found that subjects who had experienced severe physical discipline as children were more likely to recommend physical punishment for transgressing children in a set of hypothetical scenarios than subjects who had been treated with mild physical or no discipline. Research by Dodge and his associates (Weiss et al. 1992) suggests an intervening mechanism that may mediate at least some of the effects of harsh parental discipline on adult aggression: development of inadequate and biased patterns of social information-processing by the child. In this research, physically harmed chil-dren manifested many of the signs of processing deficits reviewed earlier in this review, such as inattention to relevant cues, the hostile attribution bias and lack of effective behavioural strategies for solving interpersonal problems (p. 51). In addition, evidence was found of a relationship be-tween these processing deficits and the development of aggression.

Observation of violence between parents

Seeing parents engage in angry interchanges can also contribute to emo-tional distress and problem behaviour in children, including aggression against peers (Cummings et al. 1985), especially if the observed parental dispute tends to continue over a period of time without any effective resolution (Cummings *et al.* 1994). When disputes escalate into violent interchanges between the parents, children become vulnerable to two types of emotional/behavioural problems. Both anti-social behaviours (e.g. aggression, delinquency and impulsive lack of control) and maladjusted states like internalizing anxiety, depression and withdrawal have been shown to be positively related to the amount of interparental marital violence that children observed, particularly that of the father against the mother (e.g. O'Keefe 1994).

The development of behavioural and adjustment problems in connection with seeing parental violence involves both affective and cognitive processes. Grych and Fincham (1990) argue that children actively attempt to understand the meaning of conflicts between their parents, and that their appraisals lead them to form beliefs about what roles they might have played in causing the dispute or in helping to end it. The child's appraisals may therefore produce feelings of threat, guilt and self-blame, and these feelings mediate subsequent problems of adjustment (Kerig 1998). The child's perceptions of personal control can also mediate unfortunate outcomes. Children who think that they can control conflicts between their parents are at an especially high risk of emotional maladjustment, particularly if their attempts at control fail and they blame themselves. In addition, by seeking to exercise control they may be drawn into the violence and become victims (Rossman and Rosenberg 1992). There is also evidence that children develop different ways of coping with the angry behaviour of their parents and that these coping methods have some effect on subsequent emotionality. El-Sheikh *et al.* (1989) found that children who responded to their parents' anger without becoming emotional were later less angry in an interview than children who had reacted to their parents' outbursts with anger or distress.

The overall picture, therefore, is one in which angry conflicts between parents, which can escalate into violence, can cause children to become emotionally maladjusted and possibly aggressive. This process is mediated by the ways in which the children interpret interparental violence, the extent to which they feel anxious, threatened and guilty, and their ability to develop coping strategies that help them to ward off such feelings.

Domestic roots of delinquency

As noted elsewhere in this review, social learning theory has played a major role in explaining the development of human aggression. This theoretical approach has guided a programme of research into the origins of delinquency and adult anti-social behaviour conducted for more than thirty years by Patterson and his colleagues (e.g. Patterson *et al.* 1989). Two types of delinquency have been identified by these investigators: late-starting and early-starting. The first of these is of relatively minor importance in the study of long-term aggression; the latter has important consequences for both juvenile and adult anti-social behaviour. Patterson stresses the importance of early training in aversive behaviour as the first stage in a sequence of processes that culminates in a wide range of delinquent acts and is the basis for the emergence of an anti-social personality trait (Patterson *et al*. 1992).

Inadequate parenting

The key to this early training is a pattern of unskilled and ineffective discipline by the child's parents, including direct confrontations with the child, high levels of punishment, and a tendency to react to the child's negative actions in kind. The conflicts between parent and child grow longer and more severe, often ending in anger and physical punishment (DeBaryshe *et al*. 1993). In addition, ineffective parents give frequent negative reinforcement to the child's attempts at coercing other members of the family by ignoring small and relatively trivial acts like whining and backtalk (Snyder and Patterson 1986). As the parent–child interaction continues (Patterson and his associates aptly call this 'coercion training'), the nature of the child's aggressive and coercive behaviour evolves from high-frequency, low-intensity actions to less frequent, but more serious, transgressions (Patterson *et al*. 1992). In addition, the child's anti-social and coercive behaviour begins to generalize from the home setting to the school (Loeber and Dishion 1984).

The ineffective parenting skills that underlie coercion training are related to certain antecedent variables. Parents who are themselves anti-social are more likely than other parents to use ineffective discipline and monitoring practices with their children (Patterson and Capaldi 1991). This finding suggests that one process underlying intergenerational correlations in anti-social behaviour may be ineffective parenting from one generation to the next. Variables related to employment, education and intelligence that place the parents at a social disadvantage have also been shown to affect the style of parenting that is used (DeBaryshe *et al*. 1993).

Generalization of effects

Once anti-social tendencies have generalized to the school, they can, by impairing the child's development of normal social skills, have two serious consequences. One is rejection by the child's peer group, and the other is a low level of achievement in school work (Dishion *et al*. 1991). Children who are rejected by the larger peer group react by associating with others who, like themselves, manifest generally anti-social tendencies. In this association lies the basis for delinquency, as the deviant children set standards for each other and reinforce each other's behaviours. Anti-social skills are polished, and the likelihood of more serious deviance is increased. Ultimately, the delinquent adolescent runs a serious risk of becoming an anti-social adult (Patterson *et al*. 1992). It must be emphasized that this process explains only *early-starting* delinquency (see above). Late-starting delinquency begins during adolescence and in the context of peer interaction. It is not the product of ineffective and coercive parenting and it does not involve the poor development of social skills during mid-childhood that characterized early starters. For these reasons, late-starting delinquents tend not to form close networks with deviant peers; as a consequence, they eventually drop out of the anti-social process.

BULLYING

Every so often a story appears in the newspapers of some unfortunate child who is driven to suicide by the taunting, the humiliation and the physical abuse heaped upon him or her by school classmates. Bullying among school-age children is an old and familiar practice that many people have experienced first-hand. The description of bullying experienced by the British writer George Orwell in an English public school almost a century ago still describes the practice fairly well:

> That was the pattern of school life – a continuous triumph of the strong over the weak. Virtue consisted in winning: it consisted in being bigger, stronger, handsomer, richer, more popular, more elegant, more unscrupulous than other people – in dominating them, bullying them, making them suffer pain, making them look foolish, getting the better of them in every way. Life was hierarchical and whatever happened was right. There were the strong, who deserved to win and always did win, and there were the weak, who deserved to lose and always did lose.
>
> (Orwell 1968: 359)

Bullying is grounded in such variables as status, power, competitiveness and the need that some people have to dominate others. Although it may include some hostile affect, it is mainly an instrumental form of aggressing. If the bully feels anything towards his or her victim it is more likely to be loathing than anger.

Characteristics of bullies and victims

Despite its being an old problem, bullying has been studied systematically by psychologists only since the 1970s, with the earliest investigations being those of the Norwegian psychologist Dan Olweus. Much of the psychological literature on bullying has come from the Scandinavian countries and Great Britain, although the problem has also been studied in Japan, Australia, Canada, the United States and several European countries (Smith and Brain 2000). Bullying has been shown, as observers like Orwell have long known, to be the consequence of a differential in power between the bully and the victim, and Olweus (1994) has explored the basis for this differential in the psychological characteristics of the two parties. His research has shown that victims are more anxious and insecure than the average student, with a tendency to be cautious, sensitive and withdrawn. They have a generally negative view of themselves and their everyday situations, and they tend to be to be lonely, isolated and unaggressive. Their typical reaction to being bullied is not to resist, but to withdraw and try to avoid their tormentors. Among boys, victims are physically weaker than their peers. Bullies are characterized by general aggressiveness. They attack, in one way or another, not just their victims, but teachers, parents and siblings as well. They like and admire violence. They lack empathy and have a strong need to dominate. Among boys, bullies are physically stronger than their peers. It is clear from this picture that the victim, given his or her manifest and clearly recognized weaknesses, makes a perfect target for the bully.

Reactions to being bullied

The behaviour of the bully is shaped to some extent by the reactions of the victim. Salmivalli *et al.* (1996) analysed the responses of more than 570 Finnish schoolchildren to the question of how each victim in his or her class reacted to being bullied, and determined that the reactions fell into three classes. Some responded to bullying with counteraggression (e.g. hitting back, speaking up), others by becoming helpless (e.g. crying, missing school, threatening to report the incident to the teacher) and still others by affecting an air of nonchalance (e.g. staying calm, ignoring the bullying, appearing not to be bothered). In a subsequent study, the investigators found that the reaction style most often attributed to victims by their peers was nonchalance, and this was true whether the victim was a boy or a girl. This finding suggests that submission by the victim is not the most common response to being bullied. Children in this study preferred to act as if they were not bothered by the bullying. In addition, some victims – mostly boys – responded with either physical or verbal counteraggression. In addition, girls responded with helplessness more than boys.

One reason for the apparent preference for nonchalant responding is that such a strategy may have been most effective in lessening or terminating the bullying. When students were asked to identify which of the response types was most likely to produce a reduction or termination of bullying, the one most commonly named for both girls and boys was the nonchalant. Thus, by taking an indifferent-seeming attitude to being bullied, the victim could escape or avoid a continuation or exacerbation of the treatment. The investigators point out that this does not mean that such victims actually *were* indifferent and not bothered. It suggests only that they had acquired this way of *acting* because it worked. The response strategy described as most likely to have the opposite effect, i.e. to keep the bullying behaviour going, was helplessness for girls and counteraggression for boys. Note that in each case the response that apparently aroused the bully to renewed efforts was the one contrary to sex-role expectations.

The social context of bullying

Bullies may also be influenced to some extent by social support from other children. Additional data from the study reported above indicated the ways in which students in the classes, other than the bullies and their victims, responded to the bully's behaviour. Four types of bystander were identified: *reinforcers*, who cheered the bully; *assistants*, who actively served as flunkies for the bully; *defenders* of the victim, who sought in various ways to take the victim's side; and *outsiders*, who tried not to become involved. Boys outnumbered girls in the categories of reinforcer and assistant, whereas girls were more likely than boys to be defenders or outsiders (Salmivalli *et al.* 1996). Bullying is not isolated behaviour. It is social behaviour that occurs in relatively stable groups and involves the participation of others in regular capacities. That boys should align themselves with the bully and girls with the victim suggests that traditional social roles may play some part in the overall dynamic of bullying.

Long-term effects of being bullied

Olweus (1994) has investigated the long-term effects on victims of bullying in school, Interviewing a large sample of men in their early twenties, he obtained self-reports of the extent to which each respondent felt that he was a victim of harassment by his peers at the present time. Current personality problems, such as depression, social anxiety and worry over achievement, were also assessed by means of standard tests. In addition, data were also available from school records pertaining to victimization of the respondents by bullies when they had been students in grades 6 and 9, along with personality data from those same previous periods. The results of the analyses of these manifold data allowed several conclusions about the effects of bullying on victims some seven to ten years later. First, there was no evidence that victims of bullies took on some sort of identifying characteristics that made them inviting targets for more harassment later. Being harassed as a young adult was not correlated with having victim status as a child. However, having been a victim seven to ten years earlier did have an effect on the mental health of the young men. Former victims of bullying showed higher levels of depression in their twenties than did non-victims. Victim status was also associated with high levels of overall maladjustment and anxiety, and with low levels of self-esteem, in grades 6 and 9; these characteristics continued to be elevated in former victims of bullying seven to ten years later. The clearest long-range effects of bullying therefore appear to be persistent personality problems associated with depression, anxiety and poor self-regard.

SUMMARY

1 Violence in intimate relationships, most often characterized as that of men against their female partners, is explained in terms of both proximal causes and more remote predisposing or background variables. The most common proximal cause is some act by the woman that the man perceives as a provocation to aggression, such as a challenge to his authority. The event may be trivial and innocuous, but it can evoke aggression if it is appraised as a provocation. Such hostile appraisals are a result of the aggressor's immediate affective state, his beliefs that men have more control over decisions than women, his perceptions of the general satisfactoriness of the union and transient states that may affect the accuracy of cognitive processing, such as alcohol intoxication.

2 Dispositional or background variables include a history of violence in the life of the aggressor and a clear difference in the power of the woman, compared to that of the man, with weaker women being victimized more often than those possessing power. One consequence of this power differential is that a man who is motivated to aggress against his partner often acts on that wish because he sees that the costs of spouse abuse are lower than the perceived advantages. This balance of reward to cost is often embedded in social beliefs that spousal abuse is an intrafamily matter.

3 The personality of the abuser is another background variable in spouse abuse. Impulsivity, depression and psychopathic tendencies have all been observed in male abusers. The borderline personality organization, which is manifested in disturbances in identity, a defensive approach to life and an inadequate sense of reality, has been shown to underlie the well-known cycle in domestic abuse: the slow build-up of anger and hostility, followed by the aggressive outburst and the subsequent period of contrition and tenderness that precedes the onset of the next cycle. The cyclic abuser's dysphoric state is the result of personal insecurity and fear of abandonment, which is rooted in a history of abuse and neglect by his parents.

4 Sexual violence of men against women is sometimes attributed to a high state of sexual arousal elicited in rapists by the idea of forcible sex. Another explanation is based on the finding that rapists differ from non-rapists in terms of the extent to which they attend to the suffering of the rape. Non-abusive men are inhibited from sexual aggression by their empathy for the victims, whereas abusers are not. Sexual violence is also facilitated by a callous and dehumanizing attitude towards women.

5 The confluence model describes male sexual aggression as the joint product of a state of hostility against women and an attitude of promiscuous and impersonal sexuality in which women are regarded as objects of playful exploitation. Sexual violence is a means by which the insecure and hostile male can dominate and control the woman and thereby feel less threatened by her. The factors that predict sexual aggression in young adulthood also predict more general antagonism towards, and conflict with, women later in life.

6 The 'cycle of violence' describes the common belief that adult aggressors are shaped by childhood experiences of being aggressed against. It has been related to a range of adult aggressive behaviours. Research has shown that both physical abuse and neglect in childhood are reliable predictors of criminal violence in adulthood. It has been suggested that one explanation for the cycle of violence is that childhood experiences of harsh treatment by parents leads to the development of biased and inadequate patterns of evaluating social information by the child.

7 Observation of angry interchanges and aggressive behaviour between parents can have harmful effects on children. The development of behavioural and adjustment problems is influenced by the appraisals that the child makes of the observed aggression. Feelings of being threatened by parental violence and of being to blame for it contribute to the harmful emotional outcomes – anxiety, depression and withdrawal – and the undesirable behavioural ones – aggression, delinquency and poor

inhibitory control. Children may acquire coping strategies that form part of a defensive appraisal process that forestalls some of these effects.

8 Delinquency may develop in children as a result of unskilled and ineffective parental behaviour in the home. Parents who get into conflicts with children through poor disciplinary practices, and who react to these conflicts with angry and punitive treatment of the child, provide examples of aggression that the child may internalize. In addition, parents who ignore small and relatively trivial transgressions by children within the family may thereby reinforce attempts at coercing others through these minor acts. When these behaviours generalize from the home to the school and the wider community, they can grow into more serious delinquent behaviour. A consequence of this may be the rejection of the badly behaved youngster, which drives the young delinquent to seek the company of others like himself and to receive further reinforcement from them.

9 Bullying is grounded in the needs for status and dominance. It is a form of instrumental aggression by one child upon another within the context of an immediate community of other children who take the roles of facilitators, assistants, defenders of the victim and uninvolved others. Victims of bullying show evidence of persistent personality problems, e.g. anxiety, depression and low self-esteem, years after harassment has ended.

SUGGESTIONS FOR FURTHER READING

Dutton, D. G. (1998) *The Abusive Personality: Violence and Control in Intimate Relationships.* New York: Guilford Press.

Olweus, D. (1993) *Bullying at School: What We Know and What We Can Do.* Oxford: Blackwell.

White, J. W. and Kowalski, R. M. (1998) Male violence toward women: an integrated perspective, in R. G. Geen and E. Donnerstein (eds) *Human Aggression: Theories, Research, and Implications for Social Policy.* San Diego: Academic Press, pp. 203–28.

SIX

AGGRESSION IN ENTERTAINMENT

Despite the common social concerns about aggression and its effects, many people seldom encounter such behaviour on a regular basis in their everyday lives. For them, violence is something that they mainly experience vicariously through such means as newspaper and magazine stories, the electronic communications media and spectator sports. In this chapter we review research that addresses the effects of three activities generally associated with entertainment that have the potential for evoking aggressive behaviour: films and television; violent video games; and observation of rough or aggressive sporting events.

MOTION PICTURES AND TELEVISION

The sociologist Gabriel Tarde, writing near the close of the nineteenth century, observed that 'epidemics of crime follow the line of the telegraph'. This epigram was based on the observation that highly publicized and sensational criminal acts occasionally precede outbursts of similar behaviour among the public. Tarde, whose sociology was built largely on the concepts of imitation and suggestion, explained such behaviour as a case of what we today commonly call 'copy-cat' crime, or what social psychologists describe as observational learning. Nowadays, of course, people are exposed to a level of violence in the mass media that would have been unimaginable in the nineteenth century. Much of this is in the form of fiction presented for purposes of entertainment, usually enhanced through technology and special effects to a level that the viewer never experiences in everyday life. Does violence encountered in the mass media of communication make people any more aggressive than they would otherwise be? To conclude with any certainty that observation of violence begets aggressive behaviour, we must turn to evidence from scientific investigations carried out either in the experimental laboratory or in natural settings. The purpose of this section of the chapter is to review some of this evidence.

Psychological research on violence in the mass media has been focused on two questions. The first is whether watching such violence is associated with increased aggression in the viewer. The best answer that can be given on the basis of more than thirty years of research is that considerable evidence supports such a conclusion. The second question is of greater interest to psychologists: when observation of violence is followed by aggression, what intervening processes connect the two? Nowadays we no longer explain the effect entirely in terms of imitation. As we will see, many of the variables that have been named as mediators of mass media effects – e.g. **cognitive priming**, activation of affective systems, arousal – have been discussed in other contexts in the preceding chapters of this book.

Evidence from laboratory research

The literature from laboratory experiments on the effects of media violence on aggression has been reviewed many times (e.g. Geen and Thomas 1986; Paik and Comstock 1994). The general conclusion of most reviewers has been that observation of violence is usually followed by some increase in both physical and verbal aggression. This effect is most likely to occur when the viewer has been provoked in some way and is therefore relatively likely to aggress. Because of the extensive scope of this literature, we cannot examine it in detail in a single chapter but must summarize some of the major conclusions and provide a few examples of representative studies.

Aggression as reality and fiction

When televised violence is said to depict real events it evokes more aggression from viewers than when it is described as fictitious. Geen (1975) found that subjects who had been shown a short film of two men fighting in a parking lot and told that the altercation was real not only were more aggressive to an antagonist than those who had been told that the fight was staged by actors, but showed higher levels of blood pressure as well. The finding that real violence is more exciting and that it elicits more arousal than fictitious violence suggests that the former has greater impact on the person than the latter. Possibly images of real violence are regarded as being more 'concrete' than the fictitious variety. Aggressive stimuli having a high degree of concreteness have been shown to elicit more aggression than less concrete ones (Turner and Goldsmith 1976). Realistic violence is probably processed as a more intensive informational input than is fiction. As a consequence of this it may be more likely than fictitious violence to occupy the observer's attention.

Moral justification for aggression

Media violence is more likely to elicit aggression when it is described as being morally justified by the situation than when it is less justified. This was shown in one condition of an experiment by Geen (1981). Subjects

Table 6.1 Average intensities of shocks given by subjects following observation of televised violence

Meaning of film	Treatment	
	Provocation	No provocation
Revenge	6.88[a]	4.14[b]
Professional	5.57[ab]	5.74[a]

Note: Intensity of shock is defined as the number of a button (from 1 to 10) on a Buss Aggression apparatus (see Buss, 1961). Cells having common superscripts are not significantly different from each other.
Source: Geen and Stonner (1973).

were shown a scene from the futurist movie *Rollerball*, in which one member of a professional sports team is viciously attacked by several players from the opposing team. Some subjects were told that the attackers had been goaded into their act by the victim's previous dirty play, whereas others were told that the attack was without justification. When the subject was later given an opportunity to retaliate against a fellow subject who had insulted him, verbal aggression was greater when the violence that had been observed beforehand was justified than when it was not.

Motives of the aggressor

Judgements concerning the motives of the observed aggressor may also influence the way in which media violence elicits aggression. Of the many motives that may animate aggressive behaviour, vengeance is one that most people would probably agree is at least somewhat morally justified. Several studies have shown that when violence is described as motivated by a desire for revenge, it elicits more aggression from an observer than does the same violence attributed to other motives. For example, Geen and Stonner (1973) conducted an experiment in which some male subjects were provoked by an experimenter's confederate and then shown a short scene from a movie in which one prize-fighter beats another fighter severely. Others were shown the scene without first having been provoked. Some subjects were told that the winning fighter was motivated by desire for revenge because of an earlier beating by the other man. Other subjects were told that the fight was merely a professional match involving no hostility between the participants. All subjects then retaliated against the confederate by administering electric shocks.

Provoked subjects were more aggressive than non-provoked ones only after seeing what was regarded as vengeful violence (Table 6.1). Provoked subjects who observed a scene of revenge also reported themselves as feeling less restrained in aggressing than did provoked subjects who regarded the fight as merely professional. Thus, observation of a person taking vengeance successfully on an old enemy reduced inhibitions against aggression and also facilitated expression of aggressive behaviour. On the other hand, Geen and Stonner (1972) also showed that when subjects observe a media portrayal of an *unsuccessful* attempt at revenge, they are later *less* aggressive than those who see successful vengeance.

It is important to note that in these studies only subjects who had first been angered behaved aggressively after observing violence. These findings suggest that one function of observing portrayals of revenge in the media is the facilitation of a social comparison process. The prospects of attacking another person may ordinarily raise inhibitions and aggression anxiety in angry subjects, thereby prohibiting retaliation. If, however, the subject is able to observe in the media an angry character who successfully exacts revenge, the subject may consider his or her own desire to retaliate to be more appropriate. In the same way, observation of an unsuccessful attempt at revenge may remind the subject that retaliation can have punishing consequences and may thereby reinforce inhibitions.

Identification

The social comparison hypothesis is further supported by studies which have shown that when subjects are specifically instructed to imagine themselves in the role of the winner of an act of observed violence, their subsequent aggression against an antagonist is enhanced (Turner and Berkowitz 1972; Perry and Perry 1976). Thus, 'identification with the aggressor', or covert role-taking, facilitates the expression of media-engendered aggression. Such role-taking may facilitate a social comparison process wherein the subject interprets the correctness of his or her motives to aggress on the basis of what is seen on television or in a motion picture.

Arousal

Observation of violence may facilitate the expression of aggression by causing an increase in physiological arousal. Three processes may be suggested as causes for the facilitation of aggression by increased arousal. First, arousal produced by watching violence may simply raise the person's overall activity level and thereby strengthen any responses that he or she happens to be making, including aggressive ones. A second, and as yet untested, possibility is that arousal elicited by the media, especially if it is particularly strong, may be aversive to the observer. It may therefore stimulate aggression in the same way as other aversive or painful stimuli have been shown to do (see Chapter 2). Third, arousal elicited by media portrayals of aggression may be mistaken for anger in situations involving provocation, thus producing anger-motivated aggressive behaviour.

This latter point of view has been proposed by Zillmann (1971). In his study, male subjects were shown a film prior to aggressing against someone who had previously provoked them. The film was violent, erotic or neutral in content. The erotic film, moreover, had been carefully chosen to have no violent scenes. Pre-testing had shown that the erotic film elicited greater physiological arousal in subjects than did either of the other two. In addition, Zillmann found that previously provoked subjects were more aggressive after seeing the erotic film than after seeing the violent or neutral films. He concluded that arousal produced by the movie was incorrectly attributed by the subject to the provocation, so that some of the arousal due to the movie was perceived as anger (for an extended discussion of the role of attribution in aggression, see Chapter 3). Subjects who had seen the erotic film, by being more aroused than the others, therefore felt more angry as well and aggressed more as a consequence.

Symbolic catharsis

A widely cited experiment by Feshbach (1961) stands in contrast to most of the experimental studies cited in this review. Feshbach found that male subjects who had been instigated to aggress against another person by the latter's insulting remarks, and who had then watched a film of a prize fight, were *less* hostile in their verbal appraisal of the insulting person than were similarly provoked subjects who had seen a non-violent film. This difference between film conditions was not found among men who had not first been insulted. Feshbach concluded that the aggressive film had produced a symbolic draining-off, or *catharsis*, of hostility in the previously provoked subjects.

Several explanations have been offered for the discrepancy between Feshbach's results and those of other investigators. Goranson (1970) has argued that because the Feshbach experiment did not include an introduction to the violent film that justified the aggression, it may have increased subjects' restraints against aggressing. Another possible explanation is suggested by an experiment by Zillmann et al. (1973). In this study male subjects saw the same boxing film that had been used by Feshbach, but edited so as to have two possible endings. Subjects in one condition saw the film end with the defeat of the story's hero, whereas others saw it end with a happier conclusion. The latter was the conclusion of the original film that Feshbach had used. Zillmann et al. found that the subjects who saw the happy ending experienced less arousal and were also less aggressive than those who saw the tragic conclusion. Thus, the happy ending of the film may have elicited a state of positive affect that offset any desire to aggress that the subject may have had.

Evidence from non-laboratory research

Field experiments

The findings from laboratory research on media aggression have not been universally accepted. Critics have based their arguments on allegations that such studies represent only experimental analogues of real aggressive behaviour because of the artificial and contrived nature of the aggressive stimuli used, the unnatural laboratory setting and the atypical means of aggressing available to the subject. Partly because of such arguments, interest in laboratory experiments began to wane in the 1970s as research on the effects of televised violence became based more and more on studies in natural settings. Some of these studies were field experiments involving the use of experimental methodology in everyday situations. In the typical **field experiment** on observation of media aggression, videotapes of violent motion pictures are shown, along with videos of non-violent films, to people occupying normal settings, like the common room of a boarding school. Several such investigations were reported during the 1970s and, although they have been criticized as lacking internal validity (Freedman 1984), they yielded consistent findings of a positive relationship between observation of televised violence and aggression. A detailed analysis of the strengths and weaknesses of these studies has been made by Friedrich-Cofer and Huston (1986). On the positive side, the studies involved real television programmes, real-life settings and naturally occurring aggression. However, as Friedrich-Cofer and Huston conceded, the field experiments sometimes lacked convincing non-violent control programmes and were typically carried out in institutional settings such as correctional facilities, rather than in more typical environments. However, more convincing evidence of a connection between observation of media violence and aggressive behaviour is found in a meta-analytic review of 28 field experiments conducted between 1956 and 1988 (Wood *et al.* 1991). The studies included in this analysis were chosen because they investigated the effects of media violence on aggression among children and adolescents during unconstrained social interaction with strangers, classmates and friends. Wood and her colleagues concluded that media violence enhances aggression in such settings and that, because all the experiments involved short-term immediate reactions to observed violence, the effects may be due to temporary changes in affect and arousal as well as to long-term processes like modelling.

Longitudinal studies of observed violence

Longitudinal studies involve the repeated measurement of television viewing and aggressive behaviour under real-life conditions over a lengthy period of time. One such project has been reported by Eron and his associates. This work began with a study of third-grade children in a rural county in the state of New York in 1960, in which each child's aggressiveness was assessed through ratings made by the child's peers and parents and by the children themselves (Eron *et al.* 1971). Each child's preference for violent television programmes was also measured. Ten years later, measures of the same variables were obtained for a large number of the children used in the original sample (Lefkowitz *et al.* 1977).

The data from the two periods were analysed by means of **cross-lagged panel correlations**. In cross-lagged panel correlation, measures of two variables made at one time (A_1 and B_1) are correlated with measures of the same two variables made at a later time (A_2 and B_2). If the magnitude of the correlation between A_1 and B_2 is substantially greater than the magnitude of the correlation between B_1 and A_2, this is taken as an indication that cause and effect goes from A to B and not vice versa. In the study by Lefkowitz *et al.* the correlation between viewing of televised violence in grade 3 and aggression ten years later was compared with the correlation between aggression at the early age and viewing of violence ten years hence. This analysis revealed that preference for television violence among third-grade boys was positively and significantly correlated with aggressiveness ten years later, whereas aggressiveness in grade 3 was not correlated with preference for televised violence a decade later (see Figure 6.1). This pattern of correlations supports the hypothesis that, for boys, observation of television violence

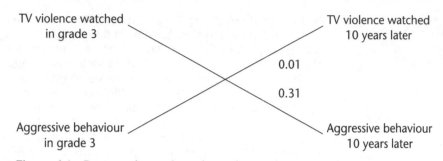

Figure 6.1 Pattern of cross-lagged correlations between amount of violent television watched and aggression over a ten-year period.
Source: data reported by Lefkowitz *et al.* (1977).

in childhood contributes to aggressiveness in young adulthood. Additional analyses showed that the pattern of results was not due to differences in the level of aggressiveness among children who did or did not like violent television in third grade. Across all levels of aggressiveness – high, moderate and low – in third-graders, an early preference for violent television was correlated significantly with aggressiveness ten years later. This relationship was not weakened by the controlling of several possible contaminating variables, such as the socio-economic status of the boys' parents, the boys' intelligence, parental aggressiveness and the total number of hours of television watched. Among girls, however, preference for violent television in grade 3 was not significantly related to aggressiveness in young adulthood.

Huesmann and his associates (1984) reported the results of a second follow-up study, involving 295 people from their original pool, 22 years after the original one. Data were gathered from interviews with the subjects, both face-to-face and mailed, interviews with spouses and children of the subjects and archival records, including criminal justice files. Childhood aggression was shown to be a predictor of both aggression and criminal behaviour even 22 years later. Furthermore, the seriousness of the crimes for which males were convicted by age 30 was shown to be significantly related to the amount of television watched as eight-year-old boys. The findings of this investigation are therefore consistent with those of the ten-year follow-up reported by Lefkowitz *et al.* (1977).

The results of a study carried out by Eron and Huesmann (1980) in the Chicago area support the conclusions of the earlier research. Cross-lagged correlations over a period of one year (1977–8) showed that among boys the correlation between frequency of observing aggression in 1977 and aggressiveness in 1978 was positive and larger than the correlation between aggression in 1977 and frequency of watching violence in 1978. Among boys, therefore, the findings were much the same as they had been in the earlier study. Among girls, however, the results were different. All correlations between observation of violence on television and aggressiveness were positive, but their pattern was the *opposite* of that found for boys. The correlation between aggressiveness in 1977 and viewing of violence in 1978 was greater than the obverse.

How may this finding for girls be explained? One possibility is that girls learn a certain set of sex roles that they are strongly encouraged to play as they mature. In part, these roles prescribe generally passive and non-aggressive behaviour in the face of conflicts rather than overt aggression. A girl who is typically aggressive must therefore find outlets for her emotions that do not include violent behaviour. One such outlet could be vicarious aggression. From year to year during childhood the aggressive girl may come more and more to turn towards violence on television as a major means of expressing her feelings. A connection between violence viewing and aggression has also been shown by Singer and Singer (1981) on the basis of a one-year study involving 141 children of nursery school age. On four occasions during the year, two-week periods were used as 'probes', during which parents kept logs of their children's television viewing. Meanwhile, observers also recorded instances of aggressive behaviour by the children in school. When data were combined across all four probes, aggressive behaviour was found to be significantly correlated with the total amount of time spent viewing 'action-adventure' television programmes (which had a high level of violence), for both boys and girls.

The pattern of cross-lagged correlations over the four probe periods again supported the conclusion that viewing violence on television produces subsequent aggression. In general, the magnitude of the correlations between violence viewing on early probes and aggression on later ones was larger than that of correlations between aggression on early probes and violence viewing on later ones (see Figure 6.2). However, this usual effect was not found during the latter stages of the study, i.e. from probe 2 to probe 3. Viewing of action-adventure programmes in the second probe period was correlated with aggression in the third ($r = 0.22$), but aggression in the second period was also correlated with viewing of action-adventure shows in the third ($r = 0.20$). This latter finding suggests that a liking for potentially aggressive television programmes may be engendered by aggressiveness in behaviour. Overall, therefore, the Singer and Singer data may indicate a circular process, by which observing violence early in the year led to subsequent aggressiveness in the children, which in turn fostered an appetite for still more of the same sort of programme.

Additional evidence of a connection between the viewing of televised violence and aggression comes from a series of longitudinal studies carried out in five countries: the United States, Australia, Finland, Poland and Israel. Two samples were studied in Israel: one from an urban setting and the other from a rural kibbutz. The findings are reported in several contributions to Huesmann and Eron (1986). The time period of the study was three years, and more than 1,000 boys and girls were tested. Aggressiveness was studied as a concomitant of such variables as the violence of preferred programmes, overall viewing of violence, identification with televised aggressors and judgements of realism of televised violence. In general, the evidence from the cross-cultural studies was consistent with that obtained from American samples in earlier research. Early television viewing was associated with aggressiveness among boys in the United States, Finland, Poland and urban Israel. Among girls, early television viewing was related to aggression in the United States and urban Israel. Moreover, early aggression was associated with increased viewing of televised violence for boys and girls in the United States and Finland, and for girls in urban Israel.

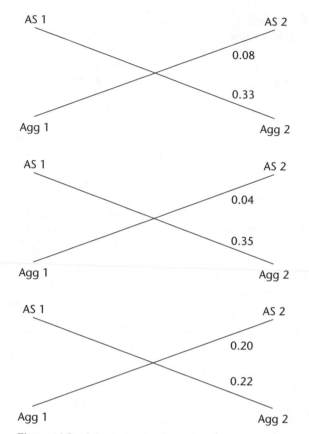

Figure 6.2 Selected cross-lagged correlations between level of viewing of action shows (AS) and aggressiveness (Agg) across three probe periods. *Source*: data reported by Singer and Singer (1981).

A final interesting finding of the studies was that children whose parents were relatively aggressive and rejecting were themselves more aggressive and more likely to watch televised violence than children with less aggressive parents. This finding led Huesmann (1986) to suggest that children who behave aggressively may thereby incur parental punishment and rejection, which in turn causes them to retreat into a fantasy world of violent television. The link between children's aggression and the viewing of violent television may therefore be less one of direct cause and effect than one mediated by parental and family variables.

Processes in media-elicited aggression

Acquisition and elaboration of aggressive scripts

Several explanations have been given for the relationship between television violence and aggression. Social learning theory states that violent action seen in the media provides both a basis for the acquisition of aggressive responses and information concerning the appropriateness of aggression as a means of settling interpersonal conflicts. An extension of the social learning approach has been developed by Huesmann (1986), who has proposed that violence on television is one source of material for the learning of mental scenarios out of which aggressive behavioural scripts are constructed (see Chapter 3). Evidence supporting this conclusion has been reported by Huesmann *et al.* (1983) in a study involving an intervention treatment with highly aggressive boys. The intervention consisted of training sessions administered during a two-year period in which the boys were taught to encode the content of violent television programmes in such a way as to render them less violent (e.g. by judging the aggressive behaviour as atypical of what people really do, or as only an illusion of violence created by special effects). By the end of the two-year period, boys who had received this treatment were significantly less aggressive than other boys in a control condition who had been equally aggressive at the beginning of the study but had subsequently not been given the encoding training received by the others.

How the violent stimulus is represented conceptually depends on a number of factors, such as the perceived justification of the observed action, the motivation of the aggressor and the realism of the aggression (Geen and Thomas 1986). The consequences for the perpetrator of violence seen in media presentations also affect the information that is assimilated to cognitive scripts. Portrayals of rewarded (i.e. successful) aggression have been found to elicit aggressiveness in viewers, whereas scenes showing punished aggression bring about an inhibition of aggression (Betsch and Dickenberger 1993). Developmental factors also play a role in the encoding of observed violence into cognitive scripts. Children's perceptions and interpretations of violence may be simpler and less responsive to subtle variations than those of adults (e.g. Collins *et al.* 1974). Adults modulate their aggression in response to television in terms of circumstances within which the violence occurs, such as the overall context of 'justification' (e.g. Geen 1981). If children are relatively insensitive to such differences in circumstances, they may, as a result, be more likely simply to react to violence with undifferentiated arousal and affect.

Cognitive and affective priming

According to the General Affective Aggression Model (Chapter 3), any stimulus that facilitates access to aggression-related cognitions and affective states in memory can become a mediator of aggressive behaviour in conditions that involve interpersonal conflict. Above we noted how this model accounts for the effects of environmental temperature on aggression (Chapter 2, p. 34). A scene from a television programme that is represented in the mind as bearing some of the characteristics listed above may therefore have the potential to engender both aggressive thoughts and feelings of anger or hostility. Berkowitz (1984) has described such processes in terms of cognitive priming: aggressive thoughts elicited by violent television programmes 'can prime other semantically related thoughts, heightening the chances that viewers will have other aggressive ideas in this period' (p. 411). With the neural networks that underlie aggressive behaviour

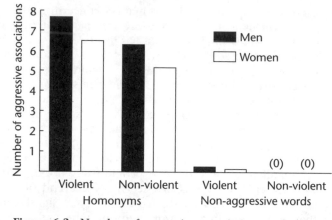

Figure 6.3 Number of aggressive associations to homonyms and non-aggressive words as a function of sex of subject and violent versus non-violent videotape.
Source: adapted from Bushman (1998).

already activated through the priming process, any provocation that occurs at this time should more readily elicit aggression as a consequence.

Two studies may be cited as examples of the priming effects of violent media presentations. Anderson (1997) measured feelings of hostility in subjects who had just watched a segment from a film that contained either violent or non-violent content and found that hostility was greater among those who had seen the violent film. Bushman (1998) carried out two similar experiments testing the hypothesis that exposure to violent films facilitates access to aggressive cognitions. In the first experiment, subjects were instructed, after first having seen either a violent or a non-violent videotape, to report immediate associations to words from two lists. One list contained homonyms (i.e. words that could have at least two different meanings), in which each homonym could have either a violent or a non-violent connotation. For example, the word 'punch' can refer to both a physical blow and a fruit drink. The other list contained words that did not suggest any violent meanings. Bushman found that subjects who had watched the violent videotape made a greater number of aggressive associations to the ambiguous homonyms than those who saw a non-violent videotape, whereas exposure to the tapes had no differential effect on the number of aggressive associations to non-aggressive words. This effect was found in both women and men, but more clearly in men (Figure 6.3). In the second experiment, subjects who had seen a violent tape recognized aggressive words more rapidly than those who had seen the non-violent video. Videotape content did not affect recognition time to non-aggressive words.

Attitudes of fear and distrust

Viewing violence in the media may have long-range effects on behaviour that do not have any obvious connection with immediate effects. In an extensive series of studies, Gerbner and his associates (e.g. Gerbner *et al.* 1980) have described one such long-range consequence of viewing violence. Briefly stated, the hypothesis of Gerbner *et al.* is that extended watching of television brings a person into contact with a high level of violence and that this violence fosters attitudes of fear, suspicion and distrust. Over time, such attitudes may contribute to the formation of a distorted view of the world in which violence is given an importance disproportionate to its prevalence. It is not the purpose of this review to discuss research on this matter. However, evidence that televised violence elicits fear in viewers would be consistent with one of the assumptions behind Gerbner's work. Some studies have shown that fear may be an immediate consequence of watching presentations of violence (e.g. Cantor 1982; Groebel and Krebs 1983). Other evidence points to the conclusion that televised aggression is more likely to be assessed as disturbing by persons who score high in neuroticism (a variable conceptually related to anxiety) than by persons who score low in this variable (Gunter and Furnham 1983).

Additional evidence of an immediate increase in fear following exposure to media violence has been presented in a study by Bryant *et al.* (1981a). Subjects received either heavy (more than four hours per day) or light (less than two hours per day) exposure to television drama over a period of days. Subjects who received the heavy exposure saw either crime dramas with socially just endings or similar dramas in which injustice prevailed. Subjects who received heavy exposure to crime drama of both types later expressed more concern about personal safety than those given lighter exposure. In addition, subjects who saw crime drama lacking justice experienced an increase in reported anxiety, whereas subjects in the other conditions did not. In fact, observation of crime stories with just endings produced a reduction in anxiety among subjects who had been highly anxious at the outset.

Thus, it is possible that fear elicited by televised violence can contribute to the 'scary' world view that Gerbner attributes to people who watch large amounts of television. Such an attitude could lead people to feel a need to protect themselves against a clear and present danger. Among the results could be public demands for punitive justice, authoritarian control and vigilantism. For example, heavy users of television are more likely than lighter users to believe that too little money is being spent on fighting crime (Gerbner *et al.* 1982).

VIDEO GAMES

Violence of game content

The popularity of video games is a relatively recent phenomenon. Prior to the 1980s these games were seldom seen, whereas now it is rare to find a person who has not had at least some exposure to them. Several studies involving large samples of children conducted in the early 1990s attest to the wide exposure of youngsters to these games. Proportions of children reporting that they had played video games either at home or in an arcade varied from 75 to 100 per cent, and the average amount of exposure per week varied between three and ten hours. Games have become not only more popular over the years, but more violent as well (Dietz 1998). Whereas video games in the 1980s tended to be relatively non-violent, like the once-popular Pac Man, increasingly violent content has characterized the newer ones. As Dill and Dill (1998) have indicated in their review of such games, the best-selling games of the 1990s have been those that involve person-to-person combat culminating in the death of one of the figures. Such games are preferred by large numbers of children to other, less aggressive one. In one large study, Buchman and Funk (1996) asked 900 boys and girls of grade-school age to choose their favourite games from among six categories (general entertainment, education, fantasy violence, human violence, non-violent sports and violent sports). Games contain-ing fantasy and human violence made up more than 50 per cent of the choices, with sports violence accounting for another 15 per cent.

Effects of video games on players

Theories of effects

Given the proliferation of games and the high level of violence in the most popular ones, it is obvious that they constitute a major source of aggressive stimulation for children. This raises the question: what effects can we expect from so much exposure to such stimulation? Direct evidence bearing on this question is relatively scarce owing to the short history of the video game phenomenon. However, Dill and Dill (1998) have suggested that video games may have effects similar to those already documented in studies of the effects of films and television. Because a person playing a video game that displays aggressive action is exposed to the same general visual and auditory stimulation as that produced in a violent film, he or she should experience some of the cognitive and motivational changes usually attributed to the latter, e.g. the priming of aggressive responses, increased accessibility of violent thoughts and feelings in memory, retrieval of aggressive behavioural scripts and increased belief in a dangerous world.

In certain other respects, playing video games is different from watching films or television, and Dill and Dill (1998) have suggested that because of certain unique features of game-playing, this pastime may be more prone to evoke aggressive actions than the other media. The most important difference between the two is that whereas observation of programmes or films is passive, the aggression that takes place in the course of a video game is interactive. The player is not only exposed to the violence of others but also an active participant in the story. This difference has several con-sequences. First, if the aggression seen in the passive media is reinforced (e.g. if the fighter is seen to be successful or otherwise rewarded for aggres-sive behaviour) the effect of this reinforcement on the viewer is indirect and vicarious. As already noted (see above, p. 102) vicarious reinforce-ment of this sort can enhance the viewer's aggressiveness. In playing a video game, however, the actor is directly reinforced for aggressive acts by the awarding of points, by sound effects or by being given access to new levels of the game. In addition to being direct rather than vicarious, the reward process in video games may also influence behaviour through the ways in which rewarding stimuli are presented. A study conducted in Canada reveals some interesting facts about the stimulus characteristics of video game rewards and punishment. Braun and Giroux (1989) analysed the 21 most popular games being played in arcades in Montreal and concluded that: (a) behaviour was rewarded considerably more often than it was punished; (b) stimuli were presented to the player so rapidly and in so many different ways that players became unconscious of how often they were being reinforced; and (c) the resulting pattern of reinforcement that the player actually experienced subjectively was one that customarily produces the rapid acquisition and maintenance of habits. Given that the most popular video games among children are those having a large content of violence, it follows that children playing such games may be learning that hitting another person or attacking with a weapon is an appropriate response to interpersonal conflict. A second consequence of the difference between exposure to violence in the passive media and in video games is that in the latter the player is subjected to multiple effects simultaneously. Modelling and direct reinforcement effects are going on together, so that the person is really *rehearsing* aggressive behaviour in the context of viewing it. Such rehearsal can strengthen aggressive scripts and make them more available in subsequent real conflict situations.

Video game playing may also enhance the player-observer's sense of identification with the actor in the aggressive drama. As noted above (p. 103), the covert role-playing that the observer goes through in watching a violent film can increase that person's aggression later on. In a video game such role-taking is *overt* because the player must actually play the role by controlling the character's behaviour. In addition, newer games feature a three-dimensional 'walking through' format, in which the viewer sees the character that he or she controls in a highly realistic setting. As Dill and Dill (1998) point out, being able to see 'oneself' in this way is not typical of everyday experience and may greatly facilitate identification with the aggressive character. Indeed, the player may, for a time, actually *become* that character. Such effects could be even further exacerbated by the next generation of 'virtual reality' video games.

Evidence of effects

As we have already noted, research on the effects of participation in video games is still in its early stages. One of the first studies reported (Silvern and Williamson 1987) compared the effects of playing a violent video game with those produced by watching an aggressive cartoon. These treatments were introduced in two separate experimental sessions, with periods of free play preceding and following the two. Instances of aggression during free play were found to be nearly twice as frequent after both exposure to the violent cartoon and participation in the video game as had been the case before the treatments. The cartoon and the game had effects of equal magnitude on the change from pre-treatment to post-treatment aggressive behaviour. In addition, the incidence of friendly and pro-social behaviours during free play decreased after game playing or observation of the cartoon. Unfortunately, this experiment did not have a

Table 6.2 Correlations among selected variables in study of
video game violence

	AB	NAB	VGV	AP
Aggressive behaviour	–	0.54	0.46	0.36
Non-aggressive behaviour		–	0.31	0.33
Video game violence			–	0.22
Aggressive personality				–

Source: adapted from Anderson and Dill (2000).

control condition in which children played non-violent video games, so
the effect of aggressive games *per se* could not be assessed.

Anderson and Dill (2000) have conducted a pair of studies in which
aggression and hostility following the playing of violent games were compared to similar effects after participation in non-violent ones. In addition,
these studies investigated possible variables and processes that might be
involved in the impact of game playing on the players. In the first study,
a self-report questionnaire was used to assess both aggressive (e.g. fighting) and non-aggressive (e.g. wilful destruction of property) delinquent
behaviour, along with the extent of exposure to video game violence,
and aggressiveness as a personality variable. Both aggressive and non-
aggressive delinquent behaviour were correlated with extent of exposure
to video game violence, with higher correlations for aggressive delinquency (Table 6.2). Exposure to violent games was also positively correlated with aggressive personality (defined in terms of a composite score
from the Caprara Irritability Scale and the Buss–Perry Aggression Scale; see
Chapter 4). This correlation probably indicates that children with aggressive personalities spend more time playing violent video games than less
aggressive children.

The link between long-term exposure to game violence and aggressive
behaviour held up even when the influences of other variables on aggression were controlled through statistical procedures. The same was found
in the case of non-aggressive delinquent behaviour. The association of
exposure to video game violence with both types of delinquency is therefore robust. Anderson and Dill also found that the effects of video game
violence on both aggressive and non-aggressive delinquency were moderated by aggressive personality, with highly aggressive subjects being more
affected by game-playing than less aggressive ones.

In the second study, subjects scoring in the top and bottom quartiles of
the Caprara Irritability Scale were instructed to play either a violent or a
non-violent video game in a laboratory setting. Immediately afterwards,
the subject's aggressive thoughts and feelings of hostility were assessed.
One week later the subject returned to the laboratory to take part in a task
in which bursts of loud noise were both received and given by the subject, ostensibly as part of a competitive task with another subject. This
situation allowed for the subject to be provoked by loud noise and then
to retaliate in kind. Subjects who had played the violent game gave
longer noise blasts after being provoked than those who had played a

non-violent game. Analysis of mediating variables revealed that subjects who had played the violent game reported more aggressive thoughts than those who had played the non-violent game. Playing a violent video game, in other words, primed aggressive thoughts. On the other hand, playing the violent game had no effect on state hostility, suggesting that the effects of playing violent games is mediated by the cognitive pathways in the GAAM.

SPECTATOR AGGRESSION AT SPORTING EVENTS

The problem of aggressive behaviour among spectators at sporting events is one that provokes considerable discussion. Aggression among spectators has been a part of sporting events since ancient times (Guttmann 1983), but it has attracted particular attention in the past few years following some unpleasant incidents at World Cup soccer matches and rioting among fans following championship series in professional sports in the United States. There is evidence that the violence level in sporting events themselves has been escalating in recent years, raising the possibility that aggression on the part of spectators could be a response to such changes (Russell 1993).

Popularity of violent sports

The hypothesis has also been put forth that the increased violence in sports may be enhancing the attractiveness of sporting events, especially among men, so that they are being observed more often than in the past. On 21 February 2000, in a widely publicized event, Marty McSorley, playing for the Boston team of the National Hockey League (the major ice hockey league in the USA and Canada), used his stick to attack an opponent, Donald Brashear of the Vancouver club, causing serious injuries to Brashear's head. In the discussions of the assault that followed, most commentators observed that violence was endemic in the game of ice hockey, and some suggested that if the fighting were forbidden, the sport would lose much of its appeal for its fans. There is some research evidence to support such anecdotes. One study that compared spectator enjoyment of aggressive and non-aggressive play was carried out by Bryant *et al.* (1981b). They showed videotapes of a large number of plays from a season of games in the National Football League (United States) to male and female observers; each videotape had been categorized prior to the study according to the level of roughness in the play. The viewers rated how much they enjoyed seeing each tape. Both male and female viewers reported enjoying the tapes of very aggressive action more than those showing less roughness, with men showing this effect more clearly than women. In another study, Bryant *et al.* (1982) showed subjects a televised tennis match on to which they had dubbed an announcer's commentary describing the two players as good friends, bitter enemies or two people who were relatively indifferent to each other. Even though all viewers saw exactly the same tennis match, those who were informed that the competitors were enemies rated the games more enjoyable than those who placed a less hostile interpretation on the event. It is of course common for sports promoters to play up real or imagined enmities among athletes to help sell the product.

Effects of violent sports on spectators

Our more immediate question is whether the proliferation of violence in sports and the enjoyment that viewers derive from it enhances aggressiveness on the part of the spectator. In many respects the behaviour of observers at sporting events, particularly those involving rough contact, is similar to that of people watching violence in the mass media. Studies carried out in natural settings indicate that spectators at aggressive sporting events often tend to become more hostile and to experience less positive affect as a result. In aggressive spectator sports, as in the case of violent television, there is little evidence of symbolic catharsis.

An early study by Goldstein and Arms (1971) exemplifies the role played by observation of aggressive sports in the expression of hostility. Male spectators were interviewed before and after a game of American football involving two traditional rivals, with males in a control condition being interviewed before and after a competitive but non-aggressive intercollegiate swimming meet. Both sets of interviews included a self-report hostility scale. Hostility after the football game was found to be greater than it had been before the game, regardless of which team the respondent had supported. The increased hostility was not, therefore, entirely due to anger over having seen a favourite team defeated. No changes in hostility were found among spectators at the swimming competition. In a subsequent study, Arms et al. (1979) found evidence of increased hostility following both an ice hockey game and a series of wrestling matches, but not after a swimming competition.

Studies such as those reviewed here indicate that merely observing sports violence can increase hostility and dispositions to aggress. Actually, several other factors seem to be involved as well, such as the identification of the spectator with a particular team. Several observers have pointed out, for example, the role played by identification with local teams in the behaviour of European football fans (Buford 1992; Armstrong 1998). Some of the normative principles in aggression discussed in Chapter 2 may contribute to the hostility and aggressiveness of spectators. It will be recalled that aggression is defined in normative terms as an act of harm that exceeds the amount required to score, to defend one's goal or to carry out other parts of the game, and that people tend to regard their own harmdoing as less aggressive than the actions of their opponents. Given these considerations, fans who identify with a team may think that their team plays 'cleaner' and is less vicious than teams against which it competes. Any violence that occurs on the field may therefore be interpreted as an affront and any penalty assessed against the favourite an injustice. In a study suggesting such possibilities, Smith (1976) conducted an analysis of 68 accounts of hostile crowd behaviour at sporting events in a Toronto newspaper between 1963 and 1973, and found that the two most common causes were, in order of occurrence, 'prior assaultive behaviour' by the opposing team, and 'unpopular officials' decisions'.

Other research has addressed the question of exactly what variables are correlated with spectators' likelihood of becoming involved in collective violence at sporting events. In each of these studies, spectators at ice hockey games in either Canada or Finland were asked how likely they would be to become involved in crowd violence should such a thing break out during the game they were watching. Other questions assessed personality traits, beliefs about the game and certain perceptions of the immediate situation.

Russell and Arms (1998), in a Canadian study, found that several personality variables were related to the likelihood of involvement in crowd aggression. Physical aggressiveness, anger and impulsivity, all assessed by means of well-established self-report scales, were significantly correlated with such likelihood. As we have already noted, these variables are typical predictors of aggressive behaviour (Chapter 4). In addition, two scales measuring sensation-seeking tendencies also correlated with the likelihood of entering into crowd aggression, though at a somewhat lesser magnitude. Sex and age of the spectator were also related to self-reported likeliness to engage in collective violence in another study in Canada, with men being more likely than women, and younger people more likely than older ones (Russell 1995). The modal personality profile of the violence-prone fan to emerge from these investigations is therefore one of a generally aggressive and angry young man with a high need for excitement and poor impulse control. Age, personal aggressiveness and sensation-seeking have also been found to be predictors of joining in crowd aggression in a study conducted in Finland (Mustonen et al. 1996).

In addition to personality variables, the respondent's reason for attending the ice hockey match has also been shown to predict the reported probability of becoming involved in fighting. People who expressed high hopes and expectations of seeing a fight break out on the ice also rated themselves as being more likely to get involved in collective violence than those who came primarily for other reasons (Russell 1995; Mustonen et al. 1996; Russell and Arms 1998). In addition, the number of people who accompanied the spectator to the game was also a factor in whether the person expected to get involved in crowd action. Russell and Arms (1998) found that the greater the number of men who came in the spectator's party, the higher was the spectator's rated likelihood of involvement. Russell and Arms (1995) also found a 'false consensus' effect, in that spectators' attraction to participating in crowd aggression was directly related to their estimates of the proportion of other fans who felt the same way.

The research reviewed here on the effects of sport violence point in some interesting directions. Consistent with the general view of human aggression taken in this book, it has shown that at least the propensities towards such behaviour are a function of both situational and background variables. But do we have any evidence that these propensities are ever followed by outright aggressive behaviour? An ambitious and systematic attempt to account for sports-related aggression with a hypothesis derived from laboratory research has been made in a series of investigations by Phillips (1986). Dealing entirely with material from public records, Phillips has sought to show a causal connection between violence-related events shown on television or reported in other news media and increments in aggression, such as suicide and murder, in the immediate aftermath. The connection is attributed by Phillips to processes of suggestion and imitation similar to those alluded to at the beginning of this chapter. The work shows a positive relationship between violence reported in the media and certain kinds of aggressive behaviour. For example, in one of the strongest demonstrations of his hypothesis, Phillips (1983) found an increased rate of murder of young African-American males following highly publicized heavyweight championship fights in which the black fighter was the loser. In a similar manner, an increased rate of murder of young Caucasian males occurred following heavyweight title fights in which the white boxer lost. Phillips concluded that some murderers imitate winning fighters by attacking men who possess certain features in common with the losing boxers. A reanalysis of the data from the Phillips (1983) study that involved more sophisticated statistical procedures (Miller *et al.* 1991) reaffirmed Phillips's conclusion of an imitative aggression effect. A related finding has been reported by White (1989), who studied the homicide rates in metropolitan areas with teams competing in play-off games of the National Football League between 1973 and 1979. Increases in homicides were found following play-off games in those areas whose teams lost their games; the home areas of winning teams revealed no such increases. White suggested that the followers of losing teams may have experienced high levels of unpleasant affect associated with the frustration of seeing their teams defeated and hence were more likely to behave violently. Obviously, we cannot draw precise causal inferences from archival data such as those surveyed in this section. These studies are important because they suggest effects that one day may be tested under more controlled conditions.

SUMMARY

1 The evidence from laboratory research has generally shown that watching violent material in motion pictures and television is associated with aggressive behaviour in viewers. Realistic violence is more likely to evoke aggressive acts than violence that is clearly fictional. Other conditions of violent movie or TV material that influence aggressive reactions are the moral justification for the violence, the motivation of the aggressor, identification of the observer with the aggressor and the degree to which the violence arouses the observer. There is little evidence for the hypothesis that observing violence makes people less aggressive through a process of **symbolic catharsis**.

2 Experiments carried out in realistic settings also tend to show that observation of aggression in the communications media promotes aggressive behaviour, thereby supporting the conclusions from laboratory experiments. The principal shortcomings of these studies have been their occasional lack of adequate control conditions and their frequent use of atypical samples and settings.

3 A few longitudinal studies have been carried out in which a relationship has been reported between exposure to media violence and aggressive behaviour over time. A significant relationship between watching violent television material during childhood and aggressive behaviour has been reported over periods varying in length between one and 22 years. Longitudinal evidence of a link between observation of violence on television and subsequent aggressiveness has been obtained in several countries.

4 Theoretical explanations of the connection between viewing violent programmes and behaving aggressively have emphasized: (a) the role of the media in shaping behavioural scripts that guide future behaviours in situations of interpersonal conflict; (b) the role played by violent stimuli in priming affective and cognitive systems, thereby facilitating the expression of aggressive acts following sufficient provocation; and (c) the influence of media presentations in fostering attitudes of social fear and distrust that motivate the mobilization of aggressive defences.

5 Playing video games having violent themes has some of the same effects as observing violence in films and television, as well as effects specific to the nature of the games. The direct involvement of the player in the violent action of the game brings about effects other than just those of observation, through vicarious effects of rewards and punishments within the game itself. Identification of the player with the fictional aggressor is also increased by the game-playing format. Engaging in violent video games also increases the likelihood of subsequent aggression by priming aggressive thoughts.

6 Aggression in the context of observing rough and aggressive sporting events can prompt the expression of hostile attitudes and a disposition to take part in aggressive crowd action. There is evidence that violence in sport enhances the popularity of such events. Self-reported likelihood of spectators taking part in aggressive behaviour is greater among men than women and among younger people than older ones. It is also enhanced by relatively high impulsiveness and the need for excitement and by a false perception that others in the situation have similar aggression-related motives. There is also some evidence that observation of violence in the context of sport can facilitate actual aggressive behaviour in observers.

SUGGESTIONS FOR FURTHER READING

Berkowitz, L. (1984) Some effects of thoughts on anti and prosocial influences of media events: a cognitive–neoassociationist analysis. *Psychological Bulletin*, 95, 410–27. A theoretical analysis of the effects of media violence in viewers derived from the cognitive-neoassociationist model.

Bryant, J., Zillmann, D. and Raney, A. A. (1998) Violence and the enjoyment of media sports, in L. A. Wenner (ed.) *Media Sport*. New York: Routledge, pp. 252–65. This chapter reviews a number of studies on the variables in sports violence that enhance the popularity of such events among the public.

Dill, K. E. and Dill, J. C. (1998) Video game violence: a review of the empirical literature. *Aggression and Violent Behavior*, 3, 407–28. A thorough empirical and conceptual review of the literature on effects of video games.

Phillips, D. P. (1986) Natural experiments on the effects of mass media violence on fatal aggression: strengths and weaknesses of a new approach, in L. Berkowitz (ed.) *Advances in Experimental Social Psychology, Volume 19*. New York: Academic Press, pp. 207–50.

SEVEN

HOSTILITY, HEALTH AND ADJUSTMENT

The emotional and affective states related to the instigation and consequences of aggression have also been linked to general health and to psycho-social adjustment. In recent years extensive research has been devoted to the question of whether hostility, anger, and trait aggressiveness play important roles in the development of such health problems as high blood pressure and coronary artery disease. Interest in this problem arises from a suspicion that such psychological risk factors may be as important in the aetiology of cardiovascular diseases as more commonly recognized physical ones, like diet, exercise and smoking. Furthermore, because these diseases indicate an increased risk of death, some investigators are studying the possibility of a correlation between aggressive affective states and mortality.

A good way to begin the study of this problem is with an analysis of the consequences of anger. A commonplace piece of folk wisdom tells us that it is unwise to hold in anger, lest we eventually explode in pent-up rage. Is there anything to this idea? Is anger accompanied by a potentially threatening increase in arousal, and, if so, does aggression – or some other type of expression – allow for a reduction in that dangerous state? Is this alleged build-up in arousal a result of active aggressiveness, or of a suspicious and hostile, but restrained, type of attitude? Furthermore, even if aggression does promote a release of potentially harmful affective arousal, does it also have a beneficial effect of psycho-social adjustment? Does aggressing when angry reduce subsequent aggressive desires and make the person less likely to be violent again? Or can the relief afforded by aggressing simply allow aggression to become habitual and subject to repetition?

In this chapter we are concerned with two aspects of aggression and its related emotional and affective states. First, we consider the possible links among anger, hostility, trait aggressiveness and physical health. We also consider whether aggressive behaviour has a beneficial effect of regulating physiological arousal associated with those affective conditions. Second, we consider whether aggression brings about a reduction in future tendencies to aggress, or whether it may under some circumstances have the exact opposite effect.

PHYSIOLOGICAL EFFECTS OF ANGER AND HOSTILITY

Physiology of anger

Cannon (1929) was among the first investigators to study the physiological concomitants of anger, noting that the pattern of autonomic activity associated with flight and withdrawal is different from that found in aggression. Similar observations were made by Ax (1953) and Schachter (1957), who carried out experiments in which fear and anger, after being experimentally induced, were shown to be accompanied by specific and different patterns of activation. In general, these investigators noted that states of fear produced a physiological reaction similar to that normally elicited by epinephrine, whereas anger appeared to be a mixed epinephrine–norepinephrine response. An important finding was also reported by Funkenstein et al. (1954), who proposed that the physiological reaction to anger depends in part on one's response to the emotion, i.e. whether anger is expressed in overt aggression or is repressed and held in. Male subjects were first harassed and provoked as they solved problems, after which they were classified into four groups: those who expressed their anger in aggression (anger-out), those who held anger in, those who showed a mixture of the two and those who manifested aggression anxiety. Physiologically, the anger-in subjects responded much like the aggression-anxious ones: both groups showed increased heart rates and systolic blood pressure. The anger-out subjects, on the other hand, showed little change in heart rate and increased diastolic blood pressure. This finding prefigured later ones which indicate that repressed hostility is related to both hypertension and cardiovascular problems.

Anger, hostility, hypertension and coronary disease

Hostility and blood pressure

The early studies reviewed above stimulated research on the possibility that one's levels of hostility may be an antecedent of hypertension, particularly if hostility is accompanied by a tendency to internalize and suppress anger. However, attempts to link individual differences in hostility to blood pressure have yielded mixed results. Some studies reveal no relationship between the two variables. Smith and Houston (1987) classified subjects in terms of levels of hostility and typical expression of anger (anger-in versus anger-out), and then gave subjects challenging mental tasks to perform. The magnitude of correlations between the various anger and hostility measures and both systolic and diastolic blood pressure during the tasks was virtually zero. Similar results have been reported by Sallis et al. (1987) in a study in which subjects were exposed to both mental and physical stressors. Again, no consistent evidence was found of a relationship between hostility and either systolic or diastolic blood pressure during the stressful tasks.

In contrast to these findings, Hardy and Smith (1988) found that subjects who participated in a role-playing analogue of a situation involving strong interpersonal conflict did show a relationship between hostility level and hypertension, at least in the case of diastolic blood pressure. Highly hostile subjects performing under these conditions revealed higher levels of diastolic blood pressure than did less hostile subjects. The main difference between the Hardy and Smith study and the other two cited here is that it involved a situational manipulation (the role-play situation) that could engender feelings of anger, whereas the others involved stressful but impersonal circumstances. Thus, hostility may be related to hypertension only when situational cues for conflict and anger are present.

Suppressed anger and blood pressure

Other studies suggest a connection between repressed anger and high blood pressure. A conclusion drawn from the evidence of early studies (e.g. Harris *et al.* 1953; Baer 1979) is that hypertension may be related to a particular personality marked by both strong anger and hostility and a need to repress and hold in such feelings out of concern for social approval and conformity.

One of the more important research programmes on the relationship between anger and hypertension is that of Harburg *et al.* (1979), who studied these variables within samples of black Americans. Harburg *et al.* speculated that suppressed hostility and anger could be contributors to the high levels of hypertension found in blacks, levels considerably higher on average than those found in whites. Black males who showed high levels of suppressed hostility were, as predicted, found to have higher diastolic blood pressure levels than those who did not reveal this pattern of suppression. In addition, males who tended to cope with stress in their lives by holding in anger and by experiencing aggression guilt were, in general, more likely to become hyptertensives than those who coped with stress more expressively. Evidence that connects anger expression with hypertension in whites as well as blacks comes from a study by Johnson *et al.* (1987). Adolescent males of both racial groups were tested for the tendency to suppress expression of anger as well as for other traditional risk factors such as smoking, excess weight and family history of hypertension. Both groups showed a clear relationship between suppression of anger and elevation in blood pressure. Among blacks, suppression of anger even outweighed the more traditional risk variables in predicting hypertension, whereas in whites the anger-in variable was less related to hypertension than was excess weight. Thus, although anger suppression appears to be a predictor of hypertension in both blacks and whites, it is a more powerful one among blacks than among whites.

Suppressed anger and coronary disease

We therefore have evidence that the connection between hostility and hypertension is probably brought about by a characteristic anger-in style of coping. The same may be true in the case of heart disorders. Some evidence exists linking suppressed hostility to coronary heart disease. Dembroski *et al.* (1985) interviewed patients undergoing diagnosis for heart problems in order to isolate two variables – the person's potential

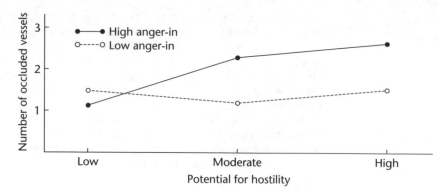

Figure 7.1   Relationship between anger expression, potential for hostility and incidence of coronary occlusion.
Source: Dembroski *et al.* (1985).

for experiencing feelings of hostility and his or her tendency to hold and suppress anger (anger-in). Potential for hostility (PH) is a component of the familiar **type A behaviour pattern** found in people who manifest a typically active, driving and impatient behavioural style. It has been shown to be correlated with hypertension and other cardiovascular disorders (e.g. McCann and Matthews 1988). Dembroski and his associates compared people who scored high in PH and in anger-in with low scorers on the same in terms of several indicators of coronary heart disease. For every indicator, PH and anger-in were found to have an interactive effect: persons who had strong tendencies to hold in anger showed progressively greater likelihood of developing coronary problems as potential for hostility increased. Figure 7.1 illustrates one of these interactions. The dependent measure is the number of coronary arteries showing blockage of 75 per cent or more. Among persons high in anger-in, the number of such arteries is greater when potential for hostility is high than when it is low. No such effect for hostility potential is found in patients low in anger-in. Coronary risk is therefore relatively high for hostile people only if they exert too much control over their anger and suppress it.

On the other hand, some investigators have concluded that coronary disease is related to the *expression* of anger and hostility rather than to suppression and restraint. Siegman and his colleagues (1987), for example, reported that coronary artery disease among patients undergoing angiogram procedures was positively correlated with high scores on a scale measuring the expression of anger and hostility but not with the experience of hostility. Coronary disease was therefore not related to feelings of hostility, but to a trait of expressing hostility in a direct and forceful manner. Siegman *et al.* (1990) supported this conclusion in an experiment in which subjects were instructed to describe several anger-arousing situations in a loud-rapid, soft-slow or normal manner of speech. They found that heart rate and blood pressure both rose as a function of style of speech, with loud-rapid expressors showing greater cardiovascular arousal than those speaking in normal or soft-slow voices. Speech style did not affect arousal when neutral situations were similarly described.

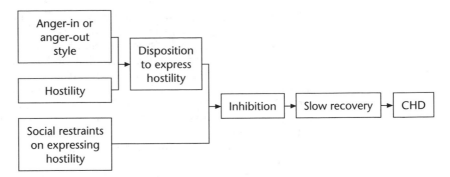

Figure 7.2 A model of anger expression, social restraints, cardiovascular recovery time and coronary heart disease.
Source: based on Brosschot and Thayer (1998).

There is, therefore, a lack of agreement on whether cardiovascular disorder is related to a tendency to hold in anger or a tendency to express it. Some studies associate such disorder with anger expression and others associate it with anger inhibition. Brosschot and Thayer (1998) have suggested a reconciliation of these conflicting findings by suggesting that individual differences in anger-in versus anger-out methods of reaction are not a matter of primary importance. Instead of concentrating on such trait factors, they argue, we should recognize that in everyday life people suppress anger far more often than they express it. For one thing, they point out, everyday stressors often take the form of minor 'hassles' that the person endures without responding; for another, society tends to discourage direct expression of anger more than it does the acting out of other emotions. Thus, dispositional inhibitors as well as expressers have one thing in common – both are highly hostile individuals who must suppress their anger more often than not.

The inhibition of anger normally mandated by society in turn leads to a slower dissipation of cardiovascular arousal than would be found if such inhibitions were not imposed. The link between heart disease and hostility is identified by Brosschot and Thayer as the result of slow **cardiovascular recovery time** (Figure 7.2). This slowdown in recovery is brought about by a low level of activity in the parasympathetic division of the autonomic nervous system, particularly the tenth cranial nerve (the vagus), which controls the action of the heart. In everyday life, they argue, such slow recovery can create a pathogenic state marked by a rapid and variable heart rate that predisposes the individual to cardiac problems.

Conclusions: hostility and cardiovascular risk

Certainly the evidence that we now have points to a conclusion that hostility is correlated with cardiovascular risk. The question remains as to what causal factors underlie this correlation. Several possibilities have been suggested. One is that hostility promotes increased reactivity to stressful situations (Smith 1992; Miller *et al.* 1996). Possibly hostile people show greater reactivity to stressful situations than less hostile ones, so that on each occasion of being angry they experience higher levels of cardiac acceleration, blood pressure, endocrine activity, muscle tension and other psychosomatic responses. Frequent experiences of anger therefore bring about a persistent high state of abnormal bodily activation that has a cumulative effect leading to hypertension and coronary disease (see Blascovich and Katkin 1993). This argument attributes the hostility–health correlation to *intrapersonal* changes. Stress and strain on the body's vital organs promote the risk of heart problems. It has also been suggested that hostility may be connected, through the same intrapersonal processes, to other diseases, such as those involving changes in the immune system (Siegman 1994).

A second possibility is that hostility, in combination with social restraints against expression of the emotion, fosters slow cardiovascular recovery following the arousal of anger (Brosschot and Thayer 1998), as discussed above. This explanation also accounts for the hostility–health correlation in intrapersonal terms. The cardiovascular risk is not so much in an absolutely high level of arousal but instead in arousal that persists at a relatively high level over an extended period of time. A third possibility is that hostile people, because of the ways in which they deal with other people, create a relatively stressful social environment for themselves. They may experience higher levels of interpersonal conflict and receive less social support than less hostile people. As a consequence, they are likely simply to encounter a greater number of specific situations that are stressful, even though they are not necessarily more reactive to those situations. This argument therefore explains the health–hostility relationship in terms of *interpersonal* causes.

A fourth possibility is that hostile people are at risk of developing poor overall health-related habits. It has been reported, for example, that hostile people exercise less, practise poorer personal hygiene, get less sleep and consume more alcohol than those who are less hostile (Leiker and Hailey 1988). Such poor preventive practices could be a factor in the development of disease, even though we do not yet know the reasons for these correlations. One possible connection has been suggested by Houston and Vavak (1991), who trace hostility to childhood experiences and attribute it to feelings of insecurity. These feelings are due to parental behaviour that lacks genuine acceptance, is overly strict and demanding, and is inconsistent in administration of discipline. Parent–child relationships may also shape the development of health habits and attitudes, such as those concerning physical activity, diet, smoking and drinking, all known to be risk factors for cardiovascular disease. This explanation therefore treats the hostility–health connection as a case of common correlation of each variable with a third factor.

AGGRESSION AND PHYSIOLOGICAL RECOVERY

Direct aggression

The literature on the relationship between the repression of anger and hostility and some of the health problems reviewed above leads us to ask whether the expression of aggression promotes the reduction of arousal and tension. A number of experimental investigations have been addressed to this problem. In each case, subjects were first provoked in some way so that arousal would be increased, after which the subjects were given an opportunity to aggress. The main dependent measure in most of the studies was blood pressure. The conclusion most warranted from this body of research is that aggression leads to autonomic recovery under some conditions but not others, and that in some cases it may actually bring about *increased* autonomic activation. Briefly stated, the data indicate that autonomic recovery after aggression is likely to occur *except* when the target person appears to be powerful and potentially threatening, aggression is considered to be an inappropriate response or the aggressor characteristically feels guilty after aggressing.

Status of the victim

When the victim of aggression is a person of high status, aggression does not produce autonomic recovery. This is true, moreover, even when that person has provoked the subject and is the cause of the subject's agitated state. Hokanson and Shetler (1961) showed this in a study in which subjects were first abused and harassed by a male experimenter, after which some were required to give electric shocks to the experimenter and others were not. The experimenter presented himself as a person of relatively low status (a student) or high status (a young member of the faculty). Subjects who were harassed showed higher levels of blood pressure following this treatment than did those in a control group who were treated in a less frustrating and provoking way. Provoked subjects who then attacked a low-status experimenter revealed a sharp decline in blood pressure after shocking, whereas those who attacked a person of high status showed no significant change in blood pressure.

The finding that aggression against a person of high status does not promote physiological recovery underlines a problem inherent in the use of blood pressure as an indicator of anger and aggressive arousal. Other studies have shown that when subjects are free to aggress or not aggress against a provocateur, they choose not to aggress against a high-status person as much as against one of low status (Hokanson 1961). However, subjects in the Hokanson and Shetler (1961) experiment were given no choice: they had to shock the high-status experimenter. Aggression in this case may have seemed inappropriate to the subjects and was therefore likely to elicit feelings of discomfort and anxiety. Blood pressure may be susceptible to influence by several emotional states in addition to anger and hostility. Thus, subjects who aggressed against a high-status person may have shown steadily high levels of blood pressure because blood pressure was in this case reflecting fear or anxiety.

Aggression guilt

People who feel guilty about behaving aggressively may also fail to show reduced autonomic arousal after aggressing. For example, Schill (1972) carried out a study in which women subjects were first classified as high or low in aggression guilt and then frustrated by an experimenter. Later, each subject was given an opportunity to aggress verbally against the experimenter. Schill found that frustration caused increased blood pressure, regardless of level of aggression guilt. However, subjects low in guilt showed greater blood pressure reduction after verbally aggressing than did subjects high in guilt. Thus, aggression guilt hindered autonomic recovery in this experiment in much the same way as did perception of the victim's high status in the Hokanson and Shetler (1961) study.

Taken together, the two studies reviewed above suggest one possible conclusion: when aggression is likely to create an emotional state of fear, anxiety or guilt, it leads to an increase in autonomic arousal which offsets any reduction in arousal that accompanies aggression. These two antagonistic processes may summate and cancel each other out, so that there is no net change in arousal. In the absence of anxiety, fear or guilt, however, arousal reduction does occur as a consequence of aggression.

The nature of the response

Fantasy and vicarious aggression

A question that has received little attention is whether or not autonomic recovery would be more likely following some kinds of aggression than following others. Although little evidence exists, a few conclusions are suggested by what is known. One is that whereas either physical or verbal aggression may promote recovery, fantasizing about aggression does not (Baker and Schaie 1969). Even though some observers have suggested that aggressive fantasy may serve a drive-reducing function (e.g. Feshbach 1955), it would appear at the very least that such fantasizing is not as effective as overt aggression. Nor does vicarious aggression lead to autonomic recovery. Geen *et al.* (1975) conducted an experiment in which subjects who had been provoked by a fellow subject either aggressed against the latter or merely observed as the experimenter aggressed against him. Subjects who aggressed personally showed a significant reduction in blood pressure, but those who observed as the experimenter aggressed remained as aroused as they had been immediately after being provoked.

Non-aggressive responses

Reacting to a provocation with a friendly prosocial response has also been found to be ineffective in bringing about autonomic recovery, at least among men. In an experiment by Hokanson and Edelman (1966), male subjects were able to react to an attack by another person by retaliating, by ignoring the attack or by making a friendly and rewarding response. Those who retaliated showed a faster return to baseline blood pressure levels than did those who made rewarding responses. The latter showed no more autonomic recovery than control subjects who were not allowed to respond to the attack at all. Refraining from retaliation and 'blessing one's enemies', while possibly being of some benefit to society, does not appear to reduce the arousal level of a provoked person as well as does aggressing.

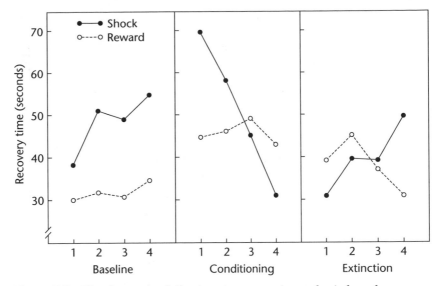

Figure 7.3 Blood pressure following non-aggressive and reinforced aggressive responses in women.
Source: Hokanson *et al.* (1968).

The study by Hokanson and Edelman shows that aggression produces autonomic recovery in men. Two questions follow from this observation. The first is whether a similar reduction in arousal is found among aggressing women. The second is why aggression has this effect in men (and possibly in women also). Both questions were addressed in an experiment by Hokanson *et al.* (1968), who concluded that a person's history of socialization and social learning is involved. These histories may differ in men and women. In the first part of the experiment, women subjects interacted with another woman who behaved in an aggressive way. Subjects could respond to her either by aggressing or by giving her a reward. Subjects showed a more rapid reduction in blood pressure after rewarding her than after attacking her. The investigators reasoned that this finding can be attributed to normal socialization *practices*, whereby girls are trained not to behave violently and, as a consequence, experience no reduction in arousal after aggressing. It is also possible that women may experience more anxiety and guilt after aggressing than do men (Frodi *et al.* 1977); as was proposed above, if anxiety and guilt produce increased arousal, this increase may overpower physiological recovery following aggression. Subsequently, Hokanson *et al.* gave their women subjects a series of rewards for behaving aggressively towards their antagonist. Following this treatment, the subjects showed more rapid autonomic recovery after aggressing than after rewarding the other person. When these rewards were later withdrawn, subjects reverted to their original pattern of recovery, showing faster recovery after rewarding responses than after aggression (See Figure 7.3).

In the second part of the experiment men served as subjects in a similar procedure. The results were almost a mirror image of those obtained with

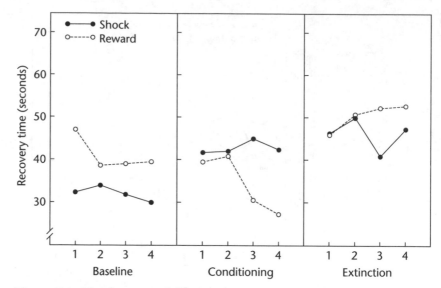

Figure 7.4 Blood pressure following aggressive and reinforced
non-aggressive responses in men.
Source: Hokanson *et al.* (1968).

women. Males originally showed more rapid autonomic recovery after
aggressing against their male antagonist than after rewarding him – the
exact opposite of what the women had shown. The males were then given
a series of rewards for behaving *non-aggressively*, with the result that they
revealed faster recovery following rewarding behaviour than after
aggressing. When rewards for non-aggression were withdrawn, the men
also reverted to their earlier pattern, this being in their case faster recovery
following aggression than following reward (see Figure 7.4). Altogether,
the study by Hokanson *et al.* indicates that people experience the optimal
degree of physiological recovery after responding to provocation in a way
that has led to reinforcement in the past. A person's history of social
learning is therefore an important contributor to the physiological outcome of aggressive behaviour.

THE BEHAVIOURAL CONSEQUENCES OF AGGRESSION

Several years ago, an American manufacturer advertised a product consisting of a short pole with large foam balls attached to each end. The device
was sold in pairs. The photograph which accompanied the advertisement
showed two men, each holding one of the instruments, squaring off in a
jousting position and apparently preparing to strike each other with the
foam balls. The text of the advertisement suggested that by using these
objects two people could work off hostility and tensions in a harmless
way. Implicit in this claim was the hypothesis that aggression helps people

reduce their violent and hostile urges and is beneficial provided that it leads to no real harm in the process.

The phenomenon by which aggressive feelings, motives and impulses are supposedly 'drained off' through violent action has been called **aggression catharsis**. It is related to an earlier theory that originated in ancient Greece. The notion that one can purge emotions by experiencing them goes back to Aristotle, who, in the *Poetics*, taught that classical tragedy induces in the viewer feelings of pity and fear, and thereby allows the viewer to experience a catharsis of these affective states. Over the years many psychologists have argued that feelings of anger and hostility may likewise be drained away through behaviour associated with these emotions. Experimental research on aggression catharsis has taken two approaches. One, already reviewed in Chapter 4, studies symbolic catharsis, whereby the angry subject is exposed to aggression carried out by others, such as actors or athletes. The other involves giving the angry subject an opportunity to attack either the antagonist or some substitute. Two questions are raised by this latter procedure: (a) does aggression reduce the attacker's level of arousal; and (b) does aggression make the person less likely to aggress again?

We have already explored evidence pertaining to the first question and have seen that under some conditions aggression does produce a reduction of the arousal state associated with anger. In this section we consider the second question and concentrate on the behavioural outcomes of aggression.

Catharsis in psychoanalytic theory

Much of the current thinking on catharsis originated in the psychoanalytic analysis of hysteria published in the 1890s by Breuer and Freud. In their book on the subject, they specifically stated that the most effective relief following traumas such as insults is obtained through direct aggression: 'The reaction of an injured person to a trauma has really only . . . a "cathartic" effect if it is expressed in an adequate reaction like revenge' (Breuer and Freud [1894]1961: 5). The form of revenge may be physical or verbal, but whatever the mode, expression of hostility is considered preferable to no expression at all: 'An insult retaliated, be it only in words, is differently recalled from one that had to be taken in silence . . . Man finds a substitute for . . . [direct aggression] in speech through which help the affect can be well-nigh abreacted.' The analytic theory of catharsis followed from the assumption that anger (with its physiological manifestations) builds up inside a person until it is released in some way. Following this cathartic relief, the person will be relatively unaggressive and will remain so until the aggressive drive builds again to a high level. Because of the widespread dissemination of pychoanalytic ideas within popular psychology, this concept has gained considerable acceptance (Bushman *et al.* 1999).

The question we must ask is whether controlled research yields any evidence for this belief. The experimental studies fall into two groups. In some studies, a subject typically aggresses against an antagonist after first having engaged in aggressive behaviour with either an inanimate object or people other than the antagonist. In other studies the subject aggresses against an antagonist twice. If the catharsis hypothesis is correct, aggression against either one's antagonist or an inanimate object should render the person less aggressive than would be the case if no such prior aggression had taken place.

Evidence bearing on the catharsis hypothesis

Aggression against inanimate objects

A claim that is often made by advocates of the catharsis hypothesis is that any sort of aggressive action (like breaking plates or hitting a pillow) can potentially drain off aggressive drive and render the actor less likely to aggress in the immediate future. In a study designed to test this possibility, Bushman et al. (1999) found results that were directly opposite to the catharsis hypothesis. Subjects in this experiment who had been made angry with another person and then allowed to punch a punching bag (which should have discharged pent-up aggressive motivation) were subsequently given an opportunity to aggress against this person in an indirect and experimentally controlled interchange. Contrary to the principle of catharsis, these subjects were *more* punitive to the other person than were control subjects who had also been angered but had not been given a chance to punch the bag.

A related idea that has attracted some attention is that taking part in vigorous physical activity such as contact sports can provide a means of discharging aggressive motives. Some evidence bearing on this idea has been found in controlled studies. In one such study, Ryan (1970) provided an opportunity for catharsis to subjects who had been angered by an experimenter's accomplice. Some subjects pounded on a box with a rubber hammer. Of these, some competed with the person who had angered them and some did not. A group of control subjects did not hammer the box. When subjects were later allowed to aggress against the accomplice, no sign of catharsis was found. Subjects who had pounded on the box, whether in competition or not, were no less aggressive than the control subjects who had not had this opportunity for catharsis.

Evidence which disputes the catharsis hypothesis has also been found in the case of the less vigorous, but perhaps more violent, act of firing a gun. Mallick and McCandless (1966) used this activity as a means of aggressive play in an experiment with children. After having been frustrated by another child, the subject engaged in either target shooting or talking with the experimenter. Half of those who conversed with the experimenter merely chatted, whereas the other half were informed that the frustration caused by the other child had not been deliberate. Later, every subject had a chance to hurt the other child by preventing that child's attainment of a valued goal. Children who had done the target-shooting were as punitive as those who had merely talked with the experimenter, and more aggressive than those to whom the other child's behaviour had been rationalized. Aggression in the form of shooting a gun had not reduced the probability of future aggression. The findings of a field study by Patterson (1974) corroborate the data from laboratory studies. High school American football players and physical education students were given hostility self-rating scales one week before the football season began and again one week after the season's end. Whereas physical education students showed a slight but non-significant decrease in hostility over the course of the season, football players showed a significant increase. Whether playing football caused this increase in hostility over the course of the season we cannot say. Of one conclusion we can, however, be certain: the experience of playing the rough and aggressive game did nothing to diminish hostility in the players.

Direct aggression against the antagonist

We must now ask whether physical aggression against another person increases or, as the catharsis hypothesis would predict, decreases the strength or likelihood of subsequent physical aggression against that person. Berkowitz (1966) showed that subjects who were first provoked and then given two opportunities to aggress against their antagonist were more aggressive on the second occasion than were other subjects not given the initial opportunity. It has also been shown that when subjects who have been provoked are given a chance to aggress over a long series of occasions, they tend to increase in their level of aggressiveness, not to decrease as the catharsis hypothesis would imply (Geen 1968).

Another investigation into the possible cathartic effects of direct aggression against an antagonist was conducted by Geen et al. (1975). In this experiment the conditions for a possible catharsis were created. In addition, the study included a measurement of physiological arousal. Subjects, all of whom were males, first interacted with an experimental confederate posing as a fellow subject. This person provoked half the subjects but not the others. Some subjects were then given a chance to deliver electric shocks to the confederate. Other subjects did not shock, but watched as the experimenter shocked the confederate. Another group of subjects merely sat and waited for a given period of time. Finally, every subject was given an opportunity to shock the confederate. The main measure of the experiment was the average intensity of shocks given during the last shocking session (in which every subject gave shocks). As Table 7.1 shows, subjects

Table 7.1 Average intensities of shocks given by subjects

Treatment of confederate	Treatment	
	Provocation	No provocation
Subject shocks	6.65[a]	3.92[bc]
Experimenter shocks	4.13[bc]	3.62[c]
No shock	5.20[b]	3.20[c]

Note: Cells having common superscripts are not significantly different from each other.
Source: Geen et al. (1975).

who had been provoked and who had also shocked the confederate previously were *more* aggressive during the final session than were both those who had not shocked previously and those who had merely watched the experimenter shock their antagonist. A second measure in the experiment was a questionnaire rating by each subject of how much he had 'held back' (i.e. been inhibited) from shocking the other person. Provoked subjects who had previously shocked felt less restrained about shocking during the second session than did those who had not shocked before. Thus, the original act of aggressing appears to have facilitated subsequent aggression instead of diminishing it. A final measure was that of blood pressure, taken at several points during the experiment. The main finding of this measurement was that provoked subjects who shocked the confederate in the first session experienced a reduction of blood pressure after this act, whereas the blood pressure of provoked subjects who did not aggress in the first session remained high until they aggressed in the second session. In other words, 'physiological catharsis' *did* occur; aggression was accompanied by a return of blood pressure to normal levels. However, 'behavioural catharsis', defined as a reduction in aggression following aggression, did not occur – in fact, the opposite was found.

Divergence of physiological catharsis and behaviour

In this chapter two questions have been raised. The first is whether aggressive behaviour promotes reduction of arousal levels that have been elevated by provocation. The other is whether aggression reduces motivation to aggress further and, as a consequence, makes further aggressive behaviour less likely. According to the hypothesis of aggression catharsis, the answer to both questions would be affirmative because the two phenomena are related. A necessary consequence of the presumed reduction in physiological arousal should be the reduced likelihood of subsequent aggression. The evidence from research tends to support the idea that aggression promotes physiological recovery following provocation, at least under conditions in which anxiety, fear or guilt are not produced. When these latter conditions are produced, they may increase arousal and offset physiological recovery. The premise that aggression reduces the likelihood of future aggression is generally not supported. Aggression, whether against an antagonist or some other target, is generally followed by *more*, not less, subsequent aggression.

Aggression and reinforcement

Despite evidence to the contrary, the catharsis hypothesis continues to have some appeal. It makes some intuitive sense to assume that a reduction in arousal following aggression should reduce motivation towards further aggression. Such an idea is also consistent with the 'aggressive drive' theory (see above, pp. 21–2). The frustration–aggression hypothesis placed catharsis at the end of a series of events related to each other in a cause–effect chain: frustration arouses aggressive drive which leads to aggression, and aggression reduces aggressive drive, thereby eliminating the motive force for further aggression. This formulation raises one important question, however: why should drive reduction reduce the probability of the behaviour that precedes it? According to the reinforcement principle, if reduction of drive is a desirable (i.e. rewarding) state, it should strengthen the preceding response and *increase* its probability. The result would therefore be that after aggressing, the person should feel less aroused than before, but more likely to react to future provocation with aggression.

One way in which aggression may be reinforced, and hence maintained, is by being successful in causing the termination or modification of the aversive conditions that produced it. When retaliatory aggression eliminates or reduces the severity of aversive conditions, it is by definition rewarded. Although this may produce a short-term reduction in the retaliator's aggression (see, for example, Epstein and Taylor 1967), receiving this sort of reinforcement for aggressive behaviour may, over the long run, make the person more and more likely to resort to aggression under similar conditions (Dengerink and Covey 1983). Dengerink and his colleagues have used an experimental procedure in which interacting partners appear to administer shocks of various intensity to each other, but in which shocks are actually under the control of the experimenter. In one such study, O'Leary and Dengerink (1973) created the impression that the intensity of shocks chosen by one subject was gradually decreased because the other subject retaliated with intense shocks of his own. In other words, the behaviour of the retaliating subject punished, and hence reduced, the aggressive behaviour of the other person. The immediate result of this was a decrease in the intensity with which the retaliator shocked the attacker.

However, in a subsequent study, Dengerink *et al.* (1978) found that subjects who experienced a decrease in their antagonist's attacks contingent on their retaliatory behaviour shocked the latter more than subjects who experienced the same reduction but did not regard it as due to their own aggressiveness. Subjects who saw their aggression as the cause of the other person's ceasing and desisting in his own violence were therefore given feedback that their aggressive behaviour was serving a useful purpose, and this feedback maintained their aggressiveness. Successful use of punishment may therefore have an undesirable side-effect for the person using it by making him or her even more likely to use such punishment in the future. For this reason Dengerink and Covey (1983: 172) have concluded that 'persons who employ aggressive means of controlling another's aversive behavior may find that successful use of such tactics [is] ultimately self-corrupting.'

Is there an alternative to aggression?

On the basis of the several topics covered in this chapter the reader may be forgiven for wondering exactly what advice psychologists would give about how to handle anger and hostility. A word or two by way of summing up may therefore be in order. First, suppressing and holding in anger is not advised. This response is closely tied to hypertension and is also a risk factor in coronary heart disease. Expressing hostile and angry feelings in some way is clearly better for overall physical health. Second, aggression is one response that can reduce tension and probably prevent a dangerous build-up of suppressed hostility. However, aggression may have an undesirable side-effect in that it may lead to a person's becoming more aggressive in the future. The angry person may therefore be faced with a difficult choice between two unattractive alternatives. Perhaps the best solution to the dilemma for someone who has been provoked and aroused to anger by another person is to express his or her feelings clearly but without hostility, and to seek a dialogue in which both persons can find mutually satisfactory outcomes to their conflict (see Holt 1970). This solution requires assertiveness, honesty and self-control on the part of both persons and may for that reason be difficult to implement. However, it may be worth the effort in that it can help to reduce undesirable tensions without risking an escalation of aggression.

SUMMARY

1 Anger and hostility influence people's lives in more ways than by serving as antecedents of aggressive behaviour. They also have consequences for health and for the overall adjustment that people make to their social environments. These emotional states can have damaging effects on the body, leading to possible hypertension and cardiovascular disease.

2 Although evidence for the relationship is not consistent, hostility has been shown to lead to increased blood pressure in some studies. Anger, particularly when it is suppressed and not acted out, may also be associated with elevated blood pressure. Coronary disease has also been linked to anger, but opinions vary as to whether inhibition or expression of the emotion is the cause. There is evidence that personal tendencies to inhibit expression (the anger-in style of reacting) are correlated with coronary problems, while other evidence points to the tendency to express anger intensely (the anger-out style) as the best predictor of the disorder. A third point of view is that inhibition of anger leads to coronary disease by increasing the amount of time needed to return to normal levels of arousal after having been provoked, and that the major cause of such inhibition is not a personal tendency towards the anger-in response, but rather social disapproval of anger expression.

3 Another theory holds that hostile and angry people may run a relatively high risk of developing coronary disease because they create hostile and non-supportive environments for themselves. By experiencing rejection and poor social support, they may place themselves under greater stress than that experienced by less hostile and angry people. Others have suggested that people who are typically hostile may place themselves at higher risk for heart disease because they also have poor habits related to the maintenance of good health.

4 Aggressive behaviour as a reaction to being provoked promotes recovery from the physiological consequences of anger under most conditions, unless the aggression creates feelings of fear, anxiety or guilt that offset recovery. Fantasizing about aggression and watching someone else aggress do not facilitate physiological recovery as much as direct aggression.

There is evidence, however, that the response which leads to the optimal physiological recovery is whatever response has been reinforced in the past.

5 Although aggression may bring about reduction in arousal, it does not necessarily produce reduced aggressiveness as predicted by the catharsis hypothesis. Aggressing may also lead to reduced inhibitions against aggression, with consequent facilitation of aggression. The facilitation of aggression by aggression has been found in verbal behaviour, aggressive play and physical retaliation.

6 If aggression is reinforced, the likelihood of future aggression is enhanced. Reinforcement may come about as a consequence of aggression itself, as is the case when aggression causes a provocateur to cease provocation.

7 The catharsis hypothesis therefore appears to be only partially supported. Aggression leads to reduction of arousal that had been elevated by provocative circumstances, but only under certain conditions. In addition, aggression may have effects other than arousal reduction, such as weakening of inhibitions, which promote further aggression.

SUGGESTIONS FOR FURTHER READING

Geen, R. G. and Quanty, M. B. (1977) The catharsis of aggression: an evaluation of a hypothesis, in L. Berkowitz (ed.) *Advances in Experimental Social Psychology, Volume 10*. New York: Academic Press, pp. 1–37. A discussion of the doctrine of catharsis and a review of evidence bearing on both physiological and behavioural effects predicted by a catharsis hypothesis.

Miller, T. Q., Smith, T. W., Turner, C. W., Guijarro, M. L. and Hallet, A. J. (1996) A meta-analytic review of research on hostility and physical health. *Psychological Bulletin*, 119, 322–48. A comprehensive review of both empirical findings and theoretical interpretations of the relation of hostility to health.

EIGHT

POSTSCRIPT

OVERVIEW

This review of human aggression from the perspective of a social psychologist has touched upon many constructs and variables. Some are more directly relevant to social psychology than others, but all are necessary to an understanding of the process that underlies aggressive behaviour. This process is obviously not simple. However, despite the complexity, we may impose a loose sort of organization on the findings. The general scheme of the organization is shown in Figure 8.1.

The sequence of events begins with some change in the person's physical or social environment (which we have called a provocation) that evokes immediately an increase in displeasure, or negative affect, as described in Berkowitz's cognitive–neoassociationist theory (1). This burst of negative affect may culminate in an immediate impulsive act of aggression, a 'striking out' against an available target that precedes any cognitive processing of the situation (2). Simultaneously, this reaction activates several associated states that have previously been established through biological inheritance and past experience: anger, hostile thoughts and memories, scripts involving aggressive plans of action, physiological arousal and motor patterns involving aggression (3). As we have noted, Anderson's General Affective Aggression Model does not involve the initial increase in negative affect, but does stipulate the activation of the associated affective, cognitive and arousal systems and is in most respects similar to Berkowitz's approach.

In both models, cognitive processing follows the initial reaction to the provoking stimulus (3). The person now makes a first appraisal of what is going on (4), by coming to some understanding of both the situation (e.g. 'What has happened to me?' 'Did this person just insult me?') and his or her own reaction to it ('I am feeling insulted and angry', 'I am having some hostile thoughts about that person'). Having assessed matters in this

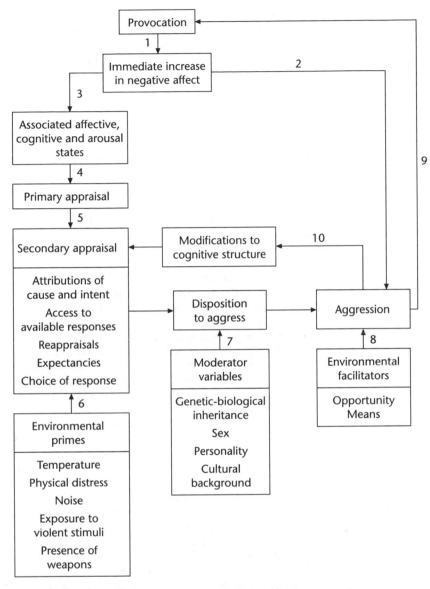

Figure 8.1 Overall schematic of processes in affective aggression.

way, the person then continues to appraise the situation by bringing in other cognitions from memory (5). These take many forms. Some are attributions of the cause of the provocation and the intent of the provoking person. Any tendencies that the person has towards the hostile attribution bias will be manifest at this point. The person may also reappraise his or her feelings at this point on the basis of the attributions of cause and intent that have been made (e.g. 'This person harmed me deliberately, so I really am angry with him'). The person will then consider the possible responses that may be made to the newly appraised situation, considering, for example, the appropriateness of each and the expectancy of successful retaliation that each provides. The response that is selected is also embedded in a cognitive script, and its retrieval is in accordance with the principles of script accessibility, including the normative beliefs about aggression that the person has formed. At this point the person is obviously engaging in intensive processing of available social information, as Crick, Dodge, Huesmann and others have described it.

We must also remember that stimuli arising in the immediate or recently experienced environment also play a part in the reappraisal process by priming certain affective and cognitive pathways and thereby making some thoughts and feelings more accessible than others (6). Environmental stressors like extreme temperature and uncontrollable noise have been shown to have such priming effects, as does physical pain. As has also been proposed, prior exposure to violent stimuli, in the form of films, television, video games, aggressive sporting events and weapons all function to facilitate access to hostile thoughts and aggression-related affective states.

Once the choice of reaction to provocation has been made, the person is disposed to aggress and probably will aggress unless restrained by inhibiting stimuli that are either personal (e.g. guilt, anxiety) or situational (e.g. threat). Inhibition of direct aggression against the provoking person may entail displaced aggression against some substitute target. Whatever the case may be, the disposition to aggress is moderated by a number of variables that interact with situational conditions (7). In this book we have discussed four classes of moderator or background variables: the person's biological inheritance, his or her sex, various personality traits and the general socio-cultural background. Lastly, even a strong disposition to aggress will eventuate in actual aggression only to the extent that the person has the opportunity and means to carry out such action (8).

Discussion of human aggression often ends at this point, but it is important to remember that aggression is an interactive process and such behaviour has consequences for both the victim and the aggressor. The immediate consequence for the victim is that the aggressor's behaviour probably serves as a provocation that initiates the same sequence described here with the roles of actor and victim reversed (9). The immediate consequence of his or her behaviour for the aggressor is a modification of some features of the cognitive structure that can influence future appraisals of provoking events (10). For example, successful retaliation following step (8) will add another reinforcing scenario to any script that exists in memory calling for retribution as a response to provocation. This should increase the retrievability of such a script on subsequent occasions of interpersonal conflict.

In the preceding paragraphs, the salient features of the work of several investigators have been shown to contribute to the overall process at different points. This overall scheme is certainly not a theory of aggression, nor is it, at this point, even a very sophisticated model. It is simply a suggestion as to how the findings of research over a number of topics may be brought together along theoretically meaningful lines, and it is presented in the hope that it may serve as a stimulus for further theoretical and empirical efforts. We must be careful to note that this general model is not intended to describe each and every instance of human aggression in detail but only to give a general arrangement of the important variables. This proviso is especially important when we shift our emphasis from theory-building to application. Take, for instance, Malamuth's highly developed model of sexual aggression discussed in Chapter 5. One would be hard-pressed to assimilate that model, or the research that lies behind it, to the scheme in Figure 8.1 in exact detail. Masculine hostility towards women is a personality moderator in Malamuth's model, but it probably enters into the process earlier than at point (6). The hostile male, who is driven towards conflict with women and who desires to master them, will undoubtedly react to any resistance on the woman's part at point (3) by labelling the woman as a false and provocative person who 'wants to be dominated', who says 'no' when she really means 'yes', and so on and on. This self-serving attribution process easily leads the aggressive male into a disposition to commit sexual aggression. But he does not commit just any aggression. He does not satisfy himself by verbally abusing the woman, by spreading lies about her or by hitting her. He may, of course, do all of these things, but his primary offence is an aggressive sexual act. Rape is therefore the *means* that he uses to carry out his aggressive purpose, and this decision is made considerably before point (7) in our scheme.

The point of this discussion is that no conceptual scheme can be applied in the same way to every case of aggressive behaviour. The careful student will therefore pay more attention to the larger issues of mediation and moderation among variables, and to the overall concept of a flow of causes and effects, than to any precise arrangement of these matters. We do well to remember a point made early in this book – that aggression is not a unitary concept, but a word taken from everyday speech to describe several functionally different behaviours.

PROSPECTS FOR THE FUTURE

One obvious conclusion to be drawn from this review is that the study of human aggression is going through a period of change. This change is reflected in the methodologies being used, in the variables and constructs being investigated, in the sophistication of research applications and in the problems that are now considered amenable to empirical study. Some of this change has been reflected, without specific reference to it, in this review. Early mechanistic models of aggression, like the original frustration–aggression hypothesis, have been displaced by social learning and social information-processing approaches. The relationship between cognition and affect has been spelled out in detail, and several alternative models of this relationship have been presented. Methodology has turned increasingly towards techniques based on correlation, thereby fostering the development of explanatory models that are not only more sweeping in their statements of interrelations among variables but also more closely tuned to the complexity of violence in society. As a result, the applied psychology of human aggression and violence has benefited from the development of newer and better theories.

Methodology

During the early years of research on human aggression, the controlled laboratory experiment was the most widely used method of investigation. In the early 1970s interest began to drift away from the laboratory experiment towards methods thought to have greater external validity, the most popular of which were cross-sectional and longitudinal observational studies, controlled experiments in everyday settings and analysis of archival materials. Numerous examples of work using these latter methods appear in the this book. That such studies make up a large proportion of the work being reported attests to the centrality of the methods that they employ. The designs of these studies are built on hypotheses that presuppose several variables operating in various combinations and interactions, and the analysis of the findings involves multivariate correlational techniques. These approaches should continue to undergo development and refinement in the years to come.

The laboratory experiment is, however, not extinct. As studies reviewed in this chapter have shown, some of the most theoretically meaningful work being reported at the present time is built on evidence from the laboratory. Nor should we forget that many of the non-experimental approaches being followed at the present time derive their approaches and working hypotheses from principles (e.g. social learning, frustration–aggression, excitation transfer) that were originally formulated in the laboratory. Few people would doubt that the best sources of information about violence in society are studies of real-life behaviour. The role that experimental researchers should play in this process is to do what they are uniquely qualified to do: generate and test causal hypotheses. The experiment is still a powerful device for clarifying theoretical issues, identifying and defining variables, and connecting variables within meaningful syntactic systems. Once this has been done, research in natural settings can be guided in theoretically meaningful directions.

Theory

Another sign of the changes alluded to above is the general agreement that the study of human aggression involves a number of interacting psychological processes. It is a many-sided phenomenon (or set of phenomena, depending on how one approaches the question of whether or not aggression is unitary). The once-respected theories that attributed aggression solely to innate determinants, to mechanisms and arousal states or to simple intervening emotional processes have been displaced by theories and models that weave cognitive, affective, biological, motivational and social variables together in ever increasing complexity. This complexity is a direct result of the growing use of the multivariate approaches mentioned above.

Many of the multivariate explanations for aggression do not rest on rigorous theoretical foundations, however. They have arisen in the context of investigations of practical problems such as domestic violence and have been addressed more to identifying antecedent variables than to building general theories. Multivariate analyses and longitudinal methods allow the generation of models that test among alternative sequences of variable effects, and from these models cause–effect relationships are inferred. Ideally, however, theory does more than explain cause and effect; it also predicts outcomes under stated conditions. A good causal model tests among various alternative paths among variables, and theories of aggression are necessary for the generation of alternatives. Research on human aggression will benefit greatly if theory-building and multivariate model-building develop together in a reciprocal relationship.

Applications

As the problems of aggression and anti-social behaviour continue to assume such importance for society, we may expect that psychological research on them will proliferate. The appearance of specialized journals like the *Journal of Family Violence* and *Violence and Victims* in the 1980s reflects a growing interest in analysing the causes of human aggression, and it would not be surprising to see similar journals being founded in the years to come. Many of the studies cited in this review originated in concern over specific problems, like spouse abuse, rape and the behaviour of spectators at sporting events, and were not, at least initially, addressed to the theory of aggression. For the most part, however, they were informed by the existing theoretical models and involved these models in the discussion and interpretation of their findings. Bringing current theory into contact with problem-centred research is an important development in the study of aggression. For one thing, conceptualizing applied research in terms of rigorous application of theory expands the scope of application by suggesting links among problem areas that may not have been apparent. If, for example, abuse in intimate relationships, sexual violence and general delinquency can all be shown to be related to a certain type of parenting, and if the link between this parenting style and these several outcomes can be explained in terms of a set of common mediating processes, the possibilities for the direction of further research into new applications are greatly enhanced. In addition, conceptually sophisticated applied research can also contribute to the development of new theory. All social behaviour is a potential source of social psychological theorizing, and the diligent psychologist will keep a sharp and watchful eye on how well his or her formal theories are playing out in the marketplace of everyday life.

GLOSSARY

Affective aggression: deliberate harmdoing that is motivated by anger or hostility.

Aggression catharsis: this term is used in two ways. It refers to physiological recovery following aggressive behaviour in instigated persons. In psychoanalytic theory, it refers to a hypothesized decrease in aggressive motivation following aggression.

Alcohol myopia: term used to describe a loss of sensitivity to social cues in intoxicated persons.

Anger-in pattern: the process of emotional control in which the expression of anger is suppressed. There is evidence that such suppression is related to hypertension and possibly to cardiovascular problems.

Arousal: physiological activation that underlies behaviour intensity. It is usually discussed in terms of activity in organs innervated by the autonomic nervous system.

Attachment style: a personal disposition to develop one of several styles of relating to persons with whom one maintains a close relationship (e.g. secure, anxious, fearful). This adult tendency generalizes from patterns of attachments to caregivers acquired during childhood.

Attribution: the subjective assignment of causes and intentions to observed events. In aggression, the term refers to judgements about the intent, maliciousness and judgements of the aggressor.

Background variables: conditions of the person, sometimes called behavioural dispositions, that provide the setting for, and interact with, situational stimuli.

Behaviour genetics: the study of the effects of biological inheritance on behaviour.

Borderline personality organization: a broad personality classification marked by intense and variable moods, typically those of dejection and depression interspersed with euphoria, irritability and intense anger. This personality is an important contributor to a major type of spouse abuse.

Cardiovascular recovery time: amount of time required for cardiovascular indicators such as heart rate to return to pre-stimulus levels.

Coercive power: power exerted by one person on another to secure the latter's compliance with the wishes of the former.

Cognitive–neoassociationism: the theory that provocation elicits negative affect which activates subsequent ideas, feelings and behaviours associated with aggression.

Cognitive priming: a term used to describe the effects of prior contexts on the interpretation of new information.

Coping: behaviour undertaken to help the person to survive stressful situations.

Cross-lagged panel correlation: a correlation between two variables assessed at two different times, sometimes used to indicate cause–effect relations.

Cycle of violence: a term used to describe the empirical observations that violent behaviour tends to run in families and that persons who are aggressed against as children have a higher probability of becoming adult aggressors than persons who have not been so treated.

Displaced aggression: aggression directed against persons other than those responsible for the instigation.

Dissipation–rumination: a personality trait describing a tendency to retain or augment feelings of anger over time following provocation.

Dizygotic twins: twins formed from two fertilized eggs; sometimes called fraternal twins.

Dysphoria: a mood state characterized by irritability and discontent; the opposite of euphoria.

Ethology: the study of animal behaviour in natural settings from a biological and evolutionary point of view.

Excitation transfer: the mistaken attribution of arousal caused by one stimulus to another, thereby exacerbating the emotion by produced the latter.

Field experiment: a quasi-controlled experiment carried out in a naturalistic setting.

Frustration: blocking or interference with goal-directed behaviour. The frustration–aggression hypothesis states that such acts are instigators of aggression.

General Affective Aggression Model: a model describing how provocation leads to aggression through three interrelated processes – cognitive, affective and physiological.

Hormone: a chemical substance secreted by glands and circulated in the body through the bloodstream. The activity of one such hormone, **testosterone**, has been found to correlate with aggression in males.

Hostile attribution bias: a tendency to attribute hostile intent to other people in situations in which the intentions of the others are ambiguous (see **social information processing**).

Hostility: an attitude or disposition towards another person characterized by feelings of dislike and rejection and by tendencies towards aggression.

Impulsivity: a personality trait characterized by tendencies to react to situations in an unrestrained manner; may be related to insufficient level of **serotonin** (q.v.) activity in the central nervous system.

Instigation: a prompt for behaviour in response to some situational stimulus (see also **provocation**).

Instrumental aggression: deliberate harmdoing to another person for purposes of obtaining rewards unrelated to the aggressive act.

Irritability: a personality trait describing a tendency to be quick-tempered, irascible, and likely to react violently to provocation.

Limbic system: a number of interrelated structures in the brain associated with the activation and regulation of emotions.

Longitudinal study: a type of study in which one sample of people is observed at successive points in time; used in the study of causal relations.

Monozygotic twins: twins formed from bifurcation of a single fertilized egg; sometimes called identical twins.

Narcissism: a personality trait describing a tendency towards both self-love and motivation to be superior to others.

Norm: a standard for behaviour, opinion or feeling in a given context agreed upon by most members of a society.

Overcontrolled aggression: excessive and pathological suppression of aggression that sometimes culminates in outbursts of extremely violent behaviour.

Passive aggression: deliberate failure to act in ways that could prevent harm to another person.

Preferred sexuality hypothesis: the contention that rapists are more sexually aroused by coercive sexual activity than by consensual sex.

Proactive aggression: aggression undertaken in the absence of apparent provocation and perceived as being under the voluntary control of the aggressor; often manifested as **instrumental aggression** (q.v.).

Provocation: a situational condition or event that produces an **instigation** (q.v.) to aggress.

Psychopathic disorder: a personality disorder characterized by a broad range of symptoms, including anti-social behaviour, narcissism, impulsiveness and absence of feelings of guilt.

Rape myth: the belief held by some men that women secretly wish to be sexually dominated and abused.

Resource exchange theory: the theory that social interaction consists of an exchange of goods (e.g. material, information) and/or services (e.g. labour, approval), and that each party is motivated to obtain an outcome (benefits minus costs) that is greater than zero.

Reactive aggression: aggression undertaken in response to a provocation.

Relational aggression: behaviour that harms others by interfering with their peer relationships or by threatening such interference.

Relative deprivation: a feeling of being unfairly short-changed of goods or services relative to the levels enjoyed by other people.

Script: an internalized description of what is normal behaviour in commonly experienced situations, acquired, maintained and elaborated through social experience.

Serotonin: the common name given to 5-hydroxytryptamine, a chemical secreted in the brain which facilitates transmission at the nerve synapses and depletion of which is correlated with aggressive behaviour.

Social information processing: the cognitive, affective, and motivational processes that connect the reception of information from others to the person's response to that information. Inaccuracies and deficits in such processing can be associated with socially dysfunctional behaviour.

Social learning: the acquisition and/or maintenance of responses through the imitation of others and socially mediated rewards and punishments.

Subcultures of violence: smaller units within the larger society (e.g. gangs, feuding families) that place a high positive value on aggressive activity.

Symbolic catharsis: a **catharsis** (q.v.) of arousal and aggressive behaviours evoked by presentation of aggression through the mass media.

Testosterone: see **hormone**.

Tomography: a technology through which brain activity may be scanned and represented graphically.

Type A behaviour pattern: an organization of personal tendencies consisting of a highly driven and competitive motivational state, heightened physiological arousal and a sense of urgency, impatience and hostility.

Violence: the use of intense force against persons or property for purposes of destruction, protest, punishment or control.

REFERENCES

Anderson, C. A. (1987) Temperature and aggression: effects on quarterly, yearly, and city rates of violent and nonviolent crime. *Journal of Personality and Social Psychology*, 52, 1161–73.

Anderson, C. A. (1997) Effects of violent movies and trait hostility on hostile feelings and aggressive thoughts. *Aggressive Behavior*, 23, 161–78.

Anderson, C. A. and Anderson, D. C. (1984) Ambient temperature and violent crime: tests of the linear and curvilinear hypotheses. *Journal of Personality and Social Psychology*, 46, 91–7.

Anderson, C. A. and Anderson, K. B. (1996) Violent crime rate studies in philosophical context: a destructive testing approach to heat and Southern culture of violence effects. *Journal of Personality and Social Psychology*, 70, 740–56.

Anderson, C. A. and Anderson, K. B. (1998) Temperature and aggression: Paradox, controversy, and a (fairly) clear picture, in R. G. Geen and E. Donnerstein (eds) *Human Aggression: Theories, Research, and Implications for Social Policy*. San Diego: Academic Press, pp. 247–98.

Anderson, C. A., Anderson, K. B. and Deuser, W. E. (1996) Examining an affective aggression framework: weapon and temperature effects on aggressive thoughts, affect, and attitudes. *Personality and Social Psychology Bulletin*, 22, 366–76.

Anderson, C. A. and Bushman, B. J. (1997) External validity of 'trivial' experiments: the case of laboratory aggression. *Review of General Psychology*, 1, 19–41.

Anderson, C. A., Bushman, B. J. and Groom, R. W. (1997) Hot years and serious and deadly assault: empirical tests of the heat hypothesis. *Journal of Personality and Social Psychology*, 73, 1213–23.

Anderson, C. A., Deuser, W. E. and DeNeve, K. M. (1995) Hot temperatures, hostile affect, hostile cognition, and arousal: tests of a general model of affective aggression. *Personality and Social Psychology Bulletin*, 21, 434–48.

Anderson, C. A. and Dill, K. E. (2000) Video games and aggressive thoughts, feelings, and behavior in the laboratory and in life. *Journal of Personality and Social Psychology*, 78, 772–90.

Anderson, C. A. and Haynes, L. (1996) Short-term effects of violent media on affect and cognition: rock music, funny songs, and movies. Paper presented to Eighth Annual Convention of the American Psychological Society.

Archer, D. (1994) American violence: how high and why? *Law Studies*, 19, 12–20.

Archer, D. and Gartner, R. (1984) *Violence and Crime in Cross-national Perspective*. New Haven, CT: Yale University Press.

Archer, D. and McDaniel, P. (1995) Violence and gender: differences and similarities across societies, in R. B. Ruback and N. A. Weiner (eds) *Interpersonal Violent Behaviors: Social and Cultural Aspects*. New York: Springer, pp. 63–87.

Archer, J. (1988) *The Behavioural Biology of Aggression*. Cambridge: Cambridge University Press.

Archer, J. (1991) The influence of testosterone on human aggression. *British Journal of Psychology*, 82, 1–28.

Archer, J. (ed.) (1994) *Male Violence*. New York: Routledge.

Archer, J. and Haigh, A. M. (1997) Beliefs about aggression among male and female prisoners. *Aggressive Behavior*, 23, 405–15.

Archer, J. and Parker, S. (1994) Social representations of aggression in children. *Aggressive Behavior*, 20, 101–14.

Arkkelin, D., Oakley, T. and Mynart, C. (1979) Effects of controllable versus uncontrollable factors on responsibility attributions: a single subject approach. *Journal of Personality and Social Psychology*, 37, 110–15.

Arms, R. L., Russell, G. W. and Sandilands, M. L. (1979) Effects of viewing aggressive sports on the hostility of spectators. *Social Psychology Quarterly*, 42, 275–9.

Armstrong, G. (1998) *Football Hooligans: Knowing the Score*. Oxford: Berg.

Averill, J. R. (1982) *Anger and Aggression: An Essay on Emotion*. New York: Springer-Verlag.

Ax, A. F. (1953) The psychophysiological differentiation between fear and anger in humans. *Psychosomatic Medicine*, 15, 433–42.

Baer, P. E., Collins, F. H., Bourianoff, G. C. and Ketchel, M. F. (1979) Assessing personality factors in essential hypertension with a brief self-report instrument. *Psychosomatic Medicine*, 16, 321–30.

Baker, J. W. and Schaie, K. W. (1969) Effects of aggressing 'alone' or 'with another' on physiological and psychological arousal. *Journal of Personality and Social Psychology*, 12, 80–6.

Bandura, A. (1983) Psychological mechanisms of aggression, in R. G. Geen and E. I. Donnerstein (eds) *Aggression: Theoretical and Empirical Reviews, Volume 1*. New York: Academic Press, pp. 1–40.

Bandura, A. (1986) *Social Foundations of Thought and Action: A Social Cognitive Theory*. Englewood Cliffs, NJ: Prentice Hall.

Barbaree, H. E. and Marshall, W. L. (1991) The role of male sexual arousal in rape: six models. *Journal of Consulting and Clinical Psychology*, 59, 621–30.

Barnett, O. W., Fagan, R. W. and Booker, J. M. (1991) Hostility and stress as mediators of aggression in violent men. *Journal of Family Violence*, 6, 217–41.

Baron, R. A. and Bell, P. A. (1975) Aggression and heat: mediating effects of prior provocation and exposure to an aggressive model. *Journal of Personality and Social Psychology*, 31, 825–32.

Baron, R. A. and Richardson, D. (1994) *Human Aggression*. New York: Plenum.

Barratt, E. S. (1994) Impulsiveness and aggression, in J. Monahan and H. J. Steadman (eds) *Violence and Mental Disorder: Developments in Risk Assessment.* Chicago: University of Chicago Press, pp. 61–79.

Bartholomew, K. and Horowitz, L. M. (1991) Attachment styles among young adults: a test of a four-category model. *Journal of Personality and Social Psychology*, 61, 236–44.

Baumeister, R. F. and Heatherton, T. F. (1996) Self-regulation failure: an overview. *Psychological Inquiry*, 7, 1–15.

Baumeister, R. F., Smart, L. and Boden, J. M. (1996) Relation of threatened egotism to violence and aggression: the dark side of high self-esteem. *Psychological Review*, 103, 5–33.

Baxter, D. J., Barbaree, H. E. and Marshall, W. L. (1986) Sexual responses to consenting and forced sex in a large sample of rapists and nonrapists. *Behavioural Research and Therapy*, 24, 513–20.

Berkowitz, L. (1983) The experience of anger as a parallel process in the display of impulsive 'angry' aggression, in R. G. Geen and E. I. Donnerstein (eds) *Aggression: Theoretical and Empirical Reviews, Volume 1*. New York: Academic Press, pp. 103–33.

Berkowitz, L. (1966) On not being able to aggress. *British Journal of Social and Clinical Psychology*, 5, 130–9.

Berkowitz, L. (1984) Some effects of thoughts on anti and prosocial influences of media events: a cognitive-neoassociationist analysis. *Psychological Bulletin*, 95, 410–27.

Berkowitz, L. B. (1993) *Aggression: Its Causes, Consequences, and Control.* New York: McGraw-Hill.

Berkowitz, L., Cochran, S. and Embree, M. (1981) Physical pain and the goal of aversively stimulated aggression. *Journal of Personality and Social Psychology*, 40, 687–700.

Berkowitz, L. and Donnerstein, E. (1982) External validity is more than skin deep: some answers to criticisms of laboratory experiments (with special reference to research on aggression). *American Psychologist*, 37, 245–57.

Berkowitz, L. and Troccoli, B. T. (1990) Feelings, direction of attention, and expressed evaluation of others. *Cognition and Emotion*, 4, 305–25.

Bersani, A., Chen, H. T., Pendleton, B. F. and Denton, R. (1992) Personality traits of convicted male batterers. *Journal of Family Violence*, 7, 123–34.

Betsch, T., and Dickenberger, D. (1993) Why do aggressive movies make people aggressive? An attempt to explain short-term effects of the depiction of violence on the observer. *Aggressive Behavior*, 19, 137–49.

Bettencourt, B. A. and Miller, N. (1996) Sex differences in aggression as a function of provocation: a meta-analysis. *Psychological Bulletin*, 119, 422–47.

Björkqvist, K., Lagerspetz, K. M. J. and Kaukiainen, A. (1992) Do girls manipulate and boys fight? Developmental trends in regard to direct and indirect aggression. *Aggressive Behavior*, 18, 117–27.

Björkqvist, K., Österman, K. and Lagerspetz, K. M. J. (1994) Sex differences in covert aggression among adults. *Aggressive Behavior*, 20, 27–33.

Blascovich, J. and Katkin, E. S. (eds) (1993) *Cardiovascular Reactivity to Psychological Stress and Disease.* Washington, DC: American Psychological Association.

Boldizar, J. P., Perry, D. G. and Perry, L. (1989) Outcome values and aggression. *Child Development*, 60, 571–9.

Bowlby, J. (1969) *Attachment and Loss. Volume 1: Attachment.* New York: Harper.

Bowlby, J. (1973) *Attachment and Loss. Volume 2: Separation.* New York: Harper.

Bowlby, J. (1980) *Attachment and Loss. Volume 3: Loss.* New York: Harper.

Bowlby, J. (1988) *A Secure Base: Parent–Child Attachment and Healthy Human Development.* New York: Basic Books.

Braun, C. and Giroux, J. (1989) Arcade video games: proxemic, cognitive, and content analyses. *Journal of Leisure Research,* 21, 92–105.

Breuer, J. and Freud, S. ([1894] 1961) *Studies in Hysteria.* Boston: Beacon Press.

Brickman, P., Ryan, K. and Wortman, C. (1975) Causal chains: attribution of responsibility as a function of immediate and prior causes. *Journal of Personality and Social Psychology,* 32, 1060–7.

Brosschot, J. F. and Thayer, J. F. (1998) Anger inhibition, cardiovascular recovery, and vagal function: a model of the link between hostility and cardiovascular disease. *Annals of Behavioral Medicine,* 20(4), 1–8.

Bryant, J., Brown, D., Comisky, P. and Zillmann, D. (1982) Sports and spectators: commentary and appreciation. *Journal of Communication,* 32, 109–19.

Bryant, J., Carveth, R. A. and Brown, D. (1981a) Television viewing and anxiety: an experimental examination. *Journal of Communication,* 31, 106–19.

Bryant, J., Comisky, P. and Zillman, D. (1981b) The appeal of rough-and-tumble play in televised professional football. *Communication Quarterly,* 29, 256–62.

Bryant, J. and Zillmann, D. (1979) Effect of intensification of annoyance through unrelated residual excitation on substantially delayed hostile behavior. *Journal of Experimental Social Psychology,* 15, 470–80.

Buchman, D. D. and Funk, J. B. (1996) Video and computer games in the 90s: children's time commitment and game preference. *Children Today,* 24, 12–16.

Buford, B. (1992) *Among the Thugs.* New York: Norton.

Bushman, B. J. (1995) Moderating role of trait aggressiveness in the effects of violent media on aggression. *Journal of Personality and Social Psychology,* 69, 950–60.

Bushman, B. J. (1996) Individual differences in the extent and development of aggressive cognitive-associative networks. *Personality and Social Psychology Bulletin,* 22, 811–19.

Bushman, B. J. (1998) Priming effects of media violence on the accessibility of aggressive constructs in memory. *Personality and Social Psychology Bulletin,* 24, 537–45.

Bushman, B. J. and Anderson, C. A. (1998) Methodology in the study of aggression: integrating experimental and nonexperimental findings, in R. G. Geen and E. Donnerstein (eds) *Human Aggression: Theories, Research, and Implications for Social Policy.* San Diego: Academic Press, pp. 23–48.

Bushman, B. J. and Baumeister, R. F. (1998) Threatened egotism, narcissism, self-esteem, and direct and displaced aggression: does self-love or self-hate lead to violence? *Journal of Personality and Social Psychology,* 75, 219–29.

Bushman, B. J., Baumeister, R. F. and Stack, A. D. (1999) Catharsis, aggression, and persuasive influence: self-fulfilling or self-defeating prophecies? *Journal of Personality and Social Psychology,* 76, 367–76.

Bushman, B. J. and Cooper, H. M. (1990) Effects of alcohol on human aggression: an integrative research review. *Psychological Bulletin,* 107, 341–54.

Bushman, B. J., Cooper, H. M. and Lemke, K. M. (1991) Meta-analysis of factor analyses: an illustration using the Buss–Durkee Hostility Inventory. *Personality and Individual Differences,* 17, 344–9.

Bushman, B. J. and Geen, R. G. (1990) Role of cognitive-emotional mediators and individual differences in the effects of media violence on aggression. *Journal of Personality and Social Psychology*, 58, 156–63.

Buss, A. H. (1961) *The Psychology of Aggression*. New York: Wiley.

Buss, A. H. and Durkee, A. (1957) An inventory for assessing different kinds of hostility. *Journal of Consulting Psychology*, 21, 343–9.

Buss, A. H. and Perry, M. (1992) The Aggression Questionnaire. *Journal of Personality and Social Psychology*, 63, 452–9.

Campbell, A. (1993) *Men, Women, and Aggression*. New York: Basic Books.

Campbell, A. and Muncer, S. (1987) Models of anger and aggression in the social talk of women and men. *Journal for the Theory of Social Behavior*, 17, 489–512.

Campbell, A. and Muncer, S. (1994) Sex differences in aggression: social representation and social roles. *British Journal of Social Psychology*, 33, 233–40.

Campbell, A., Muncer, S. and Coyle, E. (1992) Social representation of aggression as an explanation of gender differences: a preliminary study. *Aggressive Behavior*, 18, 95–108.

Campbell, A., Muncer, S., and Odber, J. (1997) Aggression and testosterone: testing a bio-social model. *Aggressive Behavior*, 23, 229–38.

Cannon, W. B. (1929) *Bodily Changes in Pain, Hunger, Fear, and Rage*. New York: Appleton-Century.

Cantor, J. R. (1982) Adolescent fright reactions from TV programming. *Journal of Communication*, 32, 87–99.

Cantor, J. R., Zillmann, D. and Bryant, J. (1975) Enhancement of experienced sexual arousal in response to erotic stimuli through misattribution of unrelated residual excitation. *Journal of Personality and Social Psychology*, 32, 69–75.

Caprara, G. V. (1982) A comparison of the frustration–aggression and emotional susceptibility hypotheses. *Aggressive Behavior*, 8, 234–6.

Caprara, G. V. (1986) Indicators of aggression: the Dissipation–Rumination Scale. *Personality and Individual Differences*, 7, 763–9.

Caprara, G. V., Barbaranelli, C., Pastorelli, C. and Perugini, M. (1994) Individual differences in the study of aggression. *Aggressive Behavior*, 20, 291–303.

Caprara, G. V., Cinanni, V., D'Imperio, G., Passerini, S., Renzi, P. and Travaglia, G. (1985) Indicators of impulsive aggression: present status of research on Irritability and Emotional Susceptibility Scales. *Personality and Individual Differences*, 6, 665–74.

Caprara, G. V., Gargaro, T., Pastorelli, C., Prezza, M., Renzi, P. and Zelli, A. (1987) Individual differences and measures of aggression in laboratory studies. *Personality and Individual Differences*, 8, 885–93.

Caprara, G. V., Renzi, P., Alcini, P., D'Imperio, G. and Travaglia, G. (1983) Instigation to aggress and escalation of aggression examined from a personological perspective: the role of irritability and emotional susceptibility. *Aggressive Behavior*, 9, 345–51.

Carlsmith, J. M. and Anderson, C. A. (1979) Ambient temperature and the occurrence of collective violence: a new analysis. *Journal of Personality and Social Psychology*, 37, 337–44.

Carmelli, D., Swan, G. E. and Rosenman, R. H. (1990) The heritability of the Cook and Medley Hostility Scale revisited. *Journal of Social Behavior and Personality*, 5, 107–16.

Caspi, A., Elder, G. H. Jr and Bem, D. J. (1987) Moving against the world: Life-course patterns of explosive children. *Developmental Psychology*, 23, 308–13.

Catalano, R., Dooley, D., Novaco, R. W., Wilson, G. and Hough, R. (1993) Using ECA survey data to examine the effect of job layoffs on violent behavior. *Hospital and Community Psychiatry*, 44, 874–9.

Check, J. V. P. and Guloien, T. H. (1989) Reported proclivity for coercive sex following repeated exposure to sexually violent pornography, nonviolent dehumanizing pornography, and erotica, in D. Zillmann and J. Bryant (eds) *Pornography: Research Advances and Policy Considerations*. Hillsdale, NJ: Erlbaum, pp. 159–84.

Chen, P. Y. and Spector, P. E. (1992) Relationships of work stressors with aggression, withdrawal, theft and substance abuse: an exploratory study. *Journal of Occupational and Organizational Psychology*, 65, 177–84.

Claes, J. A. and Rosenthal, D. M. (1990) Men who batter women: a study in power. *Journal of Family Violence*, 5, 215–24.

Coccaro, E. F. (1992) Impulsive aggression and central serotonergic system function in humans: an example of a dimensional brain-behavioral relationship. *International Journal of Clinical Psychopharmacology*, 7, 3–12.

Cohen, D. and Nisbett, R. E. (1994) Self-protection and culture of honor: explaining Southern violence. *Personality and Social Psychology Bulletin*, 20, 551–67.

Collins, W. A., Berndt, T. J. and Hess, V. L. (1974) Observational learning of motives and consequences for television aggression: a developmental study. *Child Development*, 45, 799–802.

Cook, W. W. and Medley, D. M. (1954) Proposed hostility and pharasaic-virtue scales for the MMPI. *Journal of Applied Psychology*, 38, 414–18.

Cooper, M. L., Shaver, P. R. and Collins, N. L. (1998) Attachment styles, emotion regulation, and adjustment in adolescence. *Journal of Personality and Social Psychology*, 74, 1380–97.

Crick, N. R. (1995) Relational aggression: the role of intent attributions, feelings of distress, and provocation type. *Development and Psychopathology*, 7, 313–22.

Crick, N. R., Bigbee, M. A. and Howes, C. (1996) Gender differences in children's normative beliefs about aggression. How do I hurt thee? Let me count the ways. *Child Development*, 67, 1003–14.

Crick, N. R. and Dodge, K. A. (1994) A review and reformulation of social information-processing mechanisms in children's social adjustment. *Psychological Bulletin*, 115, 74–101.

Crick, N. R. and Dodge, K. A. (1996) Social information-processing mechanisms in reactive and proactive aggression. *Child Development*, 67, 993–1002.

Crick, N. R. and Grotepeter, J. K. (1995) Relational aggression, gender, and social-psychological adjustment. *Child Development*, 66, 710–22.

Crick, N. R. and Ladd, G. W. (1990) Children's perceptions of the outcomes of aggressive strategies: do the ends justify being mean? *Developmental Psychology*, 26, 612–20.

Cummings, E. M., Hennessy, K. D., Rabideau, G. J. and Cicchetti, D. (1994) Coping with anger involving a family member in physically abused and non-abused boys. *Development and Psychopathology*, 6, 31–41.

Cummings, E. M., Ianotti, R. J. and Zahn-Waxler, C. (1985) Influence of conflict between adults on the emotions and aggression of young children. *Developmental Psychology*, 21, 495–507.

Dabbs, J. M., Frady, R. F., Carr, T. S. and Besch, N. F. (1987) Saliva testosterone and criminal violence in young adult prison inmates. *Psychosomatic Medicine*, 49, 174–82.

Dabbs, J. M. Jr and Morris, R. (1990) Testosterone, social class, and antisocial behavior in a sample of 4,462 men. *Psychological Science*, 1, 209–11.

DaGloria, J. and DeRidder, R. (1977) Aggression in dyadic interaction. *European Journal of Social Psychology*, 7, 189–219.

DaGloria, J. and DeRidder, R. (1979) Sex differences in aggression: are current notions misleading? *European Journal of Social Psychology*, 9, 49–66.

Daly, M. and Wilson, M. (1988a) Evolutionary social psychology and family homicide. *Science*, 242, 519–24.

Daly, M. and Wilson, M. (1988b) *Homicide*. New York: A. de Gruyter.

Daly, M. and Wilson, M. (1989) Homicide and cultural evolution. *Ethology and Sociobiology*, 10, 99–110.

DeBaryshe, B. D., Patterson, G. R. and Capaldi, D. M. (1993) A performance model for academic achievement in early adolescent boys. *Developmental Psychology*, 29, 795–804.

Deluty, R. H. (1985a) Cognitive mediation of aggressive, assertive and submissive behavior in children. *International Journal of Behavioral Development*, 8, 355–69.

Deluty, R. H. (1985b) Consistency of aggressive, assertive, and submissive behavior for children. *Journal of Personality and Social Psychology*, 49, 1054–65.

Dembroski, T. M., MacDougall, J. M., Williams, R. B., Haney, T. L. and Blumenthal, J. A. (1985) Components of Type A, hostility, and anger-in: relationship to angiographic findings. *Psychosomatic Medicine*, 47, 219–33.

Dengerink, H. A. and Covey, M. K. (1983) Implications of an escape-avoidance theory of aggressive responses to attack, in R. G. Geen and E. I. Donnerstein (eds) *Aggression: Theoretical and Empirical Reviews, Volume 1*. New York: Academic Press, pp. 163–88.

Dengerink, H. A., Schnedler, R. S. and Covey, M. K. (1978) The role of avoidance in aggressive responses to attack and no attack. *Journal of Personality and Social Psychology*, 36, 1044–53.

DeRidder, R. (1985) Normative considerations in the labeling of harmful behavior as aggressive. *Journal of Social Psychology*, 125, 659–66.

Diamond, E. L., Schneiderman, N., Schwartz, D. *et al.* (1984) Harassment, hostility, and Type A as determinants of cardiovascular reactivity during competition. *Journal of Behavioral Medicine*, 7, 171–89.

Dietz, T. L. (1998) An examination of violence and gender role portrayals in video games: implications for gender socialization and aggressive behavior. *Sex Roles*, 38, 435–42.

Dill, K. E. and Dill, J. C. (1998) Video game violence: a review of the empirical literature. *Aggression and Violent Behavior*, 3, 407–28.

Dishion, T. J., Patterson, G. R. and Griesler, P. C. (1994) Peer adaptations in the development of antisocial behavior: a confluence model, in L. R. Huesmann (ed.) *Aggressive Behavior: Current Perspectives*. New York: Plenum, pp. 61–95.

Dishion, T. J., Patterson, G. R., Stoolmiller, M. and Skinner, M. L. (1991) Family, school, and behavioral antecedents to early adolescent involvement with antisocial peers. *Developmental Psychology*, 27, 172–80.

Dodge, K. A. (1980) Social cognition and children's aggressive behavior. *Child Development*, 51, 162–70.

Dodge, K. A. (1983) Behavioral antecedents of peer social status. *Child Development*, 54, 1386–99.

Dodge, K. A., Murphy, R. R. and Buchsbaum, K. (1984) The assessment of intention-cue detection skills in children: implications for developmental psychopathology. *Child Development*, 55, 163–73.

Dodge, K. A. and Newman, J. P. (1981) Biased decision making processes in aggressive boys. *Journal of Abnormal Psychology*, 90, 375–9.

Dodge, K. A. and Tomlin, A. M. (1987) Utilization of self-schemas as a mechanism of interpretational bias in aggressive children. *Social Cognition*, 5, 280–300.

Dollard, J., Doob, L. W., Miller, N. E., Mowrer, O. H. and Sears, R. R. (1939) *Frustration and Aggression*. New Haven, CT: Yale University Press.

Donnerstein E. and Wilson, D. W. (1976) The effects of noise and perceived control upon ongoing and subsequent aggressive behavior. *Journal of Personality and Social Psychology*, 34, 774–83.

Dutton, D. G. (1998) *The Abusive Personality*. New York: Guilford Press.

Dutton, D. G., Saunders, K., Starzomski, A. and Bartholomew, K. (1994) Intimacy-anger and insecure attachment as precursors of abuse in intimate relationships. *Journal of Applied Social Psychology*, 24, 1367–86.

Dutton, D. G. and Starzomski, A. J. (1993) Borderline personality in perpetrators of psychological and physical abuse. *Violence and Victims*, 8, 327–37.

Eagly, A. H. and Steffen, V. J. (1986) Gender and aggressive behavior: a meta-analytic review of the social psychological literature. *Psychological Bulletin*, 100, 309–30.

Edmunds, G. and Kendrick, D. C. (1980) *The Measurement of Human Aggressiveness*. New York: Halsted Press.

Eichelman, B. (1971) Effects of subcortical lesions on shock-induced aggression in the rat. *Journal of Comparative and Physiological Psychology*, 74, 331–9.

Eichelman, B. (1995) Animal and evolutionary models of impulsive aggression, in E. Hollander and D. J. Stein (eds) *Impulsivity and Aggression*. New York: Wiley, pp. 59–69.

El-Sheikh, M., Cummings, E. M. and Goetz, V. (1989) Coping with adults' angry behavior: behavioral, physiological, and verbal responses in preschoolers. *Developmental Psychology*, 25, 490–8.

Epstein, S. and Taylor, S. P. (1967) Instigation to aggression as a function of degree of defeat and perceived aggressive intent of the opponent. *Journal of Personality*, 35, 265–89.

Eron, L. D. and Huesmann, L. R. (1980) Adolescent aggression and television. *Annals of the New York Academy of Science*, 347, 319–31.

Eron, L. D. and Huesmann, L. R. (1990) The stability of aggressive behavior – even unto the third generation, in M. Lewis and S. M. Miller (eds) *Handbook of Developmental Psychopathology*. New York: Plenum, pp. 147–56.

Eron, L. D., Walder, L. O. and Lefkowitz, M. M. (1971) *Learning of Aggression in Children*. Boston: Little, Brown.

Feierabend, I. K. and Feierabend, R. L. (1972) Systemic conditions of political aggression: an application of frustration–aggression theory, in I. K. Feierabend, R. L. Feierabend and T. R. Gurr (eds) *Anger, Violence, and Politics*. Englewood Cliffs, NJ: Prentice Hall, pp. 136–83.

Ferguson, T. J. and Rule, B. G. (1980) Effects of inferential set, outcome severity, and basis for responsibility on children's evaluations of aggressive acts. *Developmental Psychology*, 16, 141–6.

Ferguson, T. J. and Rule, B. G. (1983) An attributional perspective on anger and aggression, in R. G. Geen and E. Donnerstein (eds) *Aggression: Theoretical and Empirical Reviews. Volume 1: Theoretical and Methodological Issues*. New York: Academic Press, pp. 41–74.

Feshbach, S. (1955) The drive-reducing function of fantasy behavior. *Journal of Ahnormal and Social Psychology*, 50, 3–11.

Feshbach, S. (1961) The stimulating versus cathartic effects of a vicarious aggressive activity. *Journal of Abnormal and Social Psychology*, 63, 381–5.

Finn, P. R., Young, S. N., Pihl, R. O. and Ervin, F. R. (1998) The effects of acute plasma tryptophan manipulation on hostile mood: the influence of trait hostility. *Aggressive Behavior*, 24, 173–85.

Freedman, J. L. (1984) Effect of television violence on aggressiveness. *Psychological Bulletin*, 96, 227–46.

Friedrich-Cofer, L. and Huston, A. C. (1986) Television violence and aggression: the debate continues. *Psychological Bulletin*, 100, 364–71.

Frijda, N. H. (1994) The Lex talionis: on vengeance, in S. H. M. Van Goozen, N. E. Van de Poll and J. A. Sergeant (eds) *Emotions: Essays on Emotion Theory*. Hillsdale, NJ: Erlbaum, pp. 263–89.

Frodi, A., Macaulay, J. and Thome, P. R. (1977) Are women always less aggressive than men? A review of the experimental literature. *Psychological Bulletin*, 84, 634–60.

Funkenstein, D. H., King, S. H. and Drolette, M. E. (1954) The direction of anger during a laboratory stress-inducing situation. *Psychosomatic Medicine*, 16, 404–13.

Gantner, A. B. and Taylor, S. P. (1992) Human physical aggression as a function of alcohol and threat of harm. *Aggressive Behavior*, 18, 29–36.

Geary, D. (1998) *Male, Female: The Evolution of Human Sex Differences*. Washington, DC: American Psychological Association.

Geen, R. G. (1968) Effects of frustration, attack, and prior training in aggressiveness upon aggressive behavior. *Journal of Personality and Social Psychology*, 9, 316–21.

Geen, R. G. (1975) The meaning of observed violence: real vs. fictional violence and consequent effects on aggression. *Journal of Research in Personality*, 9, 270–81.

Geen, R. G. (1978) Effects of attack and uncontrollable noise on aggression. *Journal of Research in Personality*, 12, 15–29.

Geen, R. G. (1981) Behavioral and physiological reactions to observed violence: Effects of prior exposure to aggressive stimuli. *Journal of Personality and Social Psychology*, 40, 868–75.

Geen, R. G. and O'Neal, E. C. (1969) Activation of cue-elicited aggression by general arousal. *Journal of Personality and Social Psychology*, 11, 289–92.

Geen, R. G. and Stonner, D. (1972) The context of observed violence: Inhibition of aggression through displays of unsuccessful retaliation. *Psychonomic Science*, 27, 342–4.

Geen, R. G. and Stonner, D. (1973) Context effects in observed violence. *Journal of Personality and Social Psychology*, 25, 145–50.

Geen, R. G., Stonner, D. and Shope, G. L. (1975) The facilitation of aggression by aggression: evidence against the catharsis hypothesis. *Journal of Personality and Social Psychology*, 31, 721–6.

Geen, R. G. and Thomas, S. L. (1986) The immediate effects of media violence on behavior. *Journal of Social Issues*, 42, 7–27.

Gelles, R. J. and Cornell, C. P. (1990) *Intimate Violence in Families*, 2nd edn. Newbury Park, CA: Sage.

Gerbner, G., Gross, L., Morgan, M. and Signiorelli, N. (1980) The 'main-streaming' of America: violence profile no. II. *Journal of Communication*, 30, 10–29.

Gerbner, G., Gross, L., Morgan, M. and Signiorelli, N. (1982) Charting the mainstream: television's contributions to political orientations. *Journal of Communication*, 32, 100–27.

Ghodsian-Carpey, J. and Baker, L. A. (1987) Genetic and environmental influences on aggression in 4- to 7-year-old twins. *Aggressive Behavior*, 13, 173–86.

Giancola, P. R. and Zeichner, A. (1994) Neuropsychological performance on tests of frontal-lobe functioning and aggressive behavior in men. *Journal of Abnormal Psychology*, 103, 832–5.

Gladue, B. A. (1991) Aggressive behavioral characteristics, hormones, and sexual orientation in men and women. *Aggressive Behavior*, 17, 313–26.

Gladue, B. A., Boechler, M. and McCaul, K. D. (1989) Hormonal response to competition in human males. *Aggressive Behavior*, 15, 409–22.

Goldstein, J. H. and Arms, R. L. (1971) Effects of observing athletic contests on hostility. *Sociometry*, 34, 83–90.

Goranson, R. E. (1970) Media violence and aggressive behavior: a review of experimental research, in L. Berkowitz (ed.) *Advances in Experimental Social Psychology, Volume 5*. New York: Academic Press, pp. 1–31.

Gouze, K. R. (1987) Attention and social problem solving as correlates of aggression in preschool males. *Journal of Abnormal Child Psychology*, 15, 181–97.

Gray, J. A. (1982) *The Neuropsychology of Anxiety*. Oxford: Oxford University Press.

Groebel, J. and Krebs, D. (1983) A study of the effects of television on anxiety. In C. D. Spielberger and R. Diaz-Guerrero (eds) *Cross Cultural Anxiety, Volume 2*. Washington, DC: Hemisphere, 89–98.

Grych, J. H. and Fincham, F. (1990) Marital conflict and children's adjustment: a cognitive-contextual framework. *Psychological Bulletin*, 108, 267–90.

Guerra, N. G., Huesmann, L. R. and Hanish, L. (1994a) The role of normative beliefs in children's social behavior, in N. Eisenberg (ed.) *Social Development*. Newbury Park, CA: Sage, pp. 140–58.

Guerra, N. G., Nucci, L. and Huesmann, L. R. (1994b) Moral cognition and childhood aggression, in L. R. Huesmann (ed.) *Aggressive Behavior: Current Perspectives*. New York: Plenum, pp. 13–33.

Gunter, B. and Furnham, A. (1983) Personality and the perception of TV violence. *Personality and Individual Differences*, 4, 315–22.

Gurr, T. R. (1970) *Why Men Rebel*. Princeton, NJ: Princeton University Press.

Guttmann, A. (1983) Roman sports violence, in J. H. Goldstein (ed.) *Sports Violence*. New York: Springer-Verlag, pp. 7–19.

Hall, G. C. N., and Hirschman, R. (1991) Toward a theory of sexual aggression: a quadripartite model. *Journal of Consulting and Clinical Psychology*, 59, 662–9.

Hall, G. C. N. and Proctor, W. C. (1987) Criminological predictors of recidivism in a sexual offender population. *Journal of Consulting and Clinical Psychology*, 55, 111–12.

Hall, G. C. N., Shondrick, D. D. and Hirschman, R. (1993) The role of sexual arousal in sexually aggressive behavior: a meta-analysis. *Journal of Consulting and Clinical Psychology*, 61, 1091–5.

Hamberger, L. K., and Hastings, J. E. (1991) Personality correlates of men who batter and nonviolent men: some continuities and discontinuities. *Journal of Family Violence*, 6, 131–47.

Harburg, E., Blakelock, E. H. and Roeper, P. J. (1979) Resentful and reflective coping with arbitrary authority and blood pressure: Detroit. *Psychosomatic Medicine*, 41, 189–202.

Hardy, J. and Smith, T. W. (1988) Cynical hostility and vulnerability to disease: social support, life stress, and physiological response to conflict. *Health Psychology*, 7, 447–59.

Harris, M. B. (1991) Effects of sex of aggressor, sex of target, and relationship on evaluations of physical aggression. *Journal of Interpersonal Violence*, 6, 174–86.

Harris, M. B. (1993) How provoking! What makes men and women angry? *Aggressive Behavior*, 19, 199–211.

Harris, R. E., Sokolow, M., Carpenter, L. G., Freedman, D. and Hunt, S. P. (1953) Response to psychological stress in persons who are potentially hypertensive. *Circulation*, 7, 874–9.

Harvey, M. D. and Rule, B. G. (1978) Moral evaluations and judgments of responsibility. *Personality and Social Psychology Bulletin*, 4, 583–8.

Hepworth, J. T. and West, S. G. (1988) Lynchings and the economy: a time-series reanalysis of Hovland and Sears (1940) *Journal of Personality and Social Psychology*, 55, 239–47.

Higley, J. D., Linnoila, M. and Suomi, S. J. (1994) Ethological contributions, in M. Hersen, R. T. Ammerman and L. A. Sisson (eds) *Handbook of Aggressive and Destructive Behavior in Psychiatric Patients*. New York: Plenum, pp. 17–32.

Hokanson, J. E. (1961) The effect of frustration and anxiety on overt-aggression. *Journal of Abnormal and Social Psychology*, 62, 346–51.

Hokanson, J. E. and Edelman, R. (1966) Effects of three social responses on vascular processes. *Journal of Personality and Social Psychology*, 3, 442–7.

Hokanson, J. E. and Shetler, S. (1961) The effect of overt aggression on physiological arousal. *Journal of Abnormal and Social Psychology*, 63, 446–8.

Hokanson, J. E., Willers, K. R. and Koropsak, E. (1968) The modification of autonomic responses during aggressive interchanges. *Journal of Personality*, 36, 386–404.

Holt, R. R. (1970) On the interpersonal and intrapersonal consequences of expressing or not expressing anger. *Journal of Consulting and Clinical Psychology*, 35, 8–12.

Holtzworth-Munroe, A. and Hutchinson, G. (1993) Attributing negative intent to wife behavior: the attributions of maritally violent versus nonviolent men. *Journal of Abnormal Psychology*, 102, 206–11.

Hotaling, G. T. and Sugarman, D. B. (1990) A risk marker analysis of assaulted wives. *Journal of Family Violence*, 5, 1–13.

Houston, B. K. and Vavak, C. R. (1991) Cynical hostility: developmental factors, psychosocial correlates, and health behaviors. *Health Psychology*, 10, 9–17.

Hovland, C. J. and Sears, R. R. (1940) Minor studies in aggression: VI. Correlation of lynchings with economic indices. *Journal of Psychology*, 9, 301–10.

Huesmann, L. R. (1986) Psychological processes promoting the relation between exposure to media violence and aggressive behavior by the viewer. *Journal of Social Issues*, 42, 125–39.

Huesmann, L. R. (1988) An information processing model for the development of aggression. *Aggressive Behavior*, 14, 13–24.

Huesmann, L. R. and Eron, L. D. (eds) (1986) *Television and the Aggressive Child: A Cross-national Comparison*. Hillsdale, NJ: Erlbaum.

Huesmann, L. R., Eron, L. D., Klein, R., Brice, P. and Fischer, P. (1983) Mitigating the imitation of aggressive behaviors by changing children's attitudes about media violence. *Journal of Personality and Social Psychology*, 44, 899–910.

Huesmann, L. R., Eron, L. D., Lefkowitz, M. M. and Walder, L. O. (1984) Stability of aggression over time and generations. *Developmental Psychology*, 20, 746–75.

Huesmann, L. R., Eron, L. D. and Yarmel, P. W. (1987) Intellectual functioning and aggression. *Journal of Personality and Social Psychology*, 52, 232–40.

Hyde, J. S. (1984) How large are gender differences in aggression? A developmental meta-analysis. *Developmental Psychology*, 20, 722–36.

Ito, T. A., Miller, N. and Pollock, V. E. (1996) Alcohol and aggression: a meta-analysis on the moderating effects of inhibitory cues, triggering events, and self-focused attention. *Psychological Bulletin*, 120, 60–82.

Johansson, G. G. (1981) Neural stimulation as a means for generating standardized threat under laboratory conditions, in P. F. Brain and D. Benton (eds) *Multidisciplinary Approaches to Aggression Research*. Amsterdam: Elsevier, North Holland, pp. 93–100.

Johnson, E. H., Spielberger, C. D., Worden, T. J. and Jacobs, G. A. (1987) Emotional and familial determinants of elevated blood pressure in black and white adolescent males. *Journal of Psychosomatic Research*, 31, 287–300.

Julian, T. W. and McKenry, P. C. (1993) Mediators of male violence toward female intimates. *Journal of Family Violence*, 8, 39–58.

Kanner, A. D., Coyne, J. C., Schaefer, C. and Lazarus, R. S. (1981) Comparisons of two modes of stress measurement: daily hassles and uplifts versus major life events. *Journal of Behavioral Medicine*, 4, 1–39.

Kerig, P. K. (1998) Gender and appraisals as mediators of adjustment in children exposed to interparental violence. *Journal of Family Violence*, 13, 345–63.

Kernis, M. H., Grannemann, B. D. and Barclay, L. C. (1989) Stability and level of self-esteem as predictors of anger arousal and hostility. *Journal of Personality and Social Psychology*, 56, 1013–22.

Koss, M. P., Gidycz, C. A. and Wisniewski, N. (1987) The scope of rape: incidence and prevalence of sexual aggression and victimization in a national sample of higher education students. *Journal of Consulting and Clinical Psychology*, 55, 162–70.

Lagerspetz, K. M. J. and Björkqvist, K. (1994) Indirect aggression in boys and girls. In L. R. Huesmann (ed.) *Aggressive Behavior: Current Perspectives*. New York: Plenum, pp. 131–50.

Lagerspetz, K. M. J., Björkqvist, K. and Peltonen, T. (1988) Is indirect aggression typical of females? Gender differences in aggressiveness in 11- to 12-year-old children. *Aggressive Behavior*, 14, 403–14.

Lagerspetz, K., Wahlroos, C. and Wendelin, C. (1978) Facial expressions of pre-school children while watching televised violence. *Scandinavian Journal of Psychology*, 19, 213–22.

Landau, S. F. (1988) Violent crime and its relation to subjective social stress indicators: the case of Israel. *Aggressive Behavior*, 14, 337–62.

Landau, S. F. and Raveh, A. (1987) Stress factors, social support, and violence in Israeli society: a quantitative analysis. *Aggressive Behavior*, 13, 67–85.

Lau, M. A. and Pihl, R. O. (1996) Cognitive performance, monetary incentive, and aggression. *Aggressive Behavior*, 22, 417–30.

Lefkowitz, M. M., Eron, L. D., Walder, L. O. and Huesmann, L. R. (1977) *Growing Up to Be Violent*. New York: Pergamon.

Leiker, M. and Hailey, B. J. (1988) A link between hostility and disease: poor health habits? *Behavioral Medicine*, 3, 129–33.

Linz, D., Donnerstein, E. and Penrod, S. (1984) The effects of multiple exposures to filmed violence against women. *Journal of Communication*, 34, 130–47.

Lochman, J. E., Lampron, L. B. and Rabiner, D. L. (1989) Format differences and salience effects in the social problem-solving assessment of aggressive and nonaggressive boys. *Journal of Clinical Child Psychology*, 18, 230–6.

Loeber, R. and Dishion, T. J. (1984) Boys who fight at home and school: family conditions influencing cross-setting consistency. *Journal of Consulting and Clinical Psychology*, 52, 759–68.

Lorenz, K. (1966) *On Aggression*. New York: Harcourt, Brace and World.

McCann, B. S. and Matthews, K. A. (1988) Influences of potential for hostility, Type A behavior, and parental history of hypertension on adolescents' cardiovascular responses during stress. *Psychophysiology*, 25, 503–11.

Maccoby, E. E. and Jacklin, C. N. (1974) *The Psychology of Sex Differences*. Stanford, CA: Stanford University Press.

McDonel, E. C. and McFall, R. M. (1991) Construct validity of two heterosexual perception skill measures for assessing rape proclivity. *Violence and Victims*, 6, 17–30.

MacEwen, K. E. and Barling, J. (1988) Multiple stressors, violence in the family of origin, and marital aggression: a longitudinal investigation. *Journal of Family Violence*, 3, 73–87.

McGue, M., Bacon, S. and Lykken, D. T. (1993) Personality, stability and change in early adulthood: a behavioral genetic analysis. *Developmental Psychology*, 29, 96–109.

Malamuth, N. M. (1984) Aggression against women: cultural and individual causes. In N. M. Malamuth and E. Donnerstein (eds) *Pornography and Sexual Aggression*. New York: Academic Press, pp. 19–52.

Malamuth, N. M. (1986) Predictors of naturalistic sexual aggression. *Journal of Personality and Social Psychology*, 50, 953–62.

Malamuth, N. M. and Brown, L. M. (1994) Sexually aggressive men's perceptions of women's communications: testing three explanations. *Journal of Personality and Social Psychology*, 67, 699–712.

Malamuth, N. M. and Check, J. V. P. (1983) Sexual arousal to rape depictions: individual differences. *Journal of Abnormal Psychology*, 92, 55–67.

Malamuth, N. M., Check, J. V. P. and Briere, J. (1986) Sexual arousal in response to aggression: ideological, aggressive, and sexual correlates. *Journal of Personality and Social Psychology*, 50, 330–40.

Malamuth, N. M., Linz, D., Heavey, C. L., Barnes, G. and Acker, M. (1995) Using the confluence model of sexual aggression to predict men's conflict with women: a 10-year follow-up study. *Journal of Personality and Social Psychology*, 69, 353–69.

Malamuth, N. M., Sockloskie, R. J., Koss, M. P. and Tanaka, J. S. (1991) Characteristics of aggressors against women: testing a model using a national sample of college students. *Journal of Consulting and Clinical Psychology*, 59, 670–81.

Malamuth, N. M. and Thornhill, N. W. (1994) Hostile masculinity, sexual aggression, and gender-based domineeringness in conversations. *Aggressive Behavior*, 20, 185–93.

Mallick, S. K. and McCandless, B. R. (1966) A study of catharsis of aggression. *Journal of Personality and Social Psychology*, 4, 591–6.

Marcus-Newhall, A., Pedersen, W. C., Carlson, M. and Miller, N. (2000) Displaced aggression is alive and well: a meta-analytic review. *Journal of Personality and Social Psychology*, 78, 670–89.

Mazur, A. and Lamb, T. A. (1980) Testosterone, status, and mood in human males. *Hormones and Behavior*, 14, 236–46.

Mednick, S. A., Gabrielli, W. F. and Hutchings, B. (1984) Genetic influences in criminal convictions: evidence from an adoption cohort. *Science*, 224, 891–4.

Mikulincer, M. (1998) Adult attachment style and individual differences in functional versus dysfunctional experiences of anger. *Journal of Personality and Social Psychology*, 74, 513–34.

Miles, D. R. and Carey, G. (1997) The genetic and environmental architecture of human aggression. *Journal of Personality and Social Psychology*, 72, 207–17.

Milgram, S. (1963) Behavioral study of obedience. *Journal of Abnormal and Social Psychology*, 67, 371–8.

Miller, B. L., Darby, A., Benson, D. F., Cummings, J. L. and Miller, M. H. (1997) Aggressive, socially disruptive, and antisocial behaviour associated with fronto-temporal dementia. *British Journal of Psychiatry*, 170, 150–5.

Miller, T. Q., Heath, L., Molcan, J. R. and Dugoni, B. L. (1991) Imitative violence in the real world: a reanalysis of homicide rates following championship prize fights. *Aggressive Behavior*, 17, 121–34.

Miller, T. Q., Smith, T. W., Turner, C. W., Guijarro, M. L. and Hallet, A. J. (1996) A meta-analytic review of research on hostility and physical health. *Psychological Bulletin*, 119, 322–48.

Millon, T. (1996) *Disorders of Personality: DSM-IV and Beyond*, 2nd edn. New York: Wiley-Interscience.

Moffitt, T. E. (1993) Adolescence-limited and life-course-persistent antisocial behavior: a developmental taxonomy. *Psychological Review*, 100, 674–701.

Moser, G. and Levy-Leboyer, C. (1985) Inadequate environment and situation control: is a malfunctioning phone always an occasion for aggression? *Environment and Behavior*, 17, 520–33.

Mummendey, A., Linneweber, V. and Loschper, G. (1984) Actor or victim of aggression: divergent perspectives – divergent evaluations. *European Journal of Social Psychology*, 14, 297–311.

Mummendey, A. and Mummendey, H. D. (1983) Aggressive behavior of soccer players as social interaction, in J. H. Goldstein (ed.) *Sports Violence*. New York: Springer-Verlag, pp. 111–28.

Murphy, C. M. and O'Leary, K. D. (1989) Psychological aggression predicts physical aggression in early marriage. *Journal of Consulting and Clinical Psychology*, 57, 579–82.

Murphy, W. D., Coleman, E. M. and Haynes, M. R. (1986) Factors related to coercive sexual behavior in a nonclinical sample of males. *Violence and Victims*, 1, 255–78.

Mustonen, A., Arms, R. L. and Russell, G. W. (1996) Predictors of sports spectators' proclivity for riotous behaviour in Finland and Canada. *Personality and Individual Differences*, 21, 519–25.

Nasby, W., Hayden, B. and DePaulo, B. M. (1979) Attributional bias among aggressive boys to interpret unambiguous social stimuli as displays of hostility. *Journal of Abnormal Psychology*, 89, 459–68.

Nisbett, R. E. and Cohen, D. (1996) *Culture of Honor*. Boulder, CO: Westview Press.

Novaco, R. W. (1991) Aggression on roadways, in R. Baenninger (ed.) *Targets of Violence and Aggression*. Amsterdam: Elsevier, pp. 253–326.

Novaco, R. W. (1994) Anger as a risk factor for violence among the mentally disordered, in J. Monahan and H. J. Steadman (eds) *Violence and Mental Disorder: Developments in Risk Assessment*. Chicago: University of Chicago Press, pp. 21–59.

O'Keefe, M. (1994) Linking marital violence, mother–child/father–child aggression, and child behavior problems. *Journal of Family Violence*, 9, 63–78.

Oldham, J., Clarkin, J., Appelbaum, A. *et al*. (1985) A self-report instrument for borderline personality organization, in T. H. McGlashan (ed.) *The Borderline: Current Empirical Research*. Washington, DC: American Psychiatric Press, pp. 1–18.

O'Leary, K. D. (1993) Through a psychological lens: personality traits, personality disorders, and levels of violence, in R. J. Gelles and D. R. Loseke (eds) *Current Controversies on Family Violence*. Newbury Park, CA: Sage, pp. 262–78.

O'Leary, K. D., Barling, J., Arias, I., Rosenbaum, A., Malone, J. and Tyree, A. (1989) Prevalence and stability of physical aggression between spouses: a longitudinal analysis. *Journal of Consulting and Clinical Psychology*, 57, 263–8.

O'Leary, K. D. and Vivian, D. (1990) Physical aggression in marriage, in F. Fincham and T. N. Bradbury (eds) *The Psychology of Marriage: Basic Issues and Applications*. New York: Guilford Press, pp. 323–48.

O'Leary, M. R. and Dengerink, H. A. (1973) Aggression as a function of the intensity and pattern of attack. *Journal of Research in Personality*, 7, 61–70.

Olweus, D. (1979) Stability of aggression patterns in males: a review. *Psychological Bulletin*, 86, 852–75.

Olweus, D. (1994) Bullying at school: long-term outcomes for the victims and an effective school-based intervention program, in L. R. Huesmann (ed.) *Aggressive Behavior: Current Perspectives*. New York: Plenum, pp. 97–130.

Olweus, D., Mattsson, Å., Schalling, D. and Löw, H. (1980) Testosterone, aggression, physical, and personality dimensions in normal adolescent males. *Psychosomatic Medicine*, 42, 253–69.

Orwell, G. (1968) Such, such were the joys. In *The Collected Essays, Journalism, and Letters of George Orwell, Volume 4*. New York: Harcourt Brace Jovanovich (originally published in 1947).

Paik, H. and Comstock, G. (1994) The effects of television violence on antisocial behavior: a meta-analysis. *Communication Research*, 21, 516–39.

Panksepp, J. (1998) *Affective Neuroscience: The Foundations of Human and Animal Emotions*. New York: Oxford University Press.

Patterson, A. H. (1974) Hostility catharsis: a naturalistic quasi-experiment. Paper presented to the annual convention of the American Psychological Association, New Orleans.

Patterson, G. R. and Capaldi, D. M. (1991) Antisocial parents: unskilled and vulnerable. In P. A. Cowan and M. Hetherington (eds) *Family Transitions*. Hillsdale, NJ: Erlbaum, pp. 195–218.

Patterson, G. R., DeBaryshe, B. D. and Ramsey, E. (1989) A developmental perspective on antisocial behavior. *American Psychologist*, 44, 329–35.

Patterson, G. R., Reid, J. B. and Dishion, T. J. (1992) *Antisocial Boys*. Eugene, OR: Castalia Press.

Paul, L., Foss, M. A. and Galloway, J. (1993) Sexual jealousy in young women and men: aggressive responsiveness to partner and rival. *Aggressive Behavior*, 19, 401–20.

Paul, L. and Galloway, J. (1994) Sexual jealousy: gender differences in response to partner and rival. *Aggressive Behavior*, 20, 79–100.

Perry, D. G. and Perry, L. C. (1976) Identification with film characters, covert aggressive verbalization, and reactions to film violence. *Journal of Research in Personality*, 10, 399–409.

Perry, D. G., Perry, L. C. and Rasmussen, P. (1986) Cognitive social learning mediators of aggression. *Child Development*, 57, 700–11.

Petrides, M. (1985) Deficits on conditional associative-learning tasks after frontal- and temporal-lobe lesions in man. *Neuropsychologia*, 23, 601–14.

Petrides, M. and Milner, B. (1982) Deficits on subject-ordered tasks after frontal- and temporal-lobe lesions in man. *Neuropsychologia*, 20, 249–62.

Phillips, D. P. (1983) The impact of mass media violence on US homicides. *American Sociological Review*, 48, 560–8.

Phillips, D. P. (1986) Natural experiments on the effects of mass media violence on fatal aggression: strengths and weaknesses of a new approach, in L. Berkowitz (ed.) *Advances in Experimental Social Psychology, Volume 19*. New York: Academic Press, pp. 207–50.

Plomin, R., Nitz, K. and Rowe, D. C. (1990) Behavior genetics and aggressive behavior in childhood, in M. Lewis and S. Miller (eds) *Handbook of Developmental Psychopathology*. New York: Plenum, pp. 119–33.

Podell, S. and Archer, D. (1994) Do legal changes matter? The case of gun control laws, in M. Costanzo and S. Oskamp (eds) *Violence and the Law*. Thousand Oaks, CA: Sage, pp. 37–60.

Porter, J. F. and Critelli, J. W. (1994) Self-talk and sexual arousal in sexual aggression. *Journal of Social and Clinical Psychology*, 13, 223–39.

Quiggle, N. L., Garber, J., Panak, W. F. and Dodge, K. A. (1992) Social information processing in aggressive and depressed children. *Child Development*, 63, 1305–20.

Quinsey, V. L., Chaplin, T. C. and Upfold, D. (1984) Sexual arousal to nonsexual violence and sadomasochistic themes among rapists and non-sex-offenders. *Journal of Consulting and Clinical Psychology*, 52, 651–7.

Rajecki, D. W. (1983) Animal aggression: implications for human aggression, in R. G. Geen and E. I. Donnerstein (eds) *Aggression: Theoretical and Empirical Reviews, Volume 1*. New York: Academic Press, pp. 189–211.

Reinisch, J. M. and Sanders, S. A. (1986) A test of sex differences in aggressive response to hypothetical conflict situations. *Journal of Personality and Social Psychology*, 50, 1045–9.

Rice, M. E., Chaplin, T. C., Harris, G. T. and Coutts, J. (1994) Empathy for the victim and sexual arousal among rapists and nonrapists. *Journal of Interpersonal Violence*, 9, 435–49.

Rossman, B. B. R. and Rosenberg, M. (1992) Family stress and functioning in children: the moderating effects of children's beliefs about their control over parental conflict. *Journal of Child Psychology and Psychiatry*, 33, 699–715.

Rule, B. G. (1978) The hostile and instrumental functions of human aggression, in W. W. Hartup and J. DeWit (eds) *Origins of Aggression*. The Hague: Mouton, pp. 121–41.

Rule, B. G. and Nesdale, A. R. (1976) Emotional arousal and aggressive behavior. *Psychological Bulletin*, 83, 851–63.

Rushton, J. P., Fulker, D. W., Neale, M. C., Nias, D. K. B. and Eysenck, H. J. (1986) Altruism and aggression: the heritability of individual differences. *Journal of Personality and Social Psychology*, 50, 1192–8.

Russell, G. W. (1993) *The Social Psychology of Sport*. New York: Springer.

Russell, G. W. (1995) Personalities in the crowd: those who would escalate a sports riot. *Aggressive Behavior*, 21, 91–100.

Russell, G. W. and Arms, R. L. (1998) Toward a social psychological profile of would-be rioters. *Aggressive Behavior*, 24, 219–26.

Ryan, E. D. (1970) The cathartic effect of vigorous motor activity on aggressive behavior. *Research Quarterly*, 41, 542–51.

Sallis, J. F., Johnson, C. C., Trevorrow, T. R., Kaplan, R. M. and Hovell, M. F. (1987) The relationship between cynical hostility and blood pressure reactivity. *Journal of Psychosomatic Research*, 31, 111–16.

Salmivalli, C., Karhunen, J. and Lagerspetz, K. M. J. (1996) How do the victims respond to bullying? *Aggressive Behavior*, 22, 99–109.

Salmivalli, C., Lagerspetz, K., Björkqvist, K., Österman, K. and Kaukiainen, A. (1996) Bullying as a group process: participant roles and their relations to social status within the group. *Aggressive Behavior*, 22, 1–15.

Salvador, A., Simón, V., Suay, F. and Llorens, L. (1987) Testosterone and cortisol responses to competitive fighting in human males: a pilot study. *Aggressive Behavior*, 13, 9–13.

Schachter, J. (1957) Pain, fear, and anger in hypertensives and normotensives. *Psychosomatic Medicine*, 19, 17–29.

Schill, T. R. (1972) Aggression and blood pressure responses of high- and low-guilt subjects following frustration. *Journal of Consulting and Clinical Psychology*, 38, 461.

Séguin, J. R., Pihl, R. O., Harden, P. W., Tremblay, R. E. and Boulerice, B. (1995) Cognitive and neuropsychological characteristics of physically aggressive boys. *Journal of Abnormal Psychology*, 104, 614–24.

Siegman, A. W. (1994) Cardiovascular consequences of expressing and repressing anger, in A. W. Siegman and T. W. Smith (eds) *Anger, Hostility, and the Heart*. Hillsdale, NJ: Erlbaum, pp. 173–97.

Siegman, A. W., Anderson, R. W. and Berger, T. (1990) The angry voice: its effects on the experience of anger and cardiovascular reactivity. *Psychosomatic Medicine*, 52, 631–43.

Siegman, A. W., Dembroski, T. M. and Ringel, N. (1987) Components of hostility and the severity of coronary artery disease. *Psychosomatic Medicine*, 49, 127–35.

Siever, L. J. and Davis, K. L. (1991) A psychobiological perspective on the personality disorders. *American Journal of Psychiatry*, 148, 1647–58.

Silvern, S. B. and Williamson, P. A. (1987) The effects of video game play on young children's aggression, fantasy, and prosocial behavior. *Journal of Applied Developmental Psychology*, 8, 453–62.

Simpson, J. A. (1990) Influence of attachment styles on romantic relationships. *Journal of Personality and Social Psychology*, 59, 971–80.

Singer, J. L. and Singer, D. G. (1981) *Television, Imagination, and Aggression: A Study of Preschoolers*. Hillsdale, NJ: Erlbaum.

Slaby, R. G. and Guerra, N. G. (1988) Cognitive mediators of aggression in adolescent offenders: 1. Assessment. *Developmental Psychology*, 24, 580–8.

Smith, M. A. and Houston, B. K. (1987) Hostility, anger expression, cardiovascular responsivity, and social support. *Biological Psychology*, 24, 39–48.

Smith, M. D. (1976) Precipitants of crowd violence. *Sociological Inquiry*, 48, 121–31.

Smith, P. K. and Brain, P. (2000) Bullying in schools: lessons from two decades of research. *Aggressive Behavior*, 26, 1–9.

Smith, T. W. (1992) Hostility and health: current status of a psychosomatic hypothesis. *Health Psychology*, 11, 139–50.

Snyder, J. and Patterson, G. R. (1986) The effects of consequences on patterns of social interaction: a quasi-experimental approach to reinforcement in natural interaction. *Child Development*, 57, 1257–68.

Spielberger, C. D., Johnson, E. H., Russell, S. F. *et al.* (1985) The experience and expression of anger: construction and validation of an anger expression scale, in M. A. Chesney and R. H. Rosenman (eds) *Anger and Hostility in Cardiovascular and Behavioral Disorders*. Washington, DC: Hemisphere, pp. 5–30.

Spielberger, C. D., Reheiser, E. C. and Sydeman, S. J. (1995) Measuring the experience, expression, and control of anger, in H. Kassinove (ed.) *Anger Disorders: Definition, Diagnosis, and Treatment*. Washington, DC: Taylor & Francis, pp. 49–67.

Stattin, H. and Magnusson, D. (1989) The role of early aggressive behavior in the frequency, seriousness, and types of later crime. *Journal of Consulting and Clinical Psychology*, 57, 710–18.

Steele, C. M. and Josephs, R. A. (1990) Alcohol myopia: its prized and dangerous effects. *American Psychologist*, 45, 921–33.

Stein, D. J., Towey, J. and Hollander, E. (1995) The neuropsychiatry of impulsive aggression, in E. Hollander and D. J. Stein (eds) *Impulsivity and Aggression*. New York: Wiley, pp. 91–105.

Stith, S. M. and Farley, S. C. (1993) A predictive model of male spousal violence. *Journal of Family Violence*, 8, 183–201.

Straus, M. A. (1993) Physical assaults by wives: a major social problem, in R. J. Gelles and D. R. Loseke (eds) *Current Controversies on Family Violence*. Newbury Park, CA: Sage, pp. 67–87.

Susman, E. J., Inoff-Germain, G., Nottelman, E. D. *et al.* (1987) Hormones, emotional dispositions, and aggressive attributes in young adolescents. *Child Development*, 58, 1114–34.

Tangney, J. P., Wagner, P., Fletcher, C. and Gramzow, R. (1992) Shame into anger? The relation of shame and guilt to anger and self-reported aggression. *Journal of Personality and Social Psychology*, 62, 669–75.

Taylor, S. P. and Leonard, K. E. (1983) Alcohol and human physical aggression, in R. G. Geen and E. I. Donnerstein (eds) *Aggression: Theoretical and Empirical Reviews, Volume 2*. New York: Academic Press, pp. 77–101.

Tedeschi, J. T. and Felson, R. B. (1994) *Violence, Aggression, and Coercive Actions*. Washington, DC: American Psychological Association.

Thornhill, R. and Thornhill, N. W. (1992) The evolutionary psychology of men's coercive sexuality. *Behavioral and Brain Sciences*, 15, 363–421.

Turner, C. W. and Berkowitz, L. (1972) Identification with film aggressor (covert role taking) and reactions to film violence. *Journal of Personality and Social Psychology*, 21, 256–64.

Turner, C. W. and Goldsmith, D. (1976) Effects of toy guns on children's anti-social free play behavior. *Journal of Experimental Child Psychology*, 21, 303–15.

Van Goozen, S. H. M., Cohen-Kettenis, P. T., Gooren, L. J. G., Frijda, N. H. and Van de Poll, N. E. (1995a) Gender differences in behaviour: activating effects of cross-sex hormones. *Psychoneuroendocrinology*, 20, 343–63.

Van Goozen, S. H. M., Frijda, N. H. and Van de Poll, N. E. (1994) Anger and aggression in women: Influence of sports choice and testosterone administration. *Aggressive Behavior*, 20, 213–22.

Van Goozen, S. H. M., Frijda, N. H. and Van de Poll, N. E. (1995b) Anger and aggression during role playing: gender differences between hormonally treated male and female transsexuals and controls. *Aggressive Behavior*, 21, 257–73.

Vasta, R. and Copitch, P. (1981) Simulating conditions of child abuse in the laboratory. *Child Development*, 52, 164–70.

Volkow, N. D. and Tancredi, L. (1987) Neural substrates of violent behaviour: a preliminary study with positron emission tomography. *British Journal of Psychiatry*, 151, 668–73.

Walker, I. and Mann, L. (1987) Unemployment, relative deprivation, and social protest. *Personality and Social Psychology Bulletin*, 13, 275–83.

Walker, I. and Pettigrew, T. F. (1984) Relative deprivation theory: an overview and conceptual critique. *British Journal of Social Psychology*, 23, 301–10.

Weiss, B., Dodge, K. A., Bates, J. E. and Pettit, G. S. (1992) Some consequences of early harsh discipline: child aggression and a maladaptive social information processing style. *Child Development*, 63, 1321–35.

White, G. F. (1989) Media and violence: the case of professional football championship games. *Aggressive Behavior*, 15, 423–33.

White, J. W. (1983) Sex and gender issues in aggression research, in R. G. Geen and E. I. Donnerstein (eds) *Aggression: Theoretical and Empirical Reviews, Volume 2*. New York: Academic Press, pp. 1–26.

Widiger, T. A. and Trull, T. J. (1994) Personality disorders and violence, in J. Monahan and H. J. Steadman (eds) *Violence and Mental Disorder: Developments in Risk Assessment*. Chicago: University of Chicago Press, pp. 203–26.

Widom, C. S. (1989a) Does violence beget violence? A critical examination of the literature. *Psychological Bulletin*, 106, 3–28.

Widom, C. S. (1989b) The cycle of violence. *Science*, 244, 160–6.

Wolfgang, M. E. and Ferracuti, F. (1982) *The Subculture of Violence: Towards an Integrated Theory in Criminology*. Beverly Hills, CA: Sage.

Wood, W., Wong, F. and Chachere, J. (1991) Effects of media violence on viewers' aggression in unconstrained social interaction. *Psychological Bulletin*, 109, 371–83.

Zaidi, L. Y., Knutson, J. F. and Mehm, J. G. (1989) Transgenerational patterns of abusive parenting. *Aggressive Behavior*, 15, 137–152.

Zillmann, D. (1971) Excitation transfer in communication-mediated aggressive behavior. *Journal of Experimental Social Psychology*, 7, 419–34.

Zillmann, D. (1978) Attribution and misattribution of excitatory reactions, in J. H. Harvey, W. J. Ickes and R. F. Kidd (eds) *New Directions in Attribution Research, Volume 2*. Hillsdale, NJ: Erlbaum, pp. 335–68.

Zillmann, D. (1988) Cognition–excitation interdependencies in aggressive behavior. *Aggressive Behavior*, 14, 51–64.

Zillmann, D. and Cantor, J. R. (1976) Effect of timing of information about mitigating circumstances on emotional responses to provocation and retaliatory behavior. *Journal of Experimental Social Psychology*, 12, 38–55.

Zillmann, D., Johnson, R. C. and Hanrahan, J. (1973) Pacifying effect of happy ending of communications involving aggression. *Psychological Reports*, 32, 967–70.

Zillmann, D., Katcher, A. H. and Milavsky, B. (1972) Excitation transfer from physical exercise to subsequent aggressive behavior. *Journal of Experimental Social Psychology*, 8, 247–59.

Zurbriggen, E. L. (2000) Social motives and cognitive power–sex associations: predictors of aggressive sexual behavior. *Journal of Personality and Social Psychology*, 78, 559–81.

INDEX

RELATING TO OTHERS
Second Edition

Steve Duck

Reviews of the first edition:

Concise, readable, up-to-date, this volume is an excellent introduction to a new and expanding field.

Counseling Psychology Quarterly

. . . a wonderful book.

*Newsletter of the American Association for Counseling
and Development*

. . . very exciting.

Counselling

- How do relationships get started successfully?
- How do relationships develop?
- What makes relationships decline and how can they be repaired?

As social psychologists become more aware of the ways in which
relationships underpin almost everything in the social sciences, the
need for an introductory book for students and scholars has further
increased. This long-awaited second edition of a highly successful
text summarizes the research on relationships, focusing not only on
their growth and development but also on their negative aspects,
breakdown and repair.

The author addresses the essential use of relationship issues within
applied areas such as policing, health care, and the corporate world.
He also emphasizes the importance of multidisciplinary studies and
the integration of different frameworks and methods, by focusing
less on static factors in relationships and more on the matter of
process. Finally, he examines the need to contextualize relationship
processes and take account of the daily issues of management by
relational partners.

The second edition of *Relating to Others* is strongly grounded in a
discussion of the contexts for relating, whether cultural, linguistic,
or interpersonal. It focuses on a range of relationships, friendship,
and types of marriage and is written in an engaging style for students of psychology and the wider social sciences by one of the top
authorities in the scientific research on relationships.

Contents
*The role of relationships in life – Contexts of relationships – Developing
relationships and developing people – Developing a steady and exclusive
partnership – Managing relationships – When relationships come apart –
Putting relationships right – Overview – References – Index.*

176 pp   0 335 20163 6 (paperback)   0 335 20164 4 (hardback)

SOCIAL PSYCHOLOGY AND HEALTH
Second Edition

Wolfgang Stroebe

If you are a student of social or health psychology, or if you are working in one of the health professions, you are likely at some point to address questions such as the following:

- Which behaviour patterns are detrimental to health?
- Why do people engage in such behaviour, even if they know about its negative effects?
- How can people be influenced to change their behaviour?
- What do we mean by stressful life events and how can their impact on health be mediated?

In *Social Psychology and Health* you will find these major health topics discussed from a social psychological perspective. During recent decades there have been significant changes in conceptions of health and illness, with a move towards a broader conception of health to include physical, mental and social well-being. In line with these changes, health psychology has become a dominant force in the health sciences. This relatively new field of psychology is much influenced by social psychological theory and research, and the focus of the book reflects this.

Social Psychology and Health gives an up-to-date perspective on these key health psychology questions. The book argues for an integrative approach that combines psychological, economic and environmental interventions in order to reduce the potential risks to health arising from behaviour or stressful life events.

The second edition of this highly successful textbook has been extensively revised, expanded and updated. Much new material has been added based on research done in the last five years, in particular drawing on the author's own research into obesity and sexual risk behaviour. Many of the epidemiological examples and more than a third of the references have been updated. It is essentially a new book which will make an important contribution to the literature.

Contents
Changing conceptions of health and illness – Determinants of health behaviour: a social psychological analysis – Beyond persuasion: the modification of health behaviour – Behaviour and health: excessive appetites – Behaviour and health: self-protection – Stress and health – Moderators of the stress-health relationship – The role of social psychology in health promotion – Glossary – References – Author index – Subject index.

352 pp   0 335 19921 6 (Paperback)   0 335 19922 4 (Hardback)

THE SOCIAL PSYCHOLOGY OF DRUG ABUSE

Steve Sussman and Susan L. Ames

- Is drug abuse a disease?
- What causes drug abuse?
- How can drug abuse be best prevented or treated?

This concise and comprehensive overview unravels the complexities surrounding the definition, cause and treatment of drug abuse. The authors set out the different classes of drugs of abuse, distinguish drug use from abuse, and consider whether or not drug abuse should be seen as a disease. They go on to examine other compulsive behaviours, such as eating disorders and pathological gambling, for their similarities and differences from drug abuse, and detail current methods of assessing drug abuse. Numerous extra-personal and intra-personal predictors of drug use and abuse are examined, including drug distribution systems, and biological factors, as well as social psychological factors. Finally, the authors present the wide spectrum of current prevention and treatment programmes and discuss future directions in the prevention and cessation of drug abuse. This book takes an international approach and provides vital information on key issues, presenting its material from a social psychological perspective, but drawing on work in public health, clinical psychology and sociology. Each chapter provides a summary and tables to help the reader integrate the information. It will prove invaluable not only to undergraduate and postgraduate students, but to counsellors, researchers, and policy makers.

Contents

192 pp   0 335 20618 2 (paperback)   0 335 20619 0 (hardback)

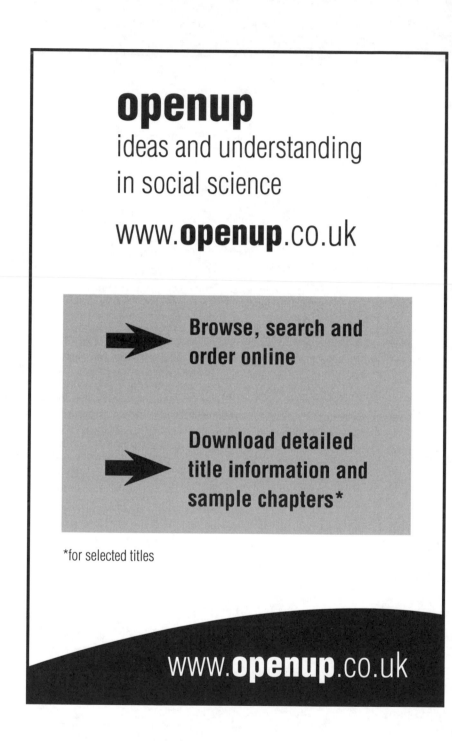